Thomas D. Marbaker

History of the Eleventh New Jersey Volunteers

Thomas D. Marbaker

History of the Eleventh New Jersey Volunteers

ISBN/EAN: 9783744760010

Printed in Europe, USA, Canada, Australia, Japan

Cover: Foto ©ninafisch / pixelio.de

More available books at **www.hansebooks.com**

HISTORY

OF THE

 Eleventh New Jersey Volunteers

FROM

Its Organization to Appomattox

TO WHICH IS ADDED

EXPERIENCES OF PRISON LIFE

AND

Sketches of Individual Members

By THOS. D. MARBAKER, SERG'T CO. E

Illustrated with Portraits from
War-time Photographs

TRENTON, N. J.:
MacCrellish & Quigley, Book and Job Printers.
1898.

The regiment took part in the following engagements:

Fredericksburg, Va., December 13th and 14th, '62.
Chancellorsville, Va., May 3d and 4th, '63.
Gettysburg, Pa., July 2d and 3d, '63.
Wapping Heights, Va., July 24th, '63.
Kelly's Ford, Va., November 8th, '63.
Locust Grove, Va., November 27th, '63.
Mine Run, Va., November 29th, '63.
Wilderness, Va., May 5th to 7th, '64.
Spottsylvania, Va., May 8th to 11th, '64.
Spottsylvania Court House, Va., May 12th to 18th, '64.
North Anna River, Va., May 23d and 24th, 64.
Tolopotomoy Creek, Va., May 30th and 31st, '64.
Cold Harbor, Va., June 1st to 5th, '64.
Barker's Mills, Va., June 10th, '64.
Before Petersburg, Va., June 16th to 23d, '64.
Deep Bottom, Va., July 26th and 27th, '64.
Mine Explosion, Va., July 30th, '64.
North Bank of James River, Va., August 14th to 18th, '64.
Ream's Station, Va., August 25th, '64.
Fort Sedgwick, Va., September 10th, '64.
Poplar Spring Church, Va., October 2d, '64.
Boynton Plank-Road, Va., October 27th, '64.
Fort Morton, November 5th, '64.
Hatcher's Run, Va., February 5th to 7th, '65.
Armstrong House, Va., March 25th, '65.
Boynton Plank-Road, Va. (capture of Petersburg), April 2d, '65.
Amelia Springs, Va., April 6th, '65.
Farmville, Va., April 6th to 7th, '65.
Lee's Surrender (Appomattox, Va.), April 9th, '65.

PREFACE.

When I began the compilation of this work, it was with the intention of making it (principally) a record of persona incidents—those happenings, grave and gay, which gave zest and variety to a soldier's life and brought out the individual characteristics of the members of the regiment. Upon stating my intention (or rather hopes) to the comrades, it was predicted that there would be such a plethora of material that I would not know what to do with it. Unfortunately the reverse has been the case. So few and tardy were the responses to solicitations for reminiscences that I became almost discouraged and practically threw the work aside. It is a strange fact that when comrades get together they can relate incident after incident, but ask them to put their recollections upon paper, then their army life seems to have been a blank. My recollections of army life are still very vivid, but memory is not infallible, and badly as this work is done, it would have been worse had it not been for the valuable assistance rendered by the late General McAllister, who gave me access to his papers, and to Colonel John Schoonover, Major Loyd, Captain John Oldershaw, Chaplain Cline, Captain William H. Meeker, Captain E. S. E. Newberry, Brevet Captain U. B. Titus, Lieutenants William Hand and E. R. Good, Quartermaster-Sergeant John Stagg, Corporals Aaron Lines, of Company B, and Bishop W. Mains, of Company E; Privates Lambert Sharp, of Company E, and John Goodman (*alias* Zuckswort), of Company B. One of my most valuable assistants has been Alonzo B Searing, of Company E, who, though but a boy at the time of his enlistment, seems to have realized the importance of keeping a full and methodical record of the happenings to himself and the regiment during those trying days from '62 to '65. His contributions have been voluminous and, in general, have well stood the test of investigation and comparison as to accuracy. One of the most important things in preparing a record of this kind is accuracy as to time and date. In some of the regimental histories that I have read, these seem to have been ignored for the sake of continuity of narrative. I may not in all cases be correct, but I have tried to be as nearly so as possible. A number of incidents have been sent me which, while they could have been made very readable and no doubt contained some elements of truth, were found to be so variant from well-known facts that I was compelled to throw them aside. The comrades have been honest, but the mists of years have obscured their memories and the recollections of the war have become so jumbled that the incidents of different periods seem to them as parts of one. I have also tried to avoid anything like bombast; I know that the Eleventh tried to do its duty ; that its contemporaries gave it credit for being brave and gallant, but it did not do it all—there were a few other troops engaged in the various battles in which it fought that rendered very efficient service.

T. D. MARBAKER.

CONTENTS.

CHAPTER I.
Organization of the Regiment.

CHAPTER II.
On to Washington—Camp Ellsworth—Guarding Convalescent Camp.

CHAPTER III.
Joining Carr's Brigade—The March to Falmouth—Battle of Fredericksburg.

CHAPTER IV.
Camp Fitzhugh—First Winter Quarters.

CHAPTER V
Hooker Takes Command—Chancellorsville.

CHAPTER VI.
The March to Gettysburg—Gettysburg.

CHAPTER VII.
Wapping Heights—March to Beverly Ford—Rappahannock.

CHAPTER VIII.
Locust Grove—Mine Run.

CHAPTER IX.
Camp at Brandy Station.

CHAPTER X.
Across the Rapidan and Southward—Wilderness—Spottsylvania—Cold Harbor.

CHAPTER XI.
Across the James—Petersburg.

CHAPTER XII.
Mahone's Attack—Major Halsey and Others Captured.

CHAPTER XIII.
Across the James—Mine Explosion—Ream's Station.

CHAPTER XIV.
Fort Davis—Poplar Spring Church—Boynton Plank Road.

CHAPTER XV
Fort Morton.

CHAPTER XVI.
With Warren to Hicksford—From December 7th to 12th, 1864.

CHAPTER XVII.
Hatcher's Run—Armstrong House.

CHAPTER XVIII.
Capture of Petersburg—Amelia Springs—Farmville—Lee's Surrender.

CHAPTER XIX.
Our Return March—Buresville—Washington—The Grand Review—Trenton—Mustered Out.

CHAPTER XX.
Southern Prisons—Imprisonment of Corporal Lines.

CHAPTER XXI.
Chaplain Cline's Letter—Lieutenant Baldwin's Headboard.

CHAPTER XXII.
Sketches.

ILLUSTRATIONS.

From War-Time Photographs.

	PAGE.
BREVET MAJOR GENERAL ROBERT MCALLISTER	FRONTISPIECE
BREVET COLONEL JOHN SCHOONOVER	1
MAJOR THOMAS G. HALSEY	10
SURGEON EDWARD L. WELLING	18
MAJOR PHILIP J. KEARNY	26
MAJOR JOHN T. HILL	34
BREVET MAJOR CHARLES F. GAGE	42
CHAPLAIN E. CLARKE CLINE	52
CAPTAIN IRA W. CORY	60
MAJOR WILLIAM H. LOYD	68
CAPTAIN SAMUEL T. SLEEPER	76
CAPTAIN D. B. LOGAN	84
CAPTAIN A. H. ACKERMAN	92
CAPTAIN S. M. LAYTON	100
ADJUTANT ALEXANDER BEACH, JR.	108
CAPTAIN CHARLES A. OLIVER	116
CAPTAIN WILLIAM H. MEEKER	124
LIEUTENANT JOSEPH C. BALDWIN	132
LIEUTENANT WILLIAM HAND	140
LIEUTENANT JOHN B. FAUSSETT	148
CAPTAIN JOHN OLDERSHAW	156
LIEUTENANT TITUS BERRY	164
SERGEANT T. O'DOANE	172
SERGEANT THOMAS D. MARBAKER	182

ILLUSTRATIONS.

	PAGE.
LIEUTENANT C. H. ROSSITER	194
LIEUTENANT WILLIAM E. ANTELL	204
SERGEANT ELIPHALET STURDEVANT	214
LIEUTENANT ALPHEUS ILIFF	226
SERGEANT JAMES McDAVITT	240
LIEUTENANT EDWIN R. GOOD	254
PRIVATE A. B. SEARING	268
CORPORAL A. S TALMAGE	282
LIEUTENANT W. H. EGAN	298
SERGEANT BLACKWOOD'S BIBLE	312
GETTYSBURG MONUMENT	326
FAC-SIMILE OF ORDER TO CAPTAIN OLIVER	336
LIEUTENANT BALDWIN'S HEADBOARD	344
GENERAL McALLISTER'S MONUMENT	348
MAJOR LOYD'S BULLET	357

Brevet-Colonel John Schoonover.

The Eleventh Regiment

CHAPTER I.

Organization of the Regiment.

THE organization of the Eleventh Regiment, New Jersey Volunteers, was begun in May, 1862, under the provisions of an act of Congress, approved July 22d, 1861, and by permission granted the Governor by the War Department to commence the raising of a regiment, in anticipation of a call, soon to be issued by the President, for more troops.

On July 7th, 1862, the President issued a call for three hundred thousand additional volunteers to serve three years or during the war. At this time about two hundred and fifty men had been recruited, and were encamped at Camp Perrine, Trenton. On the 8th of July, 1862, a telegram was received from the War Department, Washington, D. C., calling for five regiments of infantry from the State of New Jersey, and in compliance with this telegram and the provisions of General Order No. 75, Adjutant-General's office, War Department, Washington, D. C., dated July 8th, 1862, the organization of the regiment was completed. The regiment was organized, officered and equipped by the 18th day of August, 1862, at which time it was mustered into the United States service by Major Lewellyn Jones, of the First U. S. Cavalry. The strength of the regiment at time of muster was: officers, 39; non-commissioned officers and privates, 940; total, 979. The earliest enlistments in the regiment were in Company K, Charles C. Reiley, Wm. Amsden, Amon J. Foote, Jeremiah O'Brien and

George H. Porter, who enlisted on April 30th, 1862, being assigned to that company. They were followed in the same company by Edward Berden, musician, on May 5th, Jeremiah Demerest and Gershom Forate, on May 7th, and Joseph Hunton, Nicholas Maure, May 12th. By the end of June, Company K had enlisted upwards of thirty men, so it must be awarded the credit of having been the pioneer company. Before the end of June, over two hundred men had been enlisted, and camp formed along the Trenton Branch of the Camden and Amboy Railroad, opposite the New Jersey State Prison. The plot of ground used was bounded on the east by what is now Adeline street, on the south by Cass street, on the west by the railroad and the Delaware and Raritan canal, and on the north by a pond, caused by the overflow from the canal, which has since been filled in and the site occupied by a sash and blind factory and Wilson & Stokes' coal and wood yard. Across the Cass street bridge, to the westward, stands the *old* State Prison, used then as now for the State Arsenal. A part of the old campground is still vacant, but the surroundings have been so improved that, without the prison and arsenal as landmarks, it would be hard to recognize the site.

The camp was named Perrine, in honor of General Lewis Perrine, then Quartermaster-General of the State. Sibley tents were pitched, cook-houses put up, and so fast as the recruits arrived they were given quarters and inducted into the mysteries of camp-life.

No one who was with the regiment in its earliest stage, before the officers had reported to their commands, will have forgotten the self-important, tyrannical Sergeant Nolan, of Company F, who seemed for a time to have chief charge of the camp, under Major Halstead. How he strutted around, with his belt strung full of hand-cuffs, and what evident pleasure he felt when an excuse offered to punish some ignorant offender or helplessly drunken soldier! To buck-and-gag a man seemed to afford him supreme satisfaction. But the old saying, that a "tyrant is generally a coward," held good in that case, for the "noble" sergeant deserted the regiment on its way to the front, and perhaps it was well (for himself) that he did so.

The transition from the comforts of home to the comparative discomforts of Camp Perrine were not too cheerfully borne by the newly-made soldiers. We were yet to learn by experience how utterly barren of real comfort a soldier's life could be.

Among the equipments drawn from the Quartermaster's Department were small ticks, which, when well filled with straw, made not bad substitutes for the beds at home, and they were beds of down in comparison with some of our resting-places in the years that followed. We also received a tin cup, and plate of the same material. That constituted our table service, a service that many of the boys were cheated out of by the mean tricks of some of the cooks at Camp Perrine. They were told that if they would leave their cup and plate with the cook and pay twenty-five cents a week, in advance, he (the cook) would keep them clean. Many of the men did so, but when they went again for rations they were told that there was no cup and plate there for them. The only alternative was to buy new ones.

We had not been long in camp before we learned that so far as individual property was concerned each man would have to look out for his own, and, if lost, replace it as best he could.

William Hand, of Company B, lost—or, rather, had stolen—his gun, and having searched all over the camp without finding it, finally reported the loss to Lieutenant Bloomfield. Bloomfield asked why he came to him, and if he thought he had it. "No," said Hand, "but I thought you could put me in the way of finding it." The lieutenant told him that he would learn to find another gun when he had lost his, or he would find it charged against him. We soon learned that the only way for a soldier to replace a lost article was to go and find a similar one.

One day the men of Company G were overheard complaining to Lieutenant Lawrence that their property kept disappearing. "Well," said Lawrence, "here you are between Companies B and E, and I have often told you that they were the worst thieves in the regiment. Now you will either have to look out for your things, pay for them when lost, or steal others."

Colonel McAllister was a firm believer that "cleanliness was next to godliness," and, after taking command of the regiment, gave it ample opportunities for bathing. One evening the right wing and the next evening the left would be marched to the prison basin (then surrounded by a high board-fence). This event was enjoyed by all, and particularly by the boys who would get a daily swim by stealing out with some other company.

At first the camp was anything but a place of quietness. But as it filled up and officers reported to their commands, order began to appear, and drills, inspections, &c., became the daily routine. With few exceptions the men submitted quietly to the discipline that was to make them fit for the more responsible duties of a soldier's life. Every effort was made to keep intoxicating liquors out of camp, but in spite of every precaution it would be often smuggled in, with the result that some poor slave of appetite would find his way to the guard-house.

The camp was frequently visited by agents for bullet-proof vests, which articles were at first looked upon with considerable favor. A few of the men purchased, and thought they had secured a protection against the bullets of the enemy. Some of the shrewder ones suggested a practical test, to which an agent, either ignorant of the quality of his goods or strong in his belief of their invulnerability, consented. The vests were taken to the sand-bank, at the eastern end of the camp, and stood against the bank. A few well-directed shots proved their uselessness. They were thoroughly riddled, and the agent, completely crest-fallen, quietly disappeared.

At Camp Perrine Colonel McAllister inaugurated the Sunday services, which were maintained until the close of the war whenever opportunity offered. Every pleasant Sunday the regiment would be marched to the green, in front of the prison, where religious services would be held. As Chaplain Knighton did not join the regiment until near the time of its departure for Virginia, these services were conducted by visiting clergymen. The men were also allowed, under proper escort, to attend evening services in the churches of the city.

Of the thirty-nine officers of the regiment, eighteen had seen more or less service. The Colonel, Robert McAllister, had won distinction as Lieutenant-Colonel of the First New Jersey Volunteers. His fitness for command had been proven on the hard-fought battle-fields of the Peninsula. Lieutenant-Colonel Stephen Moore had held the same rank in the Third New Jersey (three months) Volunteers. Major Valentine Mutchler had been promoted from Captain of Company D, First New Jersey Volunteers. Adjutant John Schoonover was also a Peninsular veteran, having served as private and Corporal in Company D, First New Jersey, and been promoted to Commissary Sergeant of that regiment, gaining his promotion by competitive examination. Chief Surgeon E. L. Welling had been promoted from Assistant Surgeon of the Third New Jersey. Captain Luther Martin had held commission as Second Lieutenant of Company A, First New Jersey Volunteers, and Captain William Meeker had been promoted from Corporal of the same company. Captain William B. Dunning had served as Captain of Company K, Second New Jersey (three months) Volunteers.

Among the Lieutenants, Andrew Ackerman and John F Buckley had been promoted from privates in Company I, Second New Jersey Volunteers; Lott Bloomfield, from private in the Twentieth Indiana; Alexandre Beach, from private in Company K, Second New Jersey; Sydney M. Layton had held a like commission in the President's Guard; Milton S. Lawrence had come from the Fourteenth Indiana, where he had held the rank of private; Ira W Corey was promoted from Sergeant of Company K, Seventh New Jersey Volunteers; Wm. S. Provost from Sergeant-Major of the First; John Oldershaw had been connected with the famous Seventh New York, and E. S. E. Newberry had distinguished himself while a private in Company D, Third New Jersey. In an encounter with a raiding party of the enemy's cavalry he had been severely wounded in the left side and arm, and when commissioned First Lieutenant of Company E, of the Eleventh, his left arm was practically useless.

Beside these, many of the non-commissioned officers and privates had been out with the various three-months organizations, so that the regiment was not entirely lacking in knowledge gained in the school of the soldier.

To be sure, the majority when they enlisted were practically ignorant of military matters. They knew that soldiers were expected to fight, and that infantry carried muskets, but they had yet to learn how to handle them according to the rules of the Manual. The majority were young and willing to learn, and by the time the regiment left Trenton the awkwardness peculiar to recruits had in a great measure disappeared.

Perhaps no regiment that ever left the State of New Jersey presented greater physical contrasts than did the Eleventh.

In it was seen the strong, broad-shouldered man, whom years of toil and endurance had hardened, and the slender, unformed youth who had yet to feel the first weight of life's burden. Two-thirds of those composing the regiment had not reached the age of twenty-one, and many were under seventeen—in fact so many were the youths that it was called a regiment of boys—and many people laughed at the idea of such troops doing efficient service. They did not stop to think that the spirit that prompted those boys to leave the love and comfort of home would sustain them through the weariness of the march and the dangers of the battle better than the brawn and muscle of their older comrades. It was a regiment of boys until Fredericksburg and Chancellorsville made it a regiment of men. After the desperate fighting at Chancellorsville there was no more sneering at the youthful *personnel* of the Eleventh.

CHAPTER II.

On to Washington—Camp Ellsworth—Guarding Convalescent Camp.

AFTER the final muster into the United States service, the regiment was in daily expectancy of being ordered to the front. At last the order came to move on August 25th. Many of the friends and relatives had learned the date of the regiment's departure, and when the morning came they hastened to the camp to bid the departing ones farewell.

The Trenton and Bordentown Branch of the Camden and Amboy Railroad ran along the southwestern side of the camp, and there the cars were halted that were to bear the regiment southward. About eleven o'clock the order was given to board the cars, farewells were quickly spoken, and amid mingled cheers and tears, the train moved toward Camden.

Philadelphia was reached about three o'clock. After an abundant dinner at the Cooper refreshment saloon, the regiment marched to the Philadelphia and Wilmington depot, where it took train for Washington, followed by the cheers and well-wishes of many patriotic citizens of Philadelphia.

It passed through Wilmington about six o'clock, crossed the Susquehanna at eleven, and reached Baltimore at one o'clock on the morning of the 26th. There the regiment left the cars, and after being refreshed with very poor rations, the men made themselves as comfortable as possible until seven o'clock, when they once more took the cars for the last stage of their journey to the capital, which was reached about eleven A. M.

After dining at the soldiers' retreat the regiment fell into line, marched through the city and crossed the long bridge to Arlington Heights. The streets of Washington being very dusty, and the day extremely warm, this first march resulted in a number of sun-strokes.

The regiment's first encampment south of the Potomac overlooked the capital, and, in honor of the Secretary of State, it was named Camp Seward.

The stay at Arlington was not destined to be a very long one. On August 27th the regiment received orders to be in readiness for marching. Tents were struck, knapsacks packed, and all things made ready; but the 28th found us still in the same position. A heavy shower of rain coming up on the 28th, tents were hastily pitched again. At three A. M. on the morning of the 29th marching orders were renewed, and by daylight the camp had disappeared, breakfast had been eaten, and the regiment was on the move. The line of march led down to and up the Potomac to the aqueduct; across the aqueduct to Georgetown; then up the Potomac to the chain bridge. There we found a New York regiment on guard, who, in anticipation of an advance of the enemy in that direction, had removed the flooring of the bridge. The planks were temporarily relaid, and the regiment quickly crossed to the Virginia side, where the march was resumed in the direction of Leesburg. After marching some miles it filed to the right of the road and stacked arms. The officers were called to the front and center and addressed by the Colonel, who gave some words of advice and caution, companies were inspected and the ammunition equally distributed.

Far away on the famous field of Bull Run the two armies were again struggling for the mastery. All day long we could hear the boom of artillery. What would be the result? And why should we lie there inactive while comrades were being swept away by the tide of the enemy? Such were the questions we asked each other. With the zeal of inexperience we were anxious to measure strength with the foe. We did not stop to think that perhaps it was as important to have us occupying the position we then held as it would to have had us upon the battlefield.

The next day Pope's shattered and defeated forces marched by us, and as regiment after regiment filed past, with tattered battle-flags and soiled and bloody clothing, the majority of us, perhaps for the first time, began to realize what war really meant.

Dejected by defeat, tired and footsore, hungry and dusty, the heroes of the Peninsula and Bull Run soon dispelled any exalted idealisms that we may have held in regard to the life of a soldier.

Fresh from the comfort and plenty of home, possessing yet an abundance of all things necessary for comfort and cleanliness, it was hard to realize that we should in a short time be as destitute of these things as were the shattered and tired troops then marching past us.

While in this position along the Leesburg road the regiment was made acquainted with the condition of army bacon after long service in government store-houses. A quantity of it was issued to the regiment, but it took a vigilant guard to keep it from taking French leave and marching out of camp. I doubt if much of it was used, for at that early period the boys had not become accustomed to eating their meat alive.

At nine P M. the regiment was ordered to move. It was an all-night trip, for it was not until sunrise that it went into camp near Fort Marcy. No particular name was given to that encampment. It was generally denominated "Camp near Fort Marcy" While there the time was employed in drilling, guard, picket and other duties. An occasional detail was sent to Fort Ethan Allen, which lay some distance to the left.

Near the camp was a field of growing corn, which the boys soon found was about right for roasting, and though orders were given not to touch it and guards were placed to watch it, yet many a mess of green corn found its way to camp. There the old Austrian rifles that had been issued by the State were exchanged for the Harper's Ferry or Springfield musket, which carried a ball and three buckshot.

One evening, while in the vicinity of Fort Marcy, a detail consisting of a corporal and two privates was called for from Company B, and Corporal Aaron Lines and Privates William and Henry Hand were sent. Their instructions were to go up the

Major Thomas J. Hulsey.

road about one mile, where they were told they would find a hay-stack, guard it through the night, and keep the horses of the cavalry from eating the hay. They found the stack, and near it a house where a woman was selling pies and cakes to the passing soldiers. They informed her that they had been sent there to guard her house and would like some supper, whereat she furnished them an excellent meal. After eating they proceeded to the hay-stack, climbed on top and went to sleep. The entire party slept soundly and until long after daylight. When awakened they had but little trouble in getting off the stack, as it had diminished in height to about four feet and had spread out amazingly Around it stood about twenty horses busily engaged in putting away the fodder, while a short distance away lay the riders on beds of hay. They returned to camp and reported no hay-stack within four miles.

At two o'clock on the afternoon of September 7th the regiment broke camp and marched to Alexandria; passing through the city it took a position near Fort Lyons, on the heights beyond Hunting creek. On September 12th a member of Company H was wounded in the foot by the accidental discharge of his gun. From there it moved in the direction of Mount Vernon, and established "Camp Advance," where it did picket duty in connection with the Second New Jersey Brigade.

On September 14th it was moved to a point on the Alexandria and Fairfax road near Fort Worth, where it established "Camp Grover"; there, in addition to the ordinary routine of camp duty, it was made acquainted with the pick and shovel as applied to the building of fortifications. A mile or two out on the Fairfax road stood an old cider-mill, which no doubt some of the boys will call to mind from the fact that, having stolen from camp and stolen some apples, they were caught, while busily engaged in making cider, by Colonel McAllister, who happened to be passing that way with a picket detail. He took their names and sent them to camp, with the promise of punishment when he should return; but the offense was either forgotten or forgiven, for no punishment followed.

On September 30th the regiment moved to near Fort Ellsworth. The special duty to which it was assigned was that of guarding the convalescent camp and camp of paroled prisoners. An incident occurred here which served to indicate that fearlessness of danger and obedience to duty for which the regiment was afterwards characterized. The camp of paroled prisoners contained at that time between three and four thousand men—men from many States and from many regiments—men of various dispositions and temperaments. In a collection of this number many can always be found who are impatient of restraint, and who deem it an insult to be kept within bounds by troops who have seen less service than themselves.

It occurred that, while Lieutenant John Oldershaw with a detail of twenty-five men were on duty at the camp—the Colonel commanding it being absent, and a young and inexperienced officer had been left in charge—a large number of men had been sent to Alexandria to be transported to their regiments, but by some mistake no means of transportation was ready, and they were ordered back to the camp. Without waiting for orders, they broke ranks and scattered all over the country, yelling and howling, the worst characters inciting the rest. As soon as the old guard had been relieved and the reserve placed in position in rear of the Colonel's tent, the commanding officer approached Lieutenant Oldershaw and told him that they expected to have trouble in the camp that night. Oldershaw then instructed his men to rally with the reserve in case there should be a riot.

There were several chests of arms in the Colonel's tent, and also a number of axes. The new sutler had just brought up a quantity of stores and erected a new building in which to put them.

It was learned that it was the intention of the men to set fire to the store-house; in fact, toward night the situation began to look serious, and the guards were doubled around the store-house and instructions given to shoot any one who showed a disposition to commit depredations, and, in case of an alarm, all were to rally on the reserve. Everything remained quiet until between twelve and one o'clock, when two or three shots were fired, and almost immediately the store-house was in a blaze. Oldershaw, with some of his men, hurried quickly to the fire and tried to save some of the goods, but the building burned so fiercely that it was impossible to save anything.

By that time the camp was filled with a howling mob bent on mischief. They began to press forward toward the Colonel's tent, their object no doubt being to secure the arms and axes stored there.

The guard in the meantime, according to instructions, had left their post and rallied on the reserve.

Oldershaw posted his men in front of the Colonel's tent, then, stepping out, addressed the mob, telling them that if they did not disperse he would fire upon them. His words were met with howls of derision. Stepping back he instructed the rear rank to reserve their fire, then gave the order, ready, aim. He waited, thinking the mob would disperse, but they only pressed closer. The order was then given to fire. Echoing the volley came a cry of pain. The front rank began to re-load and the rear rank was about to fire, when the mob broke and ran to their quarters. The guards were posted again, and in a short time the regiment was upon the scene, but its services were not needed, for the riot was completely quelled.

While the regiment lay at Fort Ellsworth, it was sometimes visited by an old colored woman who made apple-dumplings a specialty, and carried them to the different camps for sale. One day as Lambert Sharp, of Company E, familiarly known "Bully," was sitting along the roadside under the shade of the locusts, Auntie appeared with her dumplings. They looked very tempting, and "Bully's" mouth fairly watered for a taste of them. She asked him if he did not want to buy some. He said "No"; he had no money. She remarked that that seemed to be the case with all the soldiers, but rather than take them back to Alexandria she would trade them for clothing. He asked her how many she would give for a pair of drawers. She answered, "Four." Stepping back among the trees "Bully" quickly divested himself of that article of underwear (the only pair that he owned, by the way) and handed them over to Aunty, who rolled them up and put them in the basket with the dumplings. She prepared his dumplings, which he quickly stored away, feeling well satisfied with the trade; and they no doubt were the only apple-dumplings he had the pleasure of eating while in Virginia.

On October 10th, while the regiment was encamped near Fort Ellsworth, Company E was sent into Alexandria to do guard duty over the commissary stores there collected. It was quartered in a long two-story brick building, formerly used for a cooper-shop. The ground floor was used for a dining-room and the upper floor for a sleeping apartment for the entire company, with the exception of the commissioned officers, who were quartered on the opposite side of the street. The company had no sinecure, as it required a detail of thirty men each day to fill all the posts.

One of the favorite places for doing duty was at the round-house of the Orange and Alexandria Railroad, then used as quarters for about three hundred contrabands who were employed around the docks. The quaint sayings and childish actions of the simple-minded Africans were a source of endless amusement to the guards.

Another post much sought after was the hay-yard. The forage stored there, by attracting the stray cows of the town, gave the boys an opportunity to get milk for their coffee.

It happened that one day, while two Hibernians, Riley O'Brian and James King, were on duty at the hay-yard, a dispute arose between them over some trivial matter. Epithets were hurled back and forth. At last they agreed to settle it according to the rules of the code duello. Muskets were to be the weapons—their positions were taken, and no doubt blood would have been shed had not one of the officers of the company opportunely arrived as the word to fire was about to be given.

Nearly opposite the quarters of Company E was a brick building occupied by a party of contrabands. Small-pox broke out among them. Several of the members of Company E caught the disease, and one of them, Gilbert Young, died of it.

On the evening of November 15th, Company E was ordered to re-join the regiment at Fort Ellsworth. Its departure was somewhat delayed, however, by the absence of a number of the men on an expedition organized by Lieutenant Newberry earlier in the evening. Some of the saloons in the city had been selling liquor to soldiers in defiance of orders to the contrary. Newberry had for a long time had his suspicions aroused in regard to one or two, situated not far from the company's quarters, and on the evening in question determined to investigate. Taking a number of men from the company as guards, he marched them to one of the suspected places and began a search. His efforts were at last rewarded by finding, snugly concealed in the bottom of a large ice-chest, a large quantity of whiskey conveniently bottled. It was the intention to destroy it, but in spite of the Lieutenant, a fair share of it found its way to the company's quarters, and as a result some of the men were not in very good shape for marching when the hour of departure came.

The regiment, in the meantime, had remained in camp near Fort Ellsworth, doing guard duty at the parole and convalescent camps, and sending escorts with troops to Washington and other points.

On October 9th, Lieutenant E. R. Good was ordered, with a detail, to escort thirteen hundred men to Harper's Ferry. He remained there over night with the Thirteenth Regiment, which was encamped on Maryland Heights, and returned to the regiment by way of Baltimore.

On October 15th, President Lincoln and body-guard, accompanied by General Heintzleman and staff, inspected the convalescent and parole camp.

On the 22d there was a review of the troops around Alexandria by President Lincoln, Vice-President Hamlin and other distinguished officers.

B

Chapter III.

Joining Carr's Brigade—The March to Falmouth—Battle of Fredericksburg.

On November 16th, the regiment was attached to the First Brigade (General Carr's), Second Division, Third Corps, and, strapping our shelter-tents on our backs for the first time, we bid farewell to the capacious Sibleys and started on the way to Falmouth. The first day's march took us to Fairfax Court House, where we lay until the 18th, when, with another regiment of infantry and a battery of artillery, we resumed our march as guards to a large train of baggage-wagons and ambulances. We were in heavy marching order, carrying three days' rations, forty rounds of ammunition, and knapsacks well packed, not only with the things necessary to a soldier's comfort, but with many mementoes of home. How we clung to all the keepsakes that loving friends had given us, fondly imagining at that stage of our experience that we would be able to keep them with us as reminders of those whom we had left behind! But few of those mementoes were ever seen again by those whose love prompted the giving.

About one o'clock it began raining, and we soon learned how contemptible the sacred soil could become when thoroughly moistened and trodden by the feet of marching columns.

It was nine o'clock in the evening when the order was given to halt for the night. Filing into a field, we soon turned field to common by converting rebel rails into Union caloric.

At half-past eight on the morning of the 19th the march was resumed. About twelve o'clock we reached the Occoquan at Wolf run shoals. The stream was about fifty or sixty yards wide and from one to two feet deep, the bottom covered with loose, slippery stones, making it somewhat difficult to ford—which was the only way to cross. The men took off their shoes and stockings, and, rolling up their trousers, rather reluctantly entered the nearly ice-cold water. After reaching the southern shore the march was continued for about half a mile, when the regiment went into camp and were told that they would remain there for several days.

Near this place were a number of abandoned rebel camps; the stockades were left standing, which seemed to indicate either a hurried departure or an intention to return and re-occupy them. In searching among the *debris* several bowie-knives were found, and numerous letters from their Southern friends which expressed anything but sentiments of love for the trespassing Yankees.

The first night of the regiment's stay near Wolf run, Company E spent upon picket.

The commissariat of the company showed a lack of meat, and consequently there was considerable grumbling. To remedy this deficiency Lieutenant Newberry took Corporal Ackerman and private A. B. Searing and started on a foraging expedition. After considerable hunting they succeeded in bagging quite a fine porker. After removing the entrails they tied its feet together and, running their guns through, carried it back to the picket-line; there it was hung to a sapling and skinned, as there were no facilities for following the usual method of scalding. It was cut up and divided among the pickets, and though not very fat it made an acceptable addition to their bill of fare.

In speaking of a *fine* Southern hog, in those days, the word was not applied as it would be in the North. Here it would mean a plethora of fat. There the points to be considered were much the same as those in a greyhound—length of leg, narrowness of back, and an ability to run away from anything slower than a minnie-ball or a streak of lightning.

There was one acquaintance we made while in the army who clung "closer than a brother." He was not exactly a permanent companion, yet his visits were so frequent and his stay at times so long that he became a bore. His disposition was surly and unappreciative, for, notwithstanding the fact that we furnished him with comfortable quarters and an abundance of rations, even at the expense of our own comfort, he would back-bite whenever he got an opportunity. He was universally known, as well by the general on his horse as the private tramping along through the mud and dust; but I can not truthfully say that he was universally respected, for he had but little respect for others. His habits were very intrusive, and no hour nor place was too sacred

Surgeon Edward L. Welling.

for his presence. He would startle the picket on his post and waken the tired soldier from his much-needed slumbers. Neither had he any regard for the personal property of others. If a soldier drew a new suit of clothing, he would appropriate it with as much nonchalance as if it had been procured for his especial benefit. He was a close student of dermatology, and took especial delight in poring over the pores of the human cuticle. His inquiries sometimes became so pointed that there would be bad blood between us. We would often try to shake him off and leave him behind, but he would return with overtures so pertinacious that we would have to come to the scratch—argument was in vain. All our efforts to turn him away proved futile.

We first met him at Alexandria, where he was introduced to us as the "old army greyback," and though not with us constantly from that time to the expiration of our service, his visits were too frequent to permit of warm friendship. He was very fond of waltzing, and his movements were particularly lively after a rain. I suppose he thought that exercise was the best preventive of colds.

The first night of our stay at Wolf run was damp and disagreeable, and large fires were kept burning. At one of these stood a member of Company E, familiarly known as "Bully." As his wet clothing began to dry and the warmth to penetrate, he was observed to gently slap one leg, and then the other, varying the slap by scratching motions up and down the seams of his trousers. This interesting pantomime was watched for some time in silence. At last one of his comrades asked, "Bully, what's the matter?" Turning upon the inquirer a look of supreme scorn, while reaching over his shoulder and trying to grasp the center of his spine, he answered, "Why, it's that confounded tetter." Comment was unnecessary; he'd just begun to make their acquaintance.

This same "Bully" (or Lambert Sharp) became one of the most notable foragers in the regiment. He became so expert that he could catch anything that was edible, and ofttimes things that were not. He began catching almost as soon as he struck Southern soil. He caught a sun-stroke while marching through Washington, which left him unconscious, and was picked up and put into a baggage-wagon, taken over the Potomac and dumped out near camp, minus everything his pockets had contained except a Testament; but he came around all right in a few days.

When in camp near Fort Lyons, "Bully" caught the black measles, which came very near ending his soldiering. While stopping at Wolf run he, with a number of others belonging to Company E, caught the varioloid, and was left there in charge of a nurse. As they began to convalesce, provisions ran short, and "Bully" started out to replenish the larder. Taking his gun he sauntered toward the creek. After hunting around for awhile he discovered a dog, and thinking it would suffice in the absence of other provisions, was about to shoot, when a wagon came in sight from the direction of Fairfax. It proved to be the regimental sutler, who gathered the party up, and, in consideration of their acting as guards to the front, fed them until they reached the regiment.

One day, while the regiment was encamped near Fort Ellsworth, a number of the men were discussing the difficulty of getting liquor from Alexandria. Sergeant Smith, of Company I, who was one of the party, volunteered the assertion that he could go into the city in broad daylight, without any pass, and bring out a dozen canteens full. Every one expressed a doubt of his being able so to do. To prove its practicability, he got a knapsack, placed the empty canteens inside, then taking an unarmed man to carry the knapsack and a file of men to guard him, he marched the man into the city as a prisoner to be delivered to the Provost Marshal. Going to a saloon he had his canteens filled, and marched back in the same manner, without being disturbed by guard or provost.

While the regiment lay at Alexandria, it was honored by having three of its officers placed on detached service. Captain Kearney, of Company A, was detailed as engineer; Grover, of Company F, as inspector of fortifications, and Lieutenant John Oldershaw as Aid to General Slough, then Military Governor of the city.

Among those left in hospital at Alexandria when the regiment started for Falmouth was William Hand and Aaron Lines, of Company B. They were anxious to be with the regiment, and though not fit for duty they deserted the hospital and started after it. They were nearly exhausted, when a drove of mules, on its way to the front, overtook them. Each mounted a mule and rode to within a short distance of camp. The first intimation that they had of nearness to the regiment was the voice of Dixon, the Company Commissary, drawing rations.

On November 25th the regiment again broke camp, and after a tiresome march of about twelve miles reached the village of Dumphries, where it went into bivouac for the night.

Dumphries was situated on the Quantico creek, about two and one-half miles from its mouth, and previous to the war had been quite a thriving and prosperous place. It contained a woolen factory, flour-mill, several stores, and two churches, and carried on quite a trade with Baltimore and Washington. But everything showed the marks of decay, scarce a hundred inhabitants remaining, and they mostly women.

The march was resumed on the morning of the 26th, and continued past Stafford Court House to Aquia Creek, where the regiment bivouacked for the night. Late in the afternoon, when passing a farm near Stafford Court House, a number of fine sheep had been noticed, quietly feeding, not far from the highway.

Lieutenant Newberry says: "The Government did not furnish mutton as a part of our menu, and the vision of roast lamb and mutton stew went and came to each one of us as we marched on and on, two miles past that farm-house. To get some of that mutton was easy enough, but from the fact that the General had placed a safe-guard over that man's house, and especially on the mutton. But mutton we must have, yet how to get it was the question. So, after going into camp, I called a council of war on mutton. Every commander knows his trusty men, and knowing my men, I called to my tent 'Croppy' George Zindle, William Henderson, Bishop W Mains and two others whose names I have forgotten, and it was decided that if I would lead the charge they would follow. But I was officer of the day, and the police duty of that camp was solely in my hands until nine o'clock next morning. But the desire for roast mutton made it possible to plan for the emergency should any arise.

Sending for Lieutenant Lawrence, I unfolded to him my plans and got him to assume my duties, and in case I was called to headquarters he was to respond and report me sick in my quarters. This very thing happened, but on Lieutenant Lawrence's reporting me sick no suspicion arose. Well, we went to the field where the sheep were quietly grazing. Henderson was sent to fire a blank at the sheep in order to draw the safe-guard away from the house, and as soon as the report was heard out came the guard on double-quick to drive off the marauders. He came up to Henderson and said to him: 'I am safe-guard here, and you must not forage here.' One at a time we went up to where the two men were, until the safe-guard was quietly and unsuspectingly surrounded, six to one. Suddenly 'Croppy' seized the rifle of the safe-guard and I rammed the muzzle of my navy revolver, unloaded, under his nose, at which he quickly surrendered. We left 'Croppy' and Henderson to guard our prisoner while we turned our attention to the mutton. I took 'Croppy's' rifle while he took the rifle of the safe-guard to stand guard over the latter. The four of us fired four shots and killed five sheep, I running and cutting the throats of the five we had shot, when to my horror I heard the voice of the Provost Marshal of our corps ordering us to halt or he would fire on us, with the three guards he had with him. I well knew that the only chance I had against Captain Bates (that was his name) was to bluff him, and as he began to swear, I met him with his own language and just as big oaths and just as many men, and when he asked my regiment and corps, I told him I had orders from General Newton, of the Sixth Corps, to forage for headquarters mess, and pulling out a folded official paper (which was nothing but my guard detail for camp duty) and showing it to him in the darkness, he begged my pardon for seeming interference with an officer of another corps, and took his departure. Meanwhile 'Croppy' and Henderson had got out, leaving the safe-guard, but taking the cap off his piece and squirting tobacco-juice in the nipple of his rifle. We four returned to the dead sheep, threw them over the fence and dragged them down into the edge of a dark swamp, cut off the heads, took out the bowels, tied and slung the sheep on our rifles—four men carrying five sheep. While killing our sheep we heard some young pigs squealing as though being smothered. On our way back to camp our two guards, 'Croppy' and Henderson, found us and our burden was made lighter. Arriving at camp, I reported to Lieutenant Lawrence and sent him one carcass of mutton, and in return he sent me one fine pig for roasting. His men were killing the pigs while we were getting the sheep. Next day a very fine quarter of mutton was served on the table of our Colonel, the lamented Robert McAllister, Eleventh New Jersey Volunteers. But that noble commander went to his eternal reward never knowing how or from whence that mutton came."

I have in mind another foraging expedition in which Newberry participated—the particulars of which I cannot now recall —but I know that among the spoil brought in were two old geese, which he afterwards described as "being too tough to even make soup."

On the morning of the 27th of November, after constructing a temporary bridge on which to cross Aquia creek (the former one having been destroyed), the march was again taken up toward Falmouth. After a tiresome march, camp was formed midway between Potomac creek and the Rappahannock river, and not far from Brooke's station, on the Richmond and Potomac Railroad.

Thinking their stay there would be a long one, the men began to make themselves as comfortable as possible by erecting log huts, &c.

Near this camp was an orchard and farm-house, which formed a convenient accessory to what then seemed a favorite manœuvre of the Colonel's when having the regiment on battalion drill. Scarcely a day passed that it was not put through the manœuvre of breaking to the right and left to pass the obstacle, and, from that circumstance, the camp came to be known as "Camp Obstacle."

On the 4th of December the regiment participated in a review of the Third Army Corps by General Hooker and others. The review was held on the heights near Falmouth, and in full view of the city of Fredericksburg.

Falmouth, the grand rendezvous of the Army of the Potomac, was situated on the left bank of the Rappahannock river, nearly opposite Fredericksburg. The land surrounding it was high, with a gradual slope to the river. Previous to the war it had a population of between four and five hundred, and contained about eighty dwelling-houses, one church, six flour and grist mills, stores, machine shops, &c.

Fredericksburg, which lay on the plain along the south bank of the river, was a city of about five thousand inhabitants. It contained numerous factories and mills, which, until the arrival of the Union army on the opposite heights, had been kept busy turning out clothing and subsistence for the rebel army.

On the 21st of November, General Sumner made a formal demand for the surrender of the city, alleging as a reason that his troops had been fired upon from the houses, and that the mills and factories were employed in giving aid and comfort to the rebel army.

Mayor Slaughter responded in behalf of the citizens, stating that the firing had been done by soldiers of the rebel army having no residence in the city; that the mills and factories should be stopped at once, but that the city could not be surrendered, as the generals in command of the rebel forces had forbidden it; that they neither intended to occupy the city themselves, nor to allow the Union army to do so.

On December 10th the monotony of the camp was broken by the receipt of orders to prepare for marching—three days' rations and sixty rounds of ammunition were issued—but it was not until the morning of the 11th when the first gun was heard that signaled the opening of the Fredericksburg slaughter, that the order came to fall-in.

While standing in line, listening to the dull boom of the cannon, and awaiting the order to march, Bishop W Mains, of

Company E, began to sing the "Star Spangled Banner." One by one the men caught up the words, and soon the morning air was musical with the strains of that grand battle-hymn.

It was a scene suggestive of the martyr's ecstacy at the stake, or the savage's indifference to the torture. Men pouring forth their voices in song while awaiting orders that were to usher them perhaps to bloody graves.

It was a beautiful morning, that morning of the first attack upon Fredericksburg; the sun rose bright in an almost unclouded sky, the slight sprinkling of snow that covered the ground sparkled like burnished silver, the air was clear and crisp—nature gave an almost perfect morning to be the harbinger of scenes that sent a thrill of horror through the nation and brought tears and sorrow to thousands of households.

At eight A. M. the order was given to move. The line of march was taken toward the river below the city. At half-past ten the regiment halted on the high ground on the north bank of the river, overlooking the field of operations.

On the 12th the regiment was marched by a circuitous route to Franklin's Crossing and halted near the pontoon bridge. The scenes there witnessed were terrible indeed to those not yet inured to the horrors of the battle-field. From the field of death beyond the river came a constant stream of wounded. Ambulance after ambulance, loaded down with shattered humanity, was driven hastily to the rear. Men with lesser wounds limped by, some using muskets for crutches, others being helped to a place of safety by comrades eager enough to leave the battle behind them.

On the morning of the 14th the regiment was ordered to cross the river and take position in the second line of battle, but it was soon ordered to the front line to relieve the Twenty-sixth Pennsylvania; two companies, D and I, Captains Luther Martin and John T. Hill commanding, being detailed to relieve the pickets of the Twenty-sixth Pennsylvania. As they marched out to take position, the enemy poured upon them a galling picket-fire. Though it was their first experience, their "baptism of fire," they did not falter, but as coolly and as steadily as veterans marched to their position, and even drove the enemy's pickets a short distance. A brisk picket-fire was kept up by the opposing lines.

Early in the morning the enemy had attempted to place a

Major Philip J. Kearney.

battery in front of their main line, so as to command the position of our brigade, but a company of riflemen from the Second New Hampshire, who had taken an advance position, made it so warm for them that they quickly sought shelter. About noon a suspension of hostilities was agreed upon, that the wounded and dead of both sides might be collected.

Then occurred one of the strange sights of the war—one that took from the battle-field a little of its horror, and seemed to turn for a while the crimson robe of carnage to the white hue of peace. From the picket-lines on either side the men advanced and held friendly converse, seemingly forgetful of the fact that but a few minutes before they had been endeavoring to take each other's lives, and in a few minutes more they would again be intent upon the same purpose. Papers and other articles that could be spared were exchanged for Southern tobacco—an article that was always in demand. In two or three instances friends of ante-war days met and discussed the situation. But soon the truce was ended and the work of death again began.

Near our skirmish line was the ruins of a house that had been destroyed by fire. The chimney remained nearly intact. One of our men, thinking it a favorable position, climbed to the second story, and, safely hidden in the remains of a capacious fire-place, picked off the enemy at leisure.

Companies D and I were relieved by other companies of the regiment in the evening, but their numbers had been lessened—Christopher Graham, of Company I, and Warren Green, of Company D, had been killed; John Williamson, of Company D, mortally wounded. He died on the 15th. The wounded were Peter Burk, George Davis, Edward B. Nelson and George Barnett, of Company D.

After the shades of night had hidden us from the watchful eyes of the enemy we took the bodies of our fallen comrades, and, wrapping their blankets around them, laid them to rest in soldiers' hastily-made graves. A few remarks, a brief prayer, and the ceremony was ended; but the solemnity of the occasion will never be forgotten, for, though disease had made vacancies in our ranks, and we had followed a number of our comrades to the grave, these were the first to die in actual conflict, and, despite any assumed carelessness, the question would arise, "Who next?"

But little fighting occurred on December 15th, and about ten o'clock P M. the regiment received orders to quietly recross the river, Burnside having determined to withdraw his army.

It was near midnight when the regiment went into bivouac on a wooded hill some distance from the river. It had begun to rain heavily, but despite the fact that but little rest was to be obtained, the men were heartily glad to be once more upon the north bank of the river, and away from the battle-field.

Previous to the truce at noon on the 14th, scarcely one of the enemy could be seen, but as soon as the truce was declared the woods seemed to swarm with rebels.

Among the members of Company B who were at that time on the skirmish-line, and about to be relieved, was an Irishman named John Smith. As the company rose to march back to the regiment, Smith discharged his gun toward the enemy. Captain Meeker grabbed him by the throat and asked him what he meant by firing upon a flag of truce. His answer was: "Begorra, Captain dear, haven't I been lying here this two hours widout a shot at the ribs, and do you think I was going back widout hitting one, if I could?" Fortunately, he did not hit one, and the company had the pleasure of marching back instead of crawling.

About noon on the 16th, the regiment resumed its march toward the old camp, which was reached about sundown. The 17th was spent in resting from the fatigue of the campaign, and in trying to restore to order the dilapidated camp.

On the 18th the regiment started on a three days' tour of picket duty. Returning to camp on the 21st, it took up the old routine of duty—drilling, guard, etc. At dress-parade on the 23d the following order was read to the regiment:

"HEADQUARTERS ELEVENTH N. J. VOLS.
"CAMP NEAR FALMOUTH, Dec. 23d, 1862.

"It is with feelings of pride that I congratulate you on your bearing on all the hard marches of the past campaign, and particularly on the bravery and gallantry you displayed on the field of battle before the heights of Fredericksburg. I would say to those of you who were under that galling picket-fire, when the eyes of thousands of our comrades were upon you, and like old veterans stood the raging storm of battle, not only holding, but gaining ground—I would say you deserve my warmest praise.

"We sorrow over the remains of our gallant dead who fell by our side, and sympathize with their loved ones at home, trusting that God will bear them up in their bereavement. We have before us the consoling fact that they died as brave soldiers, fighting for their country. And that those of *our* day and posterity will do them justice.

"To the wounded I would say, bear up under your afflictions with the cherished hope that in the providence of God you will soon be able to join us, and assist in more successful encounters to put down the rebellion and restore peace to our land.

"R. McALLISTER,
"*Col. Commanding.*
"JOHN SCHOONOVER,
"*Adjt.*"

When the regiment crossed the river to the battle-field, Thaddeus O. Doane, of Company B, accompanied it, although he was a very sick man at the time. His condition grew steadily worse, yet he kept with his company. On the night of the 15th, when the regiment re-crossed the river, he was unable to accompany it and was left on the field. Next day, however, he in some way managed to get over and to the hospital, where he spent weeks of suffering, battling with typhoid fever. He eventually recovered, but never fully regained his health.

We settled down in the old camp with the intention of making it a permanent winter quarters, and I think that few anticipated a change until the spring campaign should open. We were situated near the center of the army, conveniently to be sent either to the right or left, as the exigencies of the service might demand, close to Brooke's Station, then a field depot of supply for the army. In fact, thinking that our position would remain unchanged for at least a few months, many of the men began the construction of rather elaborate quarters. They forgot that one of the greatest essentials to a soldier's comfort in winter was day by day becoming more scarce—that was, an ample supply of fuel. It required from a hundred and fifty to two hundred fires to a regiment for the purpose of warmth and cooking. This number, multiplied by the number of regiments in a brigade, division and corps, called for the consumption of a vast quantity of wood, and forests near an encampment disappeared as if by magic.

It was the intention of the Quartermaster to have the camps supplied with fuel by the teams, but owing to the bad state of the roads they were kept busy hauling other supplies, barely enough being hauled to supply the cooks and officers. As a consequence, the men had to carry the wood for their private fires or suffer from the cold. That was no hardship so long as the forests were near, but when all within easy reach had been cut down, it became a heavy burden.

The stumps first left by the inexperienced soldiers presented a comical appearance to the skilled woodsman. Many of the boys had had but little experience in felling trees, and their first attempt would result in leaving stumps standing from two to three feet high, depending upon the height of the chopper. But the high stumps formed a desirable aftermath, for when standing trees began to grow scarce, *they* were subject to a second chopping, so that by the time the soldiers were done with them but little remained above ground.

As the forests would not move nearer the troops, it seemed necessary to move the troops to the forests. So on January 3d, 1863, the division was moved to a wooded ridge on the Fitzhugh estate, three miles below Falmouth.

CHAPTER IV.

Camp Fitzhugh—First Winter Quarters.

THE SITE selected for the new camp was on a timbered hillside, admirably located for drainage, and also well adapted to give the men a sufficiency of exercise in cleaning away the growth that obstructed the company streets, which were laid out up and down the hill, while the tents of the officers occupied the top of the ridge.

With few tools, and less experience, the men endeavored to construct habitations that would partially secure them from the winds and storms of winter. The styles of architecture were varied with the dispositions or skill of the builder. Some who were skilled in the use of the axe built for themselves log cabins, which, if not sightly, were at least comparatively comfortable. Others, with either less skill or energy, dug square pits, and placed a log or two around the top to retain an embankment sufficient to throw off the water. In either case shelter-tents formed the roof.

On January 5th, the division to which the Eleventh belonged was reviewed by General Burnside and others. Nothing again broke the routine of camp duties until the 20th of January, when the regiment received marching orders. At one o'clock P M. it started in the direction of United States ford on the Rappahannock. After marching about three miles it was ordered to halt and await orders. About 9 P. M., in the midst of a pouring rain, orders were received to return to camp.

Morning brought no abatement of the storm, but, notwithstanding, eight o'clock found the division again in motion, fairly started on what will ever be known as Burnside's "Mud March." Ten miles were made that day over roads that were neither land nor water, but the most contemptible conglomeration that it was ever the fate of men to wade through. Seldom was it less than shoe-top deep, and occasionally the men would sink nearly to their knees. It was useless to seek for solid ground, for there was none. The ten hours of rain that had preceded the movement had turned the ordinarily good roads into sluiceways of mud, in which wagons and artillery became so deeply mired that two and three times the usual number of animals could drag them only at a snail's-pace, and in many instances they had to be temporarily abandoned. The infantry took to the fields, but they found them but little better than the highways. After floundering along for ten miles, a comparatively firm spot was found and bivouac made for the night.

The regiment rested until noon of the 22d, when it, with the rest of the brigade, was ordered out to build corduroy roads, that the artillery and pontoons might return to camp. That work was continued on the 23d until noon, when orders were received to return to camp, which was reached a little after dark.

One of the results of the march was the replenishing of the hospital fund from the fines imposed on the stragglers. Every piece of woodland along the line of march was filled with those who had become tired of trying to force their way along the almost impassable roads, and had ordered a halt for themselves. The Eleventh Regiment furnished its full share of those who halted without orders, and after the movement had been abandoned, and the regiment was once more reposing in its old camp, the stragglers were called out in front of the regiment to hear their punishment, which consisted of fines of from four to ten dollars. No individual had need to feel lonesome—companions enough were there to keep him in countenance.

As the experience of one straggler was perhaps typical of all, I will give that of myself. The writer was one of eight from Company E who, when about seven miles out, became weary and halted by the wayside. We had reached an attractive piece of woodland, and concluded that it would be a good place to rest. We, at first, had no thought of remaining away from the regiment over night, but becoming convinced that the movement must prove a failure, and that the return of the regiment would be but a matter of a few hours, concluded to await it.

On the morning of the 22d it was proposed to follow on and overtake the regiment, but rumors reached us that the army was on its way back, and soon troops began to pass our bivouac. All day long and far into the night we kept a sharp lookout for the Second Division, but it did not come. In the meantime our provisions had become exhausted, with the exception of a well-filled haversack belonging to Lieutenant Newberry, which the writer had been carrying. Some of the party proposed eating what was in that, but the writer would not consent, dreading the wrath of Newberry more than the punishment he was likely to receive for straggling. So, with gnawings of hunger, we lay down to sleep. In the night, however, Gilbert, who was one of the party, helped himself to a portion of the Lieutenant's grub. Finding in the morning that the haversack had been despoiled of a portion of its contents, and the craving for something to eat being pretty strong, scruples were thrown aside and the remains shared and eaten.

About noon the head of the division came in sight. We made inquiries and found that the regiment was but a short distance behind. Thinking to beat it into camp, we started on a short cut. But, alas! for human calculations. Scarcely had we left the shelter of the wood when the mounted Provost captured us and marched us to General Patrick's headquarters. There our names and commands were taken, after which—the party having been recruited to a respectable size—we were forwarded under guard to the headquarters of General Sickles. He, with a generous allowance for the weakness of human nature and the trying circumstances, laughed at us and ordered us sent to our camps, which we reached a day or two later than the regiment. After a lecture from the Colonel and a promise of punishment, we were dismissed to our companies. There, about the first man met by the writer was Newberry, who greeted him with: "Oh you rascal! If I could have caught you that first night out, I would have almost killed you." He had cause to be angry, for he had been compelled to go among the boys and beg his supper.

Though the mud-march led to no battle, and consequently to no battle-losses, yet the loss of life that ultimately resulted was as great as that brought about by many actions. The long ex-

Major John T. Hill.

posure to the severe storm, the wearing of wet clothing day after day, and sleeping upon the sodden ground, laid the foundation of diseases that carried off many and made physical wrecks of many others.

Both men and officers were called upon to perform the most severe labor in corduroying roads, prying guns, wagons and pontoons out of the sloughs in which they were deeply mired. But, despite every effort, much valuable material had to be destroyed or abandoned; scores of mules were so deeply mired in the blue clay that it was impossible to extricate them, and they were either shot or cruelly left to their fate. One writer, speaking of the loss of animal life, says that "for months afterward, when going that route on picket, the smell from the decaying bodies was almost unendurable."

As has been stated, the regiment reached its old camp on the evening of the 23d, but the men were so nearly exhausted that they made no effort to put up tents that night, but wearily threw themselves on their roofless bunks and slept the sleep of the exhausted. On the 24th, tents were again stretched over the stockades, and the boys set about repairing the damages that had occurred during their absence.

The Adjutant, who enjoyed a little merriment occasionally, did not even permit the somber environments of the "Mud March" to stand in the way of perpetrating a joke upon the medical staff of the regiment. It came to his knowledge that the Hospital Steward, Geo. T. Ribble, afterward Assistant Surgeon of the regiment, had engineered, with the permission and connivance of the two Assistant Surgeons, the capture and slaughter of a fine young animal which had been discovered by a forager somewhere in the vicinity of the camp. Schoonover, who was somewhat of a penman, wrote the following order:

"HEADQUARTERS CARR'S BRIGADE.

"*Col. Robt. McAllister,*
"*Commanding Eleventh N. J. Vols.:*

"COLONEL.—It has been reported to these headquarters that a fine young cow, the property of a poor widow living near by, was taken from an enclosure last evening by a party in charge of the Hospital Steward of your regiment, driven into the woods and slaughtered. As this was in violation of existing orders, you will cause a thorough investigation to be made at once, and report the facts in the case to these headquarters.

"By command of
BRIG.-GEN. JOS. B. CARR.
"LEGRAND BENEDICT,
"*A. A. Gen.*"

Repairing to the Surgeon's tent, he read the order with unruffled countenance, and it is useless to add that it was listened to with profound consternation. In their seeming sad plight, they made an earnest appeal to the Adjutant to devise some means of extrication from their dilemma. After roasting them on the gridiron of anxiety for an hour or more, the "cat was let out of the bag," and so great was their joy at the happy turn of affairs that they offered no violence to the perpetrator of the joke.

About this time candles had become a scarce article, and the men had either to content themselves with the glare of pine knots or, remembering the lessons learned at home, procure tallow and make their own penny-dips; this many of them did.

Sunday, January 25th, brigade inspection was held; the day was clear, but very cold. The 27th brought rain, and what was more welcome, a visit from the paymaster. Much of the money was sent to families and friends in the north, by Colonel Cook, but the sutler, as usual, profited immensely by the coming of pay-day. The men becoming tired of the sameness of government rations—pork, beef, beans, and bread without butter—for a few days after receiving their money would live on sutler's goods, regardless of the high prices charged for them. Butter cost, then, 60 cents per pound; cheese, 40 cents; canned goods, from $1.00 to $1.25 per quart can; condensed milk, 75 cents for sizes that now sell for 10 cents, and other goods in proportion. It can readily be seen that the small pay of the private soldier did not allow a long indulgence in the luxuries of the sutler's tent. The system of giving orders upon the sutler that prevailed was a temptation to the men to spend more than they otherwise would have done. Each man was allowed orders upon the sutler for a certain amount per month. These were countersigned by the First Sergeant or some line officer. When pay-day came, the sutler would repair to the paymaster's tent and, as the men received their money, collect the amounts called for by the orders. There was seldom any friction, the men paying up willingly, and thus establishing a credit until next pay-day.

The weather became cold on the night of the 27th, and the rain turned to snow, which continued to fall during the 28th until the ground was covered to the depth of a foot. The 29th brought sunshine and warmth, and the snow melted rapidly, making the roads again almost impassable. At this period the supplies for the army of the Potomac were landed, either at Aquia Creek or Belle Plains. If at Aquia Creek, they could be brought by rail over the Fredericksburg and Aquia Creek Railroad to Brooke's Station. But from Belle Plains they had to be teamed to their various destinations. And notwithstanding the fact that an immense amount of corduroying was done, during a great part of the winter the roads were in such bad condition that the work of cartage was very heavy on both teams and teamsters.

The monotony of camp was not to remain long unbroken. On the evening of February 2d we received orders to be ready to move in light marching order at six the next morning. We were to carry three days' rations and sixty rounds of ammunition. The expedition consisted of six regiments of infantry, five batteries of artillery and two regiments of cavalry. The object of the expedition was to destroy bridges built by the enemy across the upper Rappahannock. The march began at the appointed time in the midst of a blinding snowstorm. The movement was attended with no fighting by us. But it tested pretty sorely the endurance and discipline of the troops who participated in it. Subjoined is a letter from "Quill," giving a spirited account of the movement.

"CAMP BELOW FALMOUTH, February 9th, 1863.

"On Saturday afternoon the Eleventh Regiment returned to camp from their second march above Falmouth, having experienced greater hardships than often fall to the lot of soldiers on similar expeditions.

"The order was received late on Wednesday night to provide three days' cooked rations, and be ready at six the next morning for special service.

"Accordingly, the cooks were aroused, and kept their fires burning and meat boiling all night, while the camp was far from being as quiet as usual.

"At six A. M. the regiment, in light marching trim, was formed on the parade-ground, under command of Lieutenant-Colonel Moore—Colonel McAllister being away on leave—and soon received marching orders, when it proceeded to brigade headquarters, and, joining the brigade, marched off in the direction of 'up the river.' It was soon apparent that the whole division—Sickles'—was included in the movement, and subsequently we were joined by two crack regiments of cavalry and three batteries of artillery, including Beam's Newark Battery.

"The air was exceedingly cold, and a light dry snow was falling.

"The troops marched rapidly forward until they reached the extreme picket-line of our forces on the right, where our brigade came to a halt and the Second New Jersey Brigade passed through.

"Many friends were recognized and congratulations exchanged, and the opportunity was soon after again afforded by our passing through the New Jersey Brigade.

"This movement was not understood, however, and our progress was rendered quite slow by its indulgence.

"The weather had now changed somewhat, and rain and sleet took the place of snow, but was not so well received.

"During the halts, which were many, the soldiers sought repose on the snow-covered ground, as the march had now become quite severe, and the wet and icy garments and blankets were far from adding comfort to 'the within.'

"About five P M. the expedition came to a halt and camped for the night in a wood on the Warrenton road, a little way beyond Hortwood church.

"A drizzling rain fell all night and rendered the condition of the soaked and chilled men truly miserable.

"Huge fires were made, and such shelters as green boughs could afford were erected, but little rest or sleep, however, could be obtained, and a whiskey ration, which was given out at midnight, found all awake to receive it. The old regiments from the

Peninsula admitted that they had never experienced so much exposure.

"The roll-call showed that the Eleventh had only two stragglers on this march, which was a highly gratifying circumstance to the commanding officer, who, at the outset, had made a few remarks in which he hoped that the men of the Eleventh would not be found lagging on the march. It is doubtful if any other regiment could show so clean a record.

"At six the next morning the expedition was again on foot, and after a march of about four miles the division was divided and stationed a short distance from the Rappahannock, in positions selected by Gen. Carr, who was in command of the reconnoissance.

"The Eleventh New Jersey and First Massachusetts were placed in a wood on a hillside on the right, with instructions to make as little noise as possible, keep small fires and be ready for service at a moment's notice.

"The First Massachusetts being in command of the Lieutenant-Colonel who was out-ranked by Lieutenant-Colonel Moore, the latter was in command of the movements in our vicinity until relieved by the Colonel of the Massachusetts regiment, who appeared during the day

"The weather continued remarkably stormy until near night, when it cleared off and became quite cold.

"Another uncomfortable night was passed near the camp-fires, the men vainly endeavoring to keep warm with their single blankets. The roads froze up solid, and when the order came to march on the return at early dawn, good progress was made for some hours.

"No war music was heard, and though it was said that the object of the expedition was accomplished, the men did not feel that they had performed any great feat, save in the exhibition of their powers of endurance.

"The march back to camp, so auspiciously begun, proved a very exhaustive one. An hour was lost early in the day waiting for another brigade, and so old 'Sol' soon got to work on the roads, rendering them very heavy. The loss of that golden hour was severely felt.

"The regiments all reached their quarters about four o'clock in the afternoon, but there was little stamina left in the men, as they were pushed through the mud at a pace awfully shocking to weak muscles. Never did a camp seem so much like home than when it was reached, after that tedious march and unusual exposure to the pitiless storms of mid-winter.

"We were informed by an order from the General commanding the division that the object of the movement was fully accomplished, and that the participators were entitled to the highest praise for the uncomplaining manner in which they performed a fatiguing march and suffered exposure to the severest storms of winter."

The cause of the movement was an attempted crossing of the river by a body of the enemy's cavalry. They had constructed a bridge and were about to cross, when they were met and repulsed by the Union cavalry. They made the second attempt, reinforced by a column of infantry, but were met by such a determined fire that they gave up the attempt. The bridge was destroyed and the expedition returned to camp.

On the return to camp, a ration of whiskey and a loaf of soft bread—making the third since November—revived somewhat the drooping spirits of the men.

On the 13th the regiment was ordered on picket ten miles away. Rations were issued before daylight, but when the "hard tack" came to be examined beneath the searching light of day they were found to be a curious but not very palatable combination of bread and meat, and the meat had not been killed. But as the men could not afford to be fastidious, they made the best of it, and picking out the larger "animals," shut their eyes to the smaller.

February 25th, snow again to about a foot in depth, making the roads almost impassable.

On Sunday, March 1st, a wagon loaded with boxes from home became mired about a mile from camp, but the men, to make sure of their delicacies, carried the boxes the rest of the distance.

On March 12th the regiment was again sent out on picket; it reached the lines and relieved the old pickets about noon. Those not on immediate duty busied themselves in building shelters of brush and collecting wood for the camp-fires, for the air was yet piercing enough to remind us that winter was still lingering.

An alarm in the night called all to arms, and a report that a large body of the enemy's cavalry was hovering near kept all on the *qui vive* until daylight.

It was ascertained afterward that the alarm was not entirely a groundless one, for a body of the rebel cavalry had passed swiftly to the north of us, fallen upon Fairfax Court House, captured Brigadier-General Stoughton and a portion of his brigade, and escaped before the troops in that vicinity fully realized what had occurred.

During the early part of the evening considerable excitement was caused on the reserve post by a conflagration which for a few minutes lit up the gloom of the forest.

Captain Halsey, of Company E, had caused to be erected a rather commodious shelter of pine boughs, which was fronted by a roaring fire of logs. Upon a bed of soft "Virginia feathers" the Captain lay, drinking in large draughts of soldier's comfort, when suddenly the resinous boughs around and above him went up in a blaze of glory, and it was not without difficulty that the Captain escaped a burning. Some mischievous soldier had slyly touched a brand to the inflammable material, and consequently the Captain was left without a shelter.

Camp-life was not without its pleasures and its humors. The days, although reasonably full of duties, left many idle hours to be spent as the inclinations of the men might dictate and circumstances permit. Groups would form and talk over matters current, or past, or speculate on the probabilites of the future.

Gambling was contrary to orders, yet card-playing was a favorite pastime with many, so much so that a pack of cards became known as a "soldier's testament." Bluff or poker was the favorite game, and it was not always played for beans, for the money-stakes were often sufficiently high to make the game intensely interesting to the participants. Others spent their idle hours with such literature as was obtainable in camp or conveniently forwarded by mail.

The readers, though perhaps not in the majority, constituted a large proportion of the men of the Eleventh. Books and periodicals would be passed from hand to hand until worn-out

Brevet Major Charles F. Gage.

with use or a move of the army compelled their abandonment. During the winter of '63 and '64, when at Brandy Station, Miss Anna Veghte, then of Stockton, Hunterdon county, N. J., among other things, sent the writer two years' numbers of the old "Knickerbocker Magazine." They were kept in constant circulation through the company and regiment until the breaking of camp, on May 4th, 1864, compelled their abandonment.

There were many convivial spirits among the brave men of the Eleventh, and the magnet of congeniality drew them into associations for pleasure and profit. One such was organized among the line officers during the winter of '62 and '63. And as *they* were *largely* a part of the regiment, the constitution and by-laws of that organization (which is subjoined) becomes a part of the regiment's history:

"CONSTITUTION AND BY-LAWS OF THE INDEPENDENT ORDER OF TRUMPS.

"*Preamble.*

"We, the undersigned free-born citizens of the United States, and other villages, feeling that a necessity exists for the universal development of mind, and muscle, hereby unite ourselves in a genial brotherhood, that is to say,

"'We're a band of brothers,'

having for its and our object the physical and mental welfare of man and woman, and circumstances at large, do bind ourselves by the following constitution and by-laws, being resolved to acquit ourselves like men, and other things.

"*Name.*

"The name, style and title of this association is and shall be, 'The Independent Order of Trumps.'

"*Officers.*

"The officers shall consist of a Grand Salaam, Right-Bower, Left-Bower, Drink-All, Eat-All, Smoke-All, Judge-Advocate and Door-Tender, who shall be elected at each meeting of the Order.

"*Qualifications for Membership.*

"Any white citizen who has risen above the scum of the earth, by virtue of holding a piece of sheepskin parchment, be it commission or warrant, shall be eligible to membership in this Order, save always those of loose moral character, such as Chaplains, Colonels, or senior Captains commanding. But no person shall be admitted or initiated into the mysteries and unwritten customs of the Order unless he, she or them shall produce in the presence of the Grand Salaam a box, or an authorized express certificate that a box is on the way and near at hand.

" Duties of Officers.

"It will be the duty of the G. S. to preside at all meetings and preserve order, if possible, in which he will be assisted by the Bowers Right and Left, who will be habitually posted on the right and left of the G. S. The duties of the Bowers will be to assist the G. S. and mediate between him and the members of the order. The duty of the Drink-All will be to test the quality and take note of the quantity of fluids on their arrival in the boxes of members and report to the Order, so that no swigging can take place unbeknownst to the members at large. The duty of the Eat-All will be in a like manner to test the solids contained in said boxes and make a written report. The duty of the Smoke-All will be to test all cigars, cheroots, Long Nines, Short Sixes, grape-vines, Three-for-a-Cent, Half Spanish and Principes; likewise all Nail-Rod, Nigger-Head, Fine-Cut, Turkish, Cavendish, Killikinnick, Mrs. Miller's Solace, American Boy, Benecia Boy, Yankee Blade, and other tobaccos, smoking, chewing and snuffing, together with hasheesh, opium and other somnolents, and report in manner and form specified. The duty of Judge-Advocate will be to act as general blower for the order, cuss in members, serve as counsel, pro and con, on all cases, questions and candidates for membership, render judgment as to the size, weight and probabilities of boxes in the perspective, making full report at every meeting. The duty of the Door-Tender will be to knock down and drag out (when decided to be necessary by the G. S.) all refractory and unruly members, and administer castigation to those who offend by secreting boxes for private enjoyment, to keep out all stragglers, Morganize all spies, informers, cowards and eavesdroppers, and carry out the dead men and old soldiers.

"*Meetings.*

"Meetings shallbe held frequently, at such times as the arrival of boxes shall warrant, and at such places as the G. S. may indicate.

"BY-LAWS.

"1. The G. S. may be deposed on being prolonged in his refusal to treat members to the 'ardent.'

"1½. At all meetings strict order will be observed, and the members will conduct themselves with decorum. Drinking, eating, smoking and chewing will be considered decorum.

"2. Each member is expected to wear his Sunday clothes, and bring his own spoon

"3. A student from an oyster cellar will be provided to open crackers.

"3½. Any member receiving a box will immediately notify the E. A., D. A. and S. A., under pain of being hurt.

"4. Three shutters and two tent-flies will be provided to carry off members who may become weak in the knees.

"5. Three cheers only will be given at one time.

"6. On no occasion of public ceremonies will music be allowed other than Dodsworth's brass band, sixty pieces, in white pants.

"7. At all parades in public the purses found on the line of March will be religiously appropriated towards paying the band (sixty pieces).

"8. On public occasions the band (sixty pieces) will provide its own supper.

"9. The hour for assemblage will be early candle-light.

"10. At all public suppers of the order, the following bill of fare will be provided:

"*First Course—Soups.*

"Clam Soup, Razor Soup, Ham Soup, and small white bean soup in which one bean, carefully mashed, will be placed.

"*Second Course—Roasts.*

"Roast Peanuts, Roast Pig-Tail, Roast Clams, Roast Ham, Roast Potatoes, and Roast Cow.

"*Third Course—Entrees.*

"Clams, Baked Apples, Alamode Mandrakes, Yams, Tarts, Tarrytown Stew, Herring Point, Oat Meal Cakes, B. C. Crakers, Steamed Onions, Pickled Eels' Feet, Soldiers' Buttons, and Turtles' Eggs.

"*Fourth Course—Fruits.*

"Clams, Ground Apples, Persimmons, Strawberries, Duck Weed, Fine-Cut, Greens.

"*Fifth Course—Nuts.*

"Clams, Hickory Nuts, Beach Nuts, Peanuts, Pig Nuts, Peacan Nuts, Brazil Nuts, Peach Pits, Apple Seeds, Walnuts, Horse Chestnuts, and Amsterdam Nuts.

"*Sixth Course—Pastry.*

"Clam Pie, Shad Apple Pie Horse Radish Custard, Milk Pie, Union Buttered Sandwiches, Red Flannel and Turnip Pie a la Mode Mince, and Mush and Milk.

"*Seventh Course—Wines and Liquors.*

"Clam Juice, Brandy and Water, Whiskey, Monongahela Rye, Apple and Bourbon, Buttermilk Whey, Lemonade, Lime Juice, Claret, Champagne, Gin, Bock Beer, Mead, Vinegar (vintage 1810), Cider, Port, Rhine Wine, Lager Beer, Ale, White of Egg and Molasses. No side dishes allowed.

"11. Fines will be imposed by the G. S. as follows: For being absent from a regular meeting, 1 pint whiskey ; for non-reception of box in one month, ½ gallon whiskey ; for disorder and disobedience of G. S., 1 bunch cigars ; for refusing drink to brother member, 1 bottle Otard ; for failing to divide contents of box, 10 kegs lager beer.

"11½. Under no circumstances shall there be any appeal from the decision of the Grand Salaam.

"11¾. Sutlers who are distinguished members when elected shall do their duty in the matter of boxes, and shall not charge three prices. This Society assumes to regulate all sutlers, and though it takes no commission on sales, requires the recognition of its rights as a vast brotherhood.

"12. No article of the above constitution or by-laws shall be altered or repealed, unless a motion to that effect has been made and carried."

As I have not a correct roll of the members of the above association I will not append any names; but I think the style of composition will betray the author to nearly every old member of the regiment.

Although much attention was paid to personal cleanliness and the sanitary condition of the camp, yet much sickness prevailed during the winter and early spring, and the regimental surgeons found plenty of work in the field hospital. Bowel troubles and typhoid fever were the most prevalent diseases, owing, no doubt, not so much to unaccustomed exposure as to the contamination of the water used for camp purposes. The source of water-supply was generally running streams, and these, running close to many camps, no doubt gathered up and spread the germs of disease. The deaths from disease in the field hospital during the winter and spring numbered nineteen, twelve of which were from typhoid fever. The deaths from all causes from the time of organization until the commencement of the Chancellorsville campaign had been fifty-one. Three had been killed in battle. Disease had, therefore, up to May 1st, 1863, taken forty-eight of our number.

On March 30th, the Fifth, Sixth, Seventh, Eighth and Eleventh New Jersey Regiments were again sent to the picket-line. About eleven o'clock that night it began snowing, and continued until nine o'clock the next morning.

At that time our picket-line was about eight miles from camp, and a tour of duty continued three days. The performance of duty was pleasant enough in fine weather, but March of '63 was unusually stormy, snow falling at times to the depth of a foot. Walking a picket-beat under such conditions was not very agreeable. Fortunately there was an abundance of wood, so that when not upon post, the men could make themselves quite comfortable.

Near midnight on the 31st, an alarm called all to arms, and during the remainder of the night the companies took turns in standing to their guns. Soon after daylight the booming of cannon to the right told that a brisk action was in progress—in the direction of Dumphries. The enemy had attempted to pierce the picket-line, but were driven back with the loss of several prisoners.

On April 2d the regiment returned to camp and resumed the old routine of drill. On the evening of the 3d, Colonel McAllister was serenaded by the band of the Eleventh Massachusetts.

Sunday, the 5th, brought snow again to the depth of seven inches. As a consequence, there was exemption from drill on Monday.

Just at nightfall on the 7th, President Lincoln, accompanied by General Hooker and others, rode past the camp.

On April 8th the Army of the Potomac was reviewed by President Lincoln, Secretary Seward and the general officers of the army. The review was held on the plain above Falmouth, and special care had been taken to prepare the ground for it. Stumps had been removed, gullies filled and the ground carefully staked out, so that no confusion might ensue. Nearly one hundred thousand men passed in review. They looked able to meet any emergency.

It was a magnificent sight. War at its best, in holiday attire—glitter of guns in the sunlight, waving of flags in the breeze, light, quick steps to the stirring music of bands, prancing of horses and sparkle of buttons and lace. But it was an army preparing for great deeds, nerving itself for heroic deaths.

The 9th of April ushered in a beautiful day, and also orders for the regiment to proceed once more to the picket-line.

Several of the picket-posts were near a couple of farm-houses, one of them occupied by a Union man, a former Pennsylvanian, who had two daughters attending school in Philadelphia. The surroundings looked comfortable and home-like. As the farmer was busy threshing with the flail, some of the men, who had not forgotten how to swing the "hungry club," amused themselves by helping him. The other house was occupied by a rebel, over whom a strict watch was kept, as he had been detected making signals to the enemy with lights.

A number of deserters came into the regimental picket-line, one of whom said that he was tired of waiting for his breakfast until he had gone to the river and caught it.

The river being not far away, some of the men went down to the shore and held conversation with members of the Ninth Alabama, doing duty on the other side.

The regiment returned to camp on the 12th, and instead of drill on the 13th it had target practice.

The orders of the 14th clearly indicated an early move. Eight days' rations were issued, three to be carried in haversacks and five in knapsacks. Blankets and dress-coats were turned into quartermaster's department, and each man received an extra pair of shoes. In addition to all this, one hundred and twenty rounds of ammunition were issued per man.

Another indication was the frequent reviews and inspections. On the 16th General Carr made a personal inspection of the brigade to see that each man had his supply of rations and ammunition. The paymaster made a very welcome appearance the following day and gave the regiment four months' pay, paying up to March 1st, '63. A large amount of the money received was sent to the homes of the soldiers, Colonel Cook, the State agent, being on hand to receive it.

About this time considerable amusement was afforded by a game of base-ball played between nines led by Captains Martin and Logan, with Lieutenant J. C. Baldwin as umpire. Below is the score:

CAPT. MARTIN'S SIDE.

Innings,	1	2	3	4	5	6	7	8	9	RUNS	OUTS.
Capt. L. Martin,	1			1	1	1				4	4
Adj. J Schoonover,	1	1	1	1	1	1				6	2
Lieut. W S Provost,	1	1	.	1	1					4	3
Lieut. A Beach,	1	1								2	3
Lieut. E. S. E. Newberry,	1	1					1	1		4	3
Lieut. S Leighton,	1	2		1		1	1	.	.	6	3
Capt. W. H Meeker,	1	1		1	1	1				5	4
Lieut. J. Souter,	1	1		1	1		1			5	2
Lieut. J. F Buckley,	1	1				1	1			4	3
Totals,	9	9	2	6	5	4	4	1		40	27

CAPT. LOGAN'S SIDE.

Innings,	1	2	3	4	5	6	7	8	9	RUNS	OUTS.
Capt. D. B. Logan,				1						1	4
Lieut. J. H. Oldershaw,	1	1				1		1		4	3
Capt. T. J. Halsey,	1							1		2	2
Lieut. A. H. Ackerman,								1		1	3
Capt. W. B Duning,											4
Lieut. Good,										.	3
Capt. Myres						1				1	3
Sergt -Major Mount,		1	1	1				1		4	3
Drum Major Durant,		1				1				2	2
Totals,	2	3	1	2	.	3	.	4	.	15	27

During our early experience candidates for promotion as non-commissioned officers were put through an examination as to their qualifications for the position. The custom afterwards fell into disuse. At best, it was but a mere form, the examination being very superficial, as the following report of one will show:

William Hand, of Company B, being awakened one night from a sound sleep, was told to report immediately at the Colonel's tent. He hastened to obey, wondering what he had been doing, but could not think of any misdemeanor or breach of discipline of which he had been guilty. Reaching the tent he found it occupied by several staff and line officers. He was told to be seated, and was then asked where he had received his education. He answered, "At a common country school."

"Ever at college?" "No." "Can you read?" "Yes." "Let us hear you read?" He took a book and read a page or two. "Can you write?" "Yes." "Let's see you write." He copied a page of the book from which he had been reading. He was then asked if he knew anything of Geography. He answered, "A little." "Grammar?" "No." "What, never studied grammar!" "Oh, yes," he answered, "I studied it for several years, and recited it to the satisfaction of the teacher, but I never learned any of it." All the time he was wishing they would tackle him on arithmetic—he was at home there—but it was not mentioned. After a few more questions in regard to military tactics he was dismissed. After returning to his quarters he learned that he had been recommended for the position of Fifth Sergeant, to which he was soon afterward promoted.

Among the few who received furloughs during the winter was a member of Company B, whom we will call "Joe." He was a famous fisherman when at home, and whether longing for a mess of fresh fish or not I do not know, but he was certainly very anxious for a furlough. Captain Meeker made application for him, but in the meantime orders came for the army to move, and all such papers were held at headquarters. The move proved to be the "mud march." On returning to camp "Joe" became very importunate about his furlough, questioning his officers so continually that they became weary of it and forbade his saying anything more about it. He got the impression that his company officers did not want him to go home. Finding little sympathy in his own company, he made a confidant of "Cap. Smith," of Company I. Smith was an incorrigible joker, and was never so happy as, when opportunity offered, to get the laugh on some one. He was very sympathetic, and advised "Joe," as his Captain would take no interest in the matter, to write direct to the President. As "Joe" could not write, Smith volunteered to do it for him. Of course the letter never reached President Lincoln. In course of time "Joe's" furlough came, properly approved, and he started home, highly elated with the thought of having outwitted Captain Meeker. While at home, and just before starting to rejoin his regiment, he went fishing and caught a fine lot of smelts. He sorted out a basket of the finest of them, and on reaching Washington took them to the White House. When relating the circumstance to the boys,

Chaplain E. Clarke Cline.

after his return, they asked him if he saw the President. He said no; he left the fish with a man at the door, and told him the President would know whom they were from, for he had granted him a furlough when his Captain refused it!

The wood kept getting farther and farther away from camp, until at last it was necessary to carry it nearly a mile. As a conequence the men would sometimes allow their supply to get so nearly exhausted that an extra cold snap would set them to hustling for a fresh supply. This occurred one cold night to "Bully" and his tentmates. They could not go to the distant forsest, and wood must be had for morning. Who should go on the skirmish for a supply? They decided to draw cuts, and the lot fell to "Bully." He knew that there was a plentiful supply around the officers' tents, but the thing was to get it without being caught. After some thought he decided to try the chaplain's pile, thinking no doubt that if caught there the chaplain would be more lenient than the other officers. He found a large white oak log beside the chaplain's tent and proceeded to shoulder it. Before he could do so, however, the chaplain appeared and offered to assist him, thinking no doubt to shame him from taking it. But as "Bully" wanted wood pretty badly, and already had it partly on his shoulder, he accepted the chaplain's assistance, and walked off with it. The chaplain must have been completely paralyzed at the man's audacity, for he never mentioned the matter.

Governor Joel Parker being on a visit to the front, and five regiments of New Jersey troops being in the Second division of the Third Corps, a review of the division was held in his honor on Sunday, the 26th. In the evening he visited the camp of the Eleventh, which had been decorated with evergreens in anticipation of his coming. He was greeted with three cheers, and on leaving, at the instance of Captain Halsey, three were given for little Jersey. The religious services in the evening were enlivened by the singing of a young lady who visited the camp with her father. A. B. Searing says "some of the boys wished to see her safely home, but our good old Colonel was so very gallant that he gave no one else a chance to play the agreeable."

On April 27th the entire corps was reviewed by General Sickles, Secretary Seward, Lord Lyons, and other distinguished officers.

Before entering into an account of the stirring scenes that the spring and summer of '63 ushered in it will be well to take a retrospective glance.

The regiment's losses in battle up to this date had been but three killed, and four wounded. But the change from the comforts of home to the roughness and exposure of camp-life had brought its penalty, and disease had claimed many victims. Twenty-one had died of typhoid fever alone.

Up to May 1st, '63, the deaths from all causes aggregated 51. A hundred and ten had been discharged for disability and other causes, three had been transferred to regiments from which they had deserted, and a hundred and five had been dropped from the rolls as deserters. In addition to this nearly two hundred were absent sick and on detached service, so that at the opening of the campaign the fighting strength of the regiment could have been but little more than five hundred.

The losses were not confined exclusively to the rank and file. A number of the officers had resigned during the fall and early spring: Major Valentine Mutchler on April 4th; Surgeon Young on February 5th; Surgeon Byington on March 20th; Captain Stagg, of Company G, December 28th, '62; Lieutenant Anderson, Company F, on November 14th, '62; Captain Willis, Lieutenants O. B. Fausett and Vancleve, of Company C, on March 6th, '63. Company C was thus left entirely without officers, and Colonel McAllister facetiously called them the lost children. Captain Grover, of Company F, was discharged on November 16th, '62.

Chapter V.

Hooker Takes Command—Chancellorsville.

THE COMMAND of the Army of the Potomac had been given to General Hooker on January 26th, 1863, and though the change gave rise to some jealousies in high quarters, it was looked upon with great favor by the men. His brilliant deeds upon the Peninsula had won for him the sobriquet of "Fighting Joe," and the rank and file had the utmost confidence in his ability and skill.

"He assumed command with confidence, but with distrust in the good will of Halleck, his superior at Washington," and I may here say that that distrust was not confined to Hooker alone, but was entertained by the majority of the rank and file, who looked upon Halleck as a jealous marplot and wholly unfitted for the position he held. Hooker at once set about an energetic reorganization of the army; he broke up the grand divisions and restored corps organizations. As soon as possible he set about the correction of the many abuses that had crept in, and paid special attention to the commissary and quartermaster's departments. He found the army in a demoralized condition. Desertions were numerous; it has been stated that as high as two hundred a day occurred.

The deserters and absentees were sufficient to have made a large army. The system of granting furloughs and leaves was revised; orders were issued that no leave should be granted to an officer of high rank except from headquarters; only one field and two line officers could be absent from a regiment at one time, and only two enlisted men out of a hundred, and they from those who had the best records.

This change no doubt was necessary, and perhaps worked well in general, but to some it seemed unjust, for some of the men selected to receive this especial reward of merit thought it well to close their records while they were yet good, and failed to return.

That was the case in Company E, of which the writer was a member. Daniel Talmadge, chosen by Captain Halsey as the most deserving man, concluded that "discretion was the better part of valor," and not only failed to return, but the place that then knew him as a citizen has since known him no more. As a consequence no more furloughs were granted from Company E during the winter.

The men in the ranks well knew that the frequent reviews and inspections that were held during the spring of '63, the drawing of extra rations and ammunition, indicated stirring times. They were therefore not surprised when, on April 28th at four P. M., they received orders to strike tents and be ready to move at a moment's notice.

At six P M. the order came to move. The line of march was towards Franklin's Crossing, below Fredericksburg. The march was continued until ten at night, when bivouac was formed in a wooded ravine not far from the river. The afternoon had brought a storm which continued through the night, but notwithstanding no tents were pitched the men rolled themselves in their blankets and slept as best they could.

At daylight on the 29th the regiment was astir, with orders to be ready to move at seven o'clock. A short march brought the regiment to near Franklin's Crossing, where it went into bivouac in a wood and remained the rest of the day and following night. Tents were pitched at night, as the rain continued without any sign of abatement.

About noon on the 30th the command again fell in and marched by a circuitous route back toward the old camp, which was passed at half-past one. Keeping well back from the river, and taking advantage of ravines and by-ways to escape the observation of the enemy, the march continued until twelve o'clock at night, when a halt was made about four miles from United States ford.

The march was resumed at eight A. M. on the morning of May 1st. After crossing the Rappahannock at United States ford a halt was made for dinner, after which the regiment moved about a mile and took position in a deserted rebel camp. At four P M. heavy firing was heard toward the left, and the brigade was ordered to move in that direction. Soon the order came to double-quick, and the men, supposing they were going into action, kept the ranks well closed. A short halt was made to load, and then—on again at a rapid pace. It was nearly dark when we filed into the wood to the left of the road running from the ford, and halted *en masse* a short distance from the Chancellorsville house, where General Hooker had his headquarters. We stacked arms and lay down to rest, with orders to be ready to fall in at a moment's notice.

With the Eleventh at that time were three colored servants. A solid shot that came from a rebel battery, perhaps a mile away, struck one of the servants, taking off one leg and shattering the other. The occurrence so demoralized the other two that they applied for passes and left for home the next day.

Chancellorsville, that was to give name to one of the fiercest and most sanguinary battles of the war, and that was to be the last halting-place of so many of the brave men of the Eleventh, consisted of a large brick mansion, built in the usual Southern style. Near by were a number of negro cabins, the indispensable accompaniment of Southern mansions in those days. It stood about eleven miles from Fredericksburg, near the junction of several roads, one running northward, with its branches, to United States ford and the fords of the Rapidan. The old turnpike-road from Culpepper, which joins the Orange plank-road two miles west of Chancellorsville, there diverges to the left, to meet it again half-way to Fredericksburg. To the westward stretches that desolate region of scrubs and brambles known as the Wilderness.

When the stampede of the Eleventh Corps began, on the afternoon of May 2d, Berry's division was still in reserve near the Chancellorsville house. About half-past four an aid rode up with orders to move hastily forward. Knapsacks were thrown in piles and left under guard, and the command was soon double-quicking out the Gordousville plank-road.

So dense was the mass of panic-stricken fugitives seeking safety in flight that it was almost impossible to make our way through them. One burly Teuton, making frantic efforts to reach a place of safety, cries as he runs, " Me runs mit Howard, me fights mit Sigel." Thereafter "Me fights mit Sigel" became a catch-word in the army.

Sergeant McDavitt caught one of the flying Germans by the shoulder, and pointing a revolver at him compelled him to enter the ranks of Company E and go with it to the front.

Soon General Berry came galloping back and called out excitedly: "Colonel McLaughlin, give me your regiment, quick!" That was the First Massachusetts. With a wild cheer they started on a dead-run down the road. It was nearly dark when they filed into position on the right of the plank-road; the rest of the brigade soon formed in their rear. The first position of the Eleventh was to the right of the plank-road and some distance from it, but in perfecting the alignment during the night the left of the regiment was brought to and rested upon the road. The battle continued on the first line until after dark. Then the volleys died away to fitful shots. The gloom of the forest, the dreary cry of the "Whip-poor-Wills" that came from every quarter seemed to exercise a depressing influence, and but little talk was indulged in. Suddenly, about midnight, there came a crash and glare that opened every drowsy eye. The guns posted in our rear opened a terrific fire, and for a while there was a very pandemonium of sound. The vivid flashes of the guns lighting up the gloom of the forest, the shrieking and bursting of shells and the crash of falling limbs combined to make a scene grand yet terrible. In regard to this midnight battle, General Doubleday says: "It was Sickles fighting his way home again." For a short time the battle raged furiously, then slowly died away. Officers passed to and fro, giving orders in low tones. General Berry rode along the lines to see that all was well, and spoke words of cheer, little thinking that it was to be his last battle-night.

Darkness gave opportunity for the coward to flee. I think, however, few places were vacant in the Eleventh when the light of Sunday morning, May 3d, broke upon it.

Quoting from Colonel McAllister's official report: "May 3d, before the dawn of day, I was ordered to move my command toward the plank-road, with the left resting on the road and at right-angles with it, General Carr directing the formation. The Eleventh Massachusetts, Colonel Blaisdell, came into the woods and formed on our right, in the same line of battle. At 4:30 the enemy moved on our front line in heavy force, and the battle raged furiously. The first line stood firm. After awhile the left wing of the First Massachusetts gave way. Colonel McLaughlin came back. I asked him what the matter was. He replied that his left wing had given way, but the right was standing firm, and that he was going back to rally the left wing. I sent my Adjutant to General Carr to know whether I should advance or remain in my position. I could not let my whole regiment fire on account of the right wing of the First Massachusetts being yet in place. I was ordered to throw the right of my left wing forward, which I did, and continued firing. My right wing held their fire until the enemy's volleys poured in on them, when I ordered them to fire. Very soon we discovered that the enemy was flanking us. I then ordered a right half-wheel of my regiment and fired upon and drove the enemy back. Captain Gamble, of the Eleventh Massachusetts, with eight men, reported to me, and asked the privilege of joining us, which was cheerfully granted. Both himself and his men fought bravely and deserve great credit.

"In this position we continued for some time, our men fighting bravely, holding our position in advance of the old line and checking the enemy's advance, until at last the battery in the road (a section of Dimick's) fell back, as well as the line in our rear, and also the Second New Jersey Brigade, on the left of the road. We then retreated slowly, keeping up a continual fire.

After retreating across the road we joined the Second Brigade in a charge upon the enemy, then in our cannon pits, and drove them out, but the enemy being upon our flanks, we could not hold them long and had to retreat toward the Chancellor house, where we formed another line of battle, losing several men,

Captain Ira W. Cory.

after which we were ordered to fall back to a line of battle near where we had lain *en masse* on the second. There we remained a short time supporting a battery. We then fell back and joined our own brigade. After shifting our position several times we went into the afterward fortified camp, and fought no more that day.

"Permit me to say that great credit is due to both officers and men of our regiment—they stood well and fought well in every position. To praise some might be doing injustice to others. But I cannot pass on without favorably mentioning Lieutenant-Colonel Moore, who acquitted himself with honor, and the heroic conduct of Captain Kearney and Adjutant Schoonover, who were of incalculable advantage in leading and urging the men forward. And also A. Du Puget, the color-bearer. They showed themselves every inch soldiers; they all deserve great credit, and promotion for meritorious conduct. Our loss in this battle was 20 killed and 113 wounded.

"May 4th we lay in the woods until about the middle of the day, when we marched out to the edge of the woods in front of the breastworks, as a support to the pickets, the Berdan sharpshooters. My instructions were to lie down until the pickets were driven in, then rise and resist the enemy's advance. I did as directed. Soon the enemy came down and most of the pickets came in. I went to the left to speak to the major in command of the pickets and ask if all his men were out, so that I could fire. He did not seem to hear me, but an order came which I at first supposed to have been given by him, but I afterward learned that it was given by the lieutenant who had command of the picket on the right, to fall back. Almost at the same time the enemy opened a battery with canister at short range, which was immediately answered by our batteries opening upon them with their guns at entirely too low a range, the shot sweeping the surface of the ground. My men, taking the order for mine, started back. Myself, Lieutenant-Colonel Moore and Adjutant Schoonover tried in vain to rally them, but had we succeeded we would have lost not less than a hundred men, being in direct line between the two fires. Our right wing halted in the ravine, the left went along the rifle-pits to the fortifications. We gathered the scattered forces and went back with different orders—that if the enemy opened with their batteries we should file into the rifle-pits, so that our batteries could open on the enemy without injuring us.

"The enemy did not again bring their artillery to bear upon us, but advanced with uncertainty, and before the sharpshooters were out of the woods our guns opened upon them and we remained lying on the ground—had one man wounded by our shells. Our shells ploughed the ground up where we lay.

"The 'rebs' were driven back. Trees were cut off at the roots by our shells in front of us. Between the sharpshooters and the enemy, we had one officer and twenty-three men wounded."

The official report gives in outline only the positions and work of the regiment during the memorable 3d and 4th of May. The details must be sought for elsewhere.

The entrance of the Eleventh Regiment to the battle of Chancellorsville was under circumstances well calculated to try the nerves of the most experienced veterans. As it hurried up the Gordonsville plank-road it was met by a disorganized and frightened mass of fugitives, horses, artillery, wild-eyed, hatless and unarmed men. Officers, forgetful of honor, intermingled, careless of the fate of others, thoughtless of what calamities their defection might bring upon their comrades, each individual frantically seeking a place of safety. Was it not a wonder that, green as the Eleventh was and unused to such scenes, it was not caught up by the tide of disorder and with it carried to the rear? Yet, though the shot fell around it and the exultant yells of the victorious enemy came from their advancing columns in the woods beyond, steadily as veterans the regiment kept its place.

The example of the leaders has much to do with the conduct of troops in battle. If they are fearful and timid, it is quickly noticed by the men in the ranks, and their conduct is regulated accordingly.

The conduct of the leader of the Third Corps, General Daniel E. Sickles, and of Generals Berry and Carr, was such as to inspire the men under them to deeds of daring. They were to be found at the extreme front, in the thickest of the battle, encouraging and directing the men. And the leaders of the Eleventh Regiment, Colonel McAllister, Lieutenant-Colonel Moore, Acting Major Kearney, Adjutant Schoonover, and their subordinates, by their conspicuous gallantry inspired the men to heroic deeds.

When the dawn of Sunday morning, May 3d, ushered in the battle by an advance of the enemy, and the Eleventh was ordered to advance and meet them, they did so eagerly. William Horton, of Company E, did not arise with the rest of the company, and an examination showed that he was dead, having been shot through the head by the first fire of the enemy.

The enemy advanced cautiously, the thick woods screening the opposing forces. It was supposed that a part of the First Massachusetts was still maintaining their position on the first line. To ascertain if such was the case, Colonel McAllister says: "I asked if any one would volunteer to go and find out what was in our front. A young boy (Lanterman, of Company H) stepped out of the ranks and advanced. Soon returning, he reported that only the enemy was in our front. I immediately gave the command to commence firing."

During a battle the soldier in the ranks has but little chance of seeing what is occurring on other parts of the line, even if the fighting is upon open ground. But in a wood like that of Chancellorsville, where the view was obstructed by trees and underbrush, his view is limited to the comrades immediately around him and the enemy in his front. Comrades of his own company may be shot down and he not see them fall. To those on the right of the regiment it did not seem necessary that any one should be sent out to reconnoitre, for the right wing did not commence firing until the enemy were in view. James P Myres and the writer, both of Company E, had advanced some paces in front of their company. The writer had just turned and said, "Hold on, Jim; we are getting too far ahead," when the column of the enemy, advancing at a left oblique, came into view. We raised our guns to fire. Captain Halsey called out, "Don't shoot, they are our own men." We called back, "They are rebs., Captain," and immediately began firing. The company, coming up at this instant, began firing, and soon it became general.

E

The Eleventh Regiment maintained its position after the rest of the brigade had fallen to the rear, and it was not until the enemy began closing on its flanks that it fell back and joined the Second New Jersey Brigade in a new alignment on the high ground near the Chancellorsville house, to the left of the plank-road. From that position it joined the Second Brigade in a charge upon the enemy, who were then occupying the pits that had been thrown up to protect the Union guns. The pits were re-captured, but, as our flanks were wholly unprotected, we could not hold them.

During the engagement the Second New Jersey Brigade captured a number of battle-flags, but that result would hardly have been possible had not the Eleventh maintained its position on the flank of that brigade.

McAllister says: "Colonel Sewell informed me that he had an opportunity to capture some flags, and asked me if I could protect his flank while so doing. I told him to go ahead and take them, that the Eleventh would hold its ground. Afterward, in conversation, he acknowledged his indebtedness to the Eleventh for the assistance rendered during this exploit."

When the regiment was falling back across the plank-road, the enemy kept up a terrific fire of shells. One of them struck in the bank on the roadside, just as Company B was climbing up, and exploded directly under the feet of Henry Hand, turning him completely over. Though somewhat bruised and covered with dirt, he escaped without serious injury. But he was less fortunate on the following day, when the regiment was supporting the sharpshooters. He then had the visor of his cap shot away, and a piece of shell struck his gun, breaking it against his left side. Though the skin was not broken, he received a severe internal injury, from which he never fully recovered. Since the war he has been an invalid and compelled to live in a Southern climate.

Shortly after the explosion of the shell under the feet of Henry Hand, a ricochetting shot struck in the midst of Company F, killing Corporal James Hamilton, Francis B. Wilson and Pat. Minton and wounding several others. It continued on its course (nearly spent) until it reached Captain Meeker, where it stopped against his left thigh, slightly bruising it.

The Eleventh Regiment never received the credit justly due it for the prominent part it took in the battle of May 3d. It held its position in the wood long after the troops upon its right had given way, and after all the other regiments of the brigade had fallen to the rear. And though at last outflanked and compelled to slowly retire, it would not acknowledge defeat, but joined the Second Jersey Brigade in holding the enemy in check while the lines were re-forming in rear.

While the brigade was re-forming in rear, some one asked: "Where is the Eleventh New Jersey?" The reply was: "They are out front, fighting on their own hook." The report was also circulated that the Colonel was killed and the regiment taken prisoners. But fortunately, though it passed through many narrow chances, it came out with organization still intact.

During all its after-experience the regiment never passed a more trying half hour than that passed on the evening of the 4th, while supporting Berdan's Sharpshooters—a duty it performed from the middle of the afternoon of the 4th until the afternoon of the 5th. Its position was at the edge of a wood; in rear of it and across an open field were the Union entrenchments, filled with artillery. About midway across the open field was a ravine, in which stood two large trees. In front of the regiment was Berdan's Sharpshooters, facing the enemy's sharpshooters. Back of the enemy's sharpshooters was high ground, occupied by their batteries. Toward evening the enemy ran a battery out to the edge of the wood and opened a sharp fire of canister. Our batteries in the entrenchments responded, but the guns were trained so low that their shot struck dangerously close to the regiment; trees were cut off by shot from our own guns, directly in front of it. The sharpshooters were ordered to retire. The right wing of the Eleventh, mistaking the order, also fell back, the left wing following. A part of the regiment sought shelter in the ravine; the rest continued to the breastworks. The position of those in the ravine was terrible. Forty

Union guns were firing over them, and the air above and around seemed thick with flying metal. The trees spoken of were struck at least fifty times.

For a half hour that terrible fire continued, and then the enemy withdrew, and the regiment went back to its former position near the wood.

The next day (the 5th) the rebel sharpshooters kept up an annoying fire, and several men of the Eleventh were wounded, among them Lieutenant Beach. When Beach was struck, one of Berdan's Sharpshooters asked "if that fellow hit any one." When told that Beach was struck, he replied: "I have my eye on the ———." The next instant there was a report, and the "reb" came tumbling out of a tree. During the 4th and 5th, besides Lieutenant Beach, twenty-three men were wounded. Had the regiment remained in position at the edge of the wood during the entire artillery fire it would have been almost annihilated.

The sun came out very warm on the 5th and a number of the men were sunstruck, among them Captain Meeker. He was taken to the hospital at Potomac Creek, and from there sent to the General Hospital at Newark. He returned to the regiment in July, but was taken very sick the night of his arrival and had to return to the hospital. Finding that he was not likely to be fit for duty for a long time he resigned, August 12th, '63, the regiment thus losing one of its most promising officers.

The regiment was almost constantly under fire from Saturday evening, the 2d, until 2 P M. on Tuesday, the 5th, when it was relieved and sent to the rear of the breastworks and given an opportunity to rest. At 1 o'clock on the morning of the 6th it received orders to fall in, and the march back across the river began. The old camp was reached just before dark. Though the men were nearly worn-out they passed a dreary, uncomfortable night. It was cold and rainy and the men nearly destitute, the tents, overcoats, etc., having been burned with the knapsacks on the battle-field. More than this, the excitement of the battle was over and they had time to think, and now began to realize the losses the regiment had sustained. They missed the tentmates that had become dear to them by the associations of the winter, the cheery voices that they would hear no more. It was like the return of the wanderer who finds the homestead deserted and the loved ones scattered. But the next day, the 7th, tents and blankets were issued. New families of comrades formed and the work of refitting and cleaning the camp commenced, and soon things began to appear more cheerful and home-like.

Many incidents occurred upon the campaign, many acts of bravery during the battle, that are worthy of being recorded, but, unfortunately, at this late day, either the forgetfulness or apathy of the surviving comrades renders it impossible.

The night of the 2d, though not cold, was chilly enough to make one feel the need of a blanket, but the men were entirely without protection, their blankets having been turned in previous to leaving camp, and overcoats either thrown away or left with the knapsacks in the rear. Lieutenant Bloomfield and Sergeant Hand, of Company B, were together, and, feeling the need of some covering, Bloomfield said he would go and get a blanket. He went back as far as Hooker's headquarters, where a number of horses were standing under the care of orderlies. A roll of blankets was strapped to the saddle of one. Going up to it he unstrapped the roll of blankets, all the time keeping up a conversation with the orderly in charge of it. On reaching the regiment he found that they had more blankets than they needed; so, after taking out a good double one, he re-packed the roll and returned it to the saddle. Next morning he looked for the horse, that he might return the borrowed blanket, but could not find it, and before he could do so the battle opened, and shortly afterward Bloomfield met his death, being shot in the middle of the forehead. Captain Meeker, who was near and saw Bloomfield fall, turned to Kelly, his second lieutenant, and said, "Ned, there goes poor Lot." "Eh?" said Kelly, who turned his head to look; just then a ball struck him over the left ear, and Kelly, too, fell dead—both killed within a minute. Meeker says: "The loss of both lieutenants (who were dearly loved by the men) seemed to make the men wild, and they fought as though they were determined to wipe out the whole rebel army. Joe Frazer (who was killed at Locust Grove) was determined to kill two rebel officers in retaliation,

Major William H. Loyd.

and he watched for them. Suddenly he ran up to me and said, 'Cap, there's a hen on.' I asked him where. He pointed to a tree and told me to watch it. I did watch it for a moment and saw the head of a rebel officer; but the sight was a brief one, for 'Joe' pulled and the officer dropped."

During the evening of the second, Lieutenant Oldershaw who was a member of General Carr's staff, but temporarily assigned to duty with General Berry, accompanied the General out between the lines. They came to a deserted caisson, but saw a rebel teamster approaching with two horses to take it off. General Berry asked him who had sent him. He said, "the General." They permitted him to attach the horses to the caisson, and then sent him into the Union lines. During the evening, when the firing occurred that resulted in the wounding and subsequent death of General Jackson, General Berry, attended by Oldershaw, was again at the extreme front. When returning they were accompanied by a rebel major, who in the confusion mistook General Berry for his own chief. He rode a splendid white horse, and Oldershaw, who ordered him to dismount, thought that it should be his by right of capture; but much to his chagrin he was not allowed to keep it.

No doubt, had Berry survived the battle, Oldershaw would have been shown some mark of his favor, for while riding with him through the shower of shot and shell, Berry turned to him and asked his name. Oldershaw gave his name and regiment. Berry replied, "Lieutenant, I shall not forget you." But, alas! brave, generous, noble-hearted Berry fell during Sunday morning's fight.

In Company E were two brothers, John and Charles Mann, both brave and gallant soldiers. During the Sunday morning's battle John was mortally wounded through the breast. Charles, laying down his gun, took him upon his back to carry him off the field. While so doing, Charles was knocked down by a falling limb, but not seriously injured. He succeeded in getting his brother to a place of comparative safety, and stayed with him until he died. By so doing, Charles became a prisoner, but was shortly released on parole. In less than a year Charles, too, met a soldier's death, being killed at Locust Grove.

A soldier sometimes has a premonition of coming death. Such was the case with Sergeant Daniel Bender, of Company H. Just previous to the battle, in a conversation with A. B. Searing, of

Company E, he said that he had a presentiment that he would not live to see the end of the coming battle. His presentiment proved too true, for a bullet, passing through the visor of his cap, pierced his brain. One year afterward, when bivouacking upon the battle-field of Chancellorsville, just before the battle of the Wilderness, among many ghastly relics picked up was a skull, the cap still upon it, and upon the visor was stamped " D. Bender, Co. H, 11th N. J. Vols." A. B. Searing, of Company E, cut the visor off and brought it home with him.

During or just after a battle many strange rumors find currency. I remember that after crossing the chain bridge, where no enemy was near to cause the firing of a shot, a rumor reached the North that the regiment had been hotly engaged and that a number had been wounded, among them the writer.

At Chancellorsville, among the names of the killed published in the Northern papers was that of Adjutant John Schoonover, and a single line written by moonlight on the battle-field announcing his safety, did not reach its destination until preparations had been made to go after his body.

As a further evidence of the gallant part taken by the regiment, and the esteem in which it was held by those who were in a position to know of its work, I will quote the words of Generals Hooker and Carr.

General Hooker, while visiting the wounded of the regiment, said to Surgeon Welling: " This is a gallant regiment; it fought splendidly; officers and men alike deserve great credit."

General Carr, who temporarily succeeded to the command of the division, after the death of General Berry, in a letter to the Adjutant-General of the State, under date of May 15th, '63, said: " The regiment greatly distinguished itself at the battle of Chancellorsville. It is one of which the State of New Jersey has reason to feel proud. Without a single exception the officers and men of the regiment acted in the most gallant and heroic manner." Again, in a letter dated May 18th, General Carr repeats his words of commendation.

Previous to the battle of Chancellorsville the Eleventh had been looked upon with something like contempt by the older regiments from its own State, owing to its youthful *personnel*, the average age being about seventeen. It was called "McAllister's boys," and arguing from that, they entertained the opinion that the noise of the conflict and a sight of the carnage would soon demoralize them. But its conduct at Chancellorsville won the admiration of all, and thenceforth "McAllister's boys" became a title of honor, and in the many battles that it afterward passed through it maintained its reputation and was always found ready and reliable, no matter how desperate the enterprise. During the engagement the staff of the flag carried by De Puget was shot away, and after the battle the colors showed many signs of hard usage.

The regiment lost 2 officers and 17 enlisted men killed; 11 officers and 146 enlisted men wounded, and 8 missing—a total of 184 out of the 500 taken into action.

The killed were Lieutenants Lot Bloomfield and Edward Kelly, and private Michael Butler, of B; Privates Hiram Gress and George Watson, of D; Sergeant James McDavitt and privates William Horton, Peter Hann, John Cook and Riley O'Brien, of E; Corporals James W. Hamilton, Pat. Minton and Private Francis B. Wilson, of F; Corporal William McMinn and Private Samuel Burk, of G; Sergeant Daniel Bender and Levi P Baird and Henry South, of H, and Josiah Van Schoick, of I.

The officers wounded were: Captains Halsey and Myer, and Lieutenant John B. Faussett, slightly, and Lieutenant Newberry, severely; Captains Logan, Martin and Ackerman, and Lieutenants Volk, Cory, Provost and Beach, slightly. Many of those reported wounded were so severely injured that they died either upon the field or soon after reaching the hospital. Sergeant Guy P Cox, of A, died at Washington, May 15th; Sergeant Emory Allen, of D, at Falmouth, June 11th; Thomas Murry, of E, at Washington, May 28th; John Mann, of E, at Chancellorsville, May 11th, and Daniel Palmer, of the same company, at Washington, June 23d. First Sergeant Jacob Myer, of Company G, reached his home at Allentown, N. J., where he died September 2d, '63 Joseph P Robare, of H, died on the 3d of May, and William A. Decker, of the same company, at Washington, May 30th; William Baird, of I, died at the Third Corps hospital, on the 18th of May, and William H. Disbrow, also of I, at Stafford Court House, May 7th. William Fraley, of C, who was wounded on the 4th, while supporting sharpshooters, died at Chancellorsville on the 6th of May.

Fire added another horror to the battle-field of Chancellorsville. The exploding shells ignited the dead leaves and underbrush, and many who were too severely injured to crawl from the field perished in the flames. It is not positively known whether any of the Eleventh perished in this manner or not, but it is highly probable, for fire swept that part of the wood where its severest fighting occurred, and no information was ever received of some of those who were reported missing.

The regiment lost some of its most promising men, and it is to be regretted that the data is not at hand to enable the giving of such personal notices as their bravery and heroism deserve.

A correspondent to the "Paterson Guardian," under date of May 30th, '63, says: "Among the brave men who gave their lives to their country, at Chancellorsville, was Lieutenant Lot Bloomfield. He is the second of the brothers of the family who have fallen in defense of the flag in the present war, the elder brother having been killed at Williamsburg."

From a private letter written by an officer of the Eleventh just after the battle, we glean the following: "In the early part of the battle and while the enemy's fire was very severe, Lieutenant Lot Bloomfield turned to speak to me. Just as his mouth was opened, and before he could speak a word, a minie ball crashed through his brain and he fell at my feet, dead. The shadow of death passed over his face as he was falling, and I saw it. It was terrible; but the rush and excitement of the battle left me no time to think of it until afterward."

Another private letter, written on May 20th, '63, says: "Captain Ackerman was struck in the leg by a piece of shell, but gallantly remained with his regiment until it was withdrawn from the field, and has since continued on duty. He also had his coat-tail adorned with a bullet-hole, while he received in his left boot a bullet which passed through the leg of Lieutenant Beach, of his company."

A letter written by a civilian, evidently a member of the Sanitary Commission, to the "Paterson Guardian," May 21st, '63, after giving a graphic account of the battle, says: "One man whom I noticed quietly leaning on his rifle, his face blackened with the smoke of powder and the perspiration making streaks down his cheeks, told me, when I asked what regiment, that he belonged to the Eleventh New Jersey. I very naturally took an interest in the man and asked about his regiment. He said that his regiment had been relieved; that they had 'fought like h—l'; that they had helped to capture four stand of colors. I could not help exclaiming, 'Well done, Jersey.' He asked if I was a Jerseyman, and, on my answering in the affirmative, seized my hand with such violence as to nearly drag me from my horse, and shook it for five minutes in a way that would make any town-pump tremble all over."

Among the many who fell none gave promise of greater usefulness than Sergeant James McDavit, of Company E. He was a young man of splendid physical development. His mental qualifications were quickness of decision and determination in execution. He was brave, but not foolhardy, and seemed to possess all the qualifications that tend to the making of a good soldier. When Captain Halsey was wounded, McDavit went to his assistance. While binding up the Captain's wound, he was struck in the head and died a few minutes afterward. The field remaining in the hands of the enemy, it is not known what became of his body. Like thousands of others, his resting-place is unknown.

Lieutenant E. S. E. Newberry, who had been severely wounded before being commissioned into the Eleventh, was wounded through the leg at Chancellorsville so that thereafter he was unable to perform the duties of a foot-soldier. After his recovery he served as a staff officer until January 28th, 1864, when he resigned and accepted a commission in the Veteran Reserve Corps.

Newberry was a North Carolinian by birth, and had two brothers holding commissions in the Confederate service. He was a born Abolitionist, and at the commencement of the war entered the Union service. Though having the quick temper of most Southerners, he was greatly liked by his men, for they knew that he would render exact justice. When off duty he did not stand upon dignity, but met the men on familiar terms. When duty called for strict discipline, all knew that obedience would be exacted. While lying *en masse* near the Chancellor house, orders were issued to detail men from each company to fill the canteens. Newberry ordered William Minton to take the canteens of E and fill them. For some reason—the proximity of the enemy or the dropping of occasional shot—Minton refused. Newberry drew his revolver and, taking out his watch, said: "Now, Bill, if in three minutes you have not gathered up those canteens and gone for water I will blow your brains out." Minton knew the Lieutenant would keep his word and hesitated no longer. Whether this bit of insubordination was foreign to the man's nature or the lesson taught was a lasting one, I do not know, but Minton afterward proved himself a good soldier until severely wounded in front of Petersburg.

To the northward of Chancellorsville was another clearing in which stood a small white house. To the eastward of this, and just within the timber between the Ely's Ford road and the road to United States ford, had been established the general field hospital. Hundreds of wounded lay upon the ground. The force of surgeons and hospital attendants was entirely inadequate, and before many of the injured had received the attention required, the battle had drawn close and shot and shell began to drop among them, resulting in death and additional wounds. Several of the surgeons and attendants were killed or wounded. A panic consequently ensued, and all who could possibly help themselves sought places of safety. The writer, who was among the wounded, after creeping for a distance through the wood, found himself along the river road. It was crowded with ambulances, but no one seemed to pay any attention to him, and he possibly would have been left to become a captive had not Lieutenant Morehouse, of Company F, who had been assisting a wounded officer, and was making his way to the front again, discovered him, and secured him a place in an ambulance. The ambulance was a part of the Eleventh Corps hospital train, and the writer was taken to a field hospital of that corps, established on the high ground on the north bank of the river. That hospital was also shelled by the enemy. Tuesday evening a number of the wounded were moved to a farm-house further back from the river, but the house and all the outbuildings were crowded with wounded, so that many were compelled to lie out in the heavy rain of Tuesday night. The writer and a drummer by the name of Henry (from the Fifth New Jersey, I think), who was wounded in the leg, lay side and side, and together were loaded into an ambulance, some time toward morning, and taken to Potomac creek. It would have been a rough ride for a sound man, for it was pitch dark, and the road led through forests, over stumps and gullies. The wounded were tossed about like chips upon the waves.

Lieutenant Beach, who was wounded at Chancellorsville, relates the following interesting incident, which occurred on his way to Washington:

"I was wounded early in the morning of the last day of the fight, and was put in an ambulance with a wounded Confederate belonging to an Alabama regiment. We were driven to the steamer at Aquia Creek to be transported to Washington. The Confederate was laid on a cot next to mine on the upper deck. Before we left the dock, President Lincoln telegraphed he was coming down to look after the wounded, and the vessel was detained until he arrived. As he came on our deck, grasping the hand and speaking a word of comfort to every one, the Alabamian asked me who it was coming. I told him it was President Lincoln. He then asked me if the President would speak to him. I replied I thought so. When the President came to his cot, he took his hand and asked about his comfort and if his wound had been dressed, and showed as much interest in his

Captain Samuel T. Sleeper.

welfare as he did in any of our own soldiers. When he left, the Confederate was in tears and was completely overcome by the kindly interest of the man against whose authority he was fighting. He said he hoped to live to return to his home and tell his people how the great heart of Abraham Lincoln had gone out toward him—a rebel."

CHAPTER VI.

The March to Gettysburg—Gettysburg.

AFTER the battle, what was left of the regiment soon settled down to the old routine of camp-life. The daily round of duties—the drill, the guard, the picket, the review, the reconstruction of camp, and the many details connected with the rehabilitating of a shattered army—occupied the time and thoughts through the daylight hours. But when gathered in their tents at night, or around the camp-fires on the reserve picket-post, the thoughts went back to the battle-field, and many personal experiences were related, hairbreadth escapes and deeds of daring, known only to the relator.

The comrades who were gone were not forgotten, but a soldier soon learns to realize that wounds and death are the inevitable results of war, and learns to look upon them with an indifference and seeming lack of feeling incomprehensible to those who never experienced the sights and sounds of a battle-field. The loser of a finger or a toe, or the possessor of a flesh-wound sufficiently severe to temporarily disable, were looked upon with envy or made a subject of merriment—it meant a respite from duty, and possibly a twenty or thirty days' furlough.

I do not think that the American soldier gives much consideration to the probable dangers of the future. He does not let his spirits become depressed by brooding over what may occur, consequently he rushes into danger with a carelessness, even a cheerfulness, peculiarly his own. It is only the boom of the cannon and the crack of the rifle that will scatter the cards from his pocket upon the roadside.

On May 11th the regiment participated in a review of the corps by General Daniel E. Sickles. Only its lack of numbers told of the desperate fighting through which the corps had passed. Its entire loss at Chancellorsville footed up 4,039. On the 12th the brigade was sent on picket, the Eleventh Regiment being held on reserve. While some of Company E were doing guard-duty at General Carr's headquarters, who occupied a country mansion in rear of the picket-line, a slave was brought in under guard, who, in the absence of his mistress, had entered the house, broken a portion of her furniture, stolen a gold and a silver watch, ninety dollars in money, and decamped. I do not know what disposition the General made of him.

A large number of our wounded had been left in the enemy's hands; they having scant facilities for caring for them, General Lee, after taking their parole, allowed bridges to be laid, and on the 13th the ambulances crossed and brought them within our lines.

On the 14th the regiment was placed upon the front line of pickets, where it remained until eight A. M. of the 15th, when it was relieved and marched back to camp.

The 17th, being Sunday, brought its usual regimental inspection, its round of visits from the chaplain, who distributed tracts and other reading-matter of a religious nature.

On the 18th a large detail was sent to Potomac creek, where the corps hospital had been established, to assist in the erection of tents and other work necessary to make the wounded comfortable. The Third Corps hospital lay along Potomac creek and not far from the railroad running from Aquia Creek to Falmouth, over which a large part of the supplies for the army of the Potomac were taken. This short line of road was noted for a very remarkable piece of engineering, material considered. To cross the valley of Potomac creek required a bridge four hundred feet in length and one hundred in height. When General McDowell lay at Falmouth—the original bridge having been destroyed—General Haupt caused a new one to be erected. The material was poles cut from the adjacent woods, spliced and braced together. "The bridge was finished about midnight. Early next morning President Lincoln, with his cabinet, passed over it to hold a conference with McDowell at Falmouth. On his return he remarked to members of Congress that he had seen the most remarkable structure that the human eye ever rested upon. 'That man, General Haupt, has built a bridge over Potomac creek, upon which the trains to supply the army are moving every hour; and upon my word, gentlemen, there is nothing in it but bean-poles and cornstalks.' The bridge was destroyed and rebuilt several times."*

Surgeon E. L. Welling, of the Eleventh New Jersey, was in charge of the Division Hospital, and connected with it as nurses were Miss Helen L. Gilson and Mr. Fay, of Chelsea, Massachusetts. Only those who were recipients of their care can make a just estimate of their services. Did the capricious appetite of the feverish soldier long for something not in the army bill of fare, Miss Gilson's name would bring it. And how many times her songs revived the drooping spirits! The war called forth many noble women. But Miss Gilson seemed nearer to the white diamonds—more directly the representative of that army of self-sacrificing, heroic spirits that were serving wherever suffering was to be found, some of whom gave not only time and comfort, but health and even life.

Nothing occurred to disturb the dullness of camp-life until June 11th, when marching orders were again received. Lee had concluded that an invasion of the North was practicable, and his army was headed for the rich fields of Pennsylvania. It has been said that the most positive information that General Lee was moving northward with his army was obtained through an old colored man who sold pies to the Confederate army. Some time during the battle of Chancellorsville he had come to the northern side of the river, and found himself away from home when Lee again took possession of Fredericksburg. General Sharp, who was at that time in charge of the Secret Service department, offered to send him back if he would establish a clothes-line telegraph on the other side near the shore, where his wife was accustomed to do her washing. The instructions were that if General Lee moved his troops to the north, a red article should be hung upon the northern end; if to the south, on the

---

*From History of One Hundred and Eighteenth Pennsylvania.

F

southern end; if to the rear, the red article was to hang in the center of the line, the number of articles appearing upon the line to indicate the extent of the movement. Not many days elapsed before a red article appeared upon the extreme northern end of the line. Day after day others were added, until the entire northern end was covered with red. In the daily visits of the old colored man to the army he had gained this important information and communicated it to General Sharp.

Hooker had learned, however, from his spies that an invasion was talked of, and had written to President Lincoln, on the 28th, that the enemy was about to make a movement of some kind. The movement of the rebel camps had also been noted by the commander of the Army of the Potomac; and yet, so skillful had Lee managed his movements that it was probably not until the taking of Winchester that his object was definitely known.

The regiment broke camp on June 11th, and after marching eight miles, bivouacked for the night at Harewood church. The ground was not entirely unknown, for the hurried march of the previous winter, through rain and sleet, had made the men slightly acquainted with the locality. After a good night's rest the troops were early astir, and six o'clock found them on the move. The morning was beautifully clear, and a delightful breeze tempered the heat. Morrisville, a point where four roads met, was reached about noon. The Second Division took the road to the river and reached Rappahannock Station at dark. The First Brigade, however, continued to Beverly ford, which it reached at ten P. M., making the march for the day twenty-four miles.

Doubleday says: "It would seem that it was Lee's first intention to march along the eastern base of the Blue Ridge, directly toward Washington, trusting to his cavalry to conceal his movements." The defeat of his cavalry at Brandy Station, however, compelled him to take the valley route, where his movements were entirely hidden by the mountains. In anticipation of a movement of that kind, however, Hooker had sent the Third Corps to guard the fords opposite Culpepper, while the Fifth Corps guarded those lower down.

The brigade remained at Beverly ford until the 14th, doing picket-duty along the river. At dark on the 14th the pickets were withdrawn and the march taken toward Bealton Station. The march was continued along the railroad all night, and until nine A. M. on the 15th, when a halt was made for breakfast one mile east of Warrenton Junction. At one P. M. the troops were again put in motion. The day was terribly close, and the clouds of dust made marching almost unendurable. Hundreds were compelled to fall out, and the ambulances were loaded with those who had succumbed to the heat. Many were sun-struck, some fatally. But still the march went on with few halts, until eleven o'clock at night, when Manassas Junction was reached. After rations were issued, the troops were allowed a much-needed rest. The short march of only one mile on the 16th was a God-send to the still wearied men. The day's rest gave them renewed vigor, and the march was resumed with cheerfulness on the morning of the 17th. When Bull Run was reached the column was halted and the men given an opportunity to take a much-needed bath. At three P. M., thoroughly refreshed, the march was resumed to Centerville, where bivouac was made for the night. The 18th was an easy day. The regiment having been detailed as guard to the wagon-train, only a half mile was marched, but a heavy thunder-storm that came up made shelter of any kind desirable.

The long march without adequate halts for rest, the extreme heat and the stifling clouds of dust that were encountered on the 15th caused many good soldiers to straggle. However much they may have desired to keep with their commands, they could not do so, the work required being beyond their powers of endurance.

Among the many who thus found themselves separated from their regiments was a group of four belonging to Company B, of the Eleventh New Jersey, namely, Wm. Hand, T. O'Doane and Charles and John Vorhees; and with them was a member of the Eleventh Massachusetts. They were all good soldiers, as was proven at Gettysburg, where all five were wounded. As they were marching down the railroad, a train of freight cars stopped near them. Thinking they would gain time, and also a rest, they climbed aboard and rode to Fairfax Station, where they were informed that only those having a surgeon's pass could go any further in that direction. They climbed down and bivouacked for the night near a spring. The next morning they were told by a wagon-master that the Third Corps was on a road twenty miles to the westward and was marching northward. They were then in a dilemma, as it might take them several days to overtake their commands, and they were entirely out of rations, and the surrounding country had been so often subject to forays that nothing was left to reward the forager. But Hand rose equal to the occasion. An officer of the Commissary Department was at the station issuing rations to the teamsters. Doane was already quite sick, but Hand told him to make himself look as ill as possible and he would see if he could not work upon the sympathies of the Commissary. Taking Doane with him, he proceeded to the station and told the officer that he was in charge of four sick men, with orders to take them to Alexandria; that they had given out and were out of rations, and could go no further without getting something to eat. The Commissary asked where the other three men were. Hand told him down by the railroad, not able to come up. The officer seemed to hesitate, but Doane at that moment wilted down to the ground, and, placing his head between his hands, he so nearly assumed the appearance of a man approaching dissolution that he turned the scale, and the officer, with one more look at him, ordered his Sergeant to weigh out three days' rations for five men. After getting the rations, Hand thanked him and rejoined his comrades at the spring. After getting breakfast they started toward Centerville, which they reached just as the head of the Third Corps was passing. Adjutant Schoonover was the first one to discover them as they approached the regiment, but so well did they explain their absence—I think Hand must have remained spokesman for the party—that they escaped with a light reprimand.

By a strange coincidence all five of these men were wounded at Gettysburg, Charles A. Vorhees losing both eyes and the man from the Eleventh Massachusetts a leg. Haud afterwards rose to the rank of First Lieutenant and John Vorhees to Sergeant, and both served until the close of the war. Doane became permanently disabled and was transferred to the Veteran Reserve Corps, and was discharged from it as Sergeant.

At three o'clock on the afternoon of the 19th the march was resumed and Gum Springs reached about dark. There, with the exception of a change of camp and the excitement occasioned by the cavalry fight at Aldie, the sound of which could be plainly heard, the regiment rested quietly until the 25th.

The inhabitants of Gum Springs and vicinity were intensely rebel, all the able-bodied men being either in the regular Confederate service or with Mosby's band of guerillas; consequently but little restraint was put upon foragers. A party who went out from the Eleventh on the 24th returned with twenty cows and a miscellaneous lot of sheep, geese and chickens. Two Union soldiers were found hanging in a barn, where they had been murdered by guerillas.

While lying at Gum Springs a number of those who had been left on duty at the hospital re-joined their commands. It will be remembered that the Third Corps hospital had been located at Potomac creek, and in the event of the Union army moving northward it would be exposed to capture. In view of this fact it seems strange that ample time had not been given for the removal of the wounded and the hospital stores to a place of safety. But it was not until the 13th—two days after the Corps had started on its northward march—that orders were issued to send the wounded and stores to Aquia Creek for transportation to Alexandria. Then the movement was made hastily and a large quantity of stores, such as tents, provisions, small arms, cars, etc., were destroyed. It was supposed that no troops remained between the hospital and the enemy, when in fact

Sedgwick, who had been ordered to throw a portion of his corps across the river at Franklin's crossing to ascertain if the enemy still held their old position, did not re-cross until the night of the 13th, and on the 15th was still between the Rappahannock and Potomac creek.

Captain D. B. Logan.

As the experience of those left behind with the hospital may be of interest, and as the experience of one is typical of all, I will quote the account given by A. B. Searing, of Company E, Eleventh New Jersey, who was one of the number:

"On the 13th we received orders to place all of the wounded men in our corps hospital on board the cars and send them to

Aquia Creek. Those who were able rode to the cars in ambulances, but some with fractured or amputated limbs had to be tenderly carried there on stretchers. We did not get much sleep or rest that night, as there were so many wounded to move. The next day was Sunday, and we worked hard, taking down the hospital tents and packing up. In the afternoon the surgeons left in a hurry, for there was no armed force of ours known to be stationed between us and the rebels, and, having no time to cart the hospital supplies to the cars, the Provost Marshal gave us orders to destroy them. We burned up what tents were left, and, going to the commissary building, we knocked in the heads of the vinegar and molasses barrels and let their contents run down the hill; set fire to the building containing crackers, rice, sugar, and other eatables, and, taking a lot of rifles stored near by, we broke their stocks off and threw them in the creek, so that if the rebels found them they would be of no use. In looking where the surgeons' tent had stood, one of our number found a half-gallon jug of whiskey, which he confiscated, and, noticing a box filled with sawdust, I put my hand down in it and found several bottles of blackberry brandy, which I divided among the soldiers, keeping one myself. We went around the whole camp, making sure that everything was destroyed or on fire, and about dark, not knowing how soon the rebels would advance on us, our small detail of soldiers marched down to the railroad station, and at nine P. M. left there on the last train of cars for Aquia Creek, where the locomotives were run on boats prepared for them. The cars and buildings were burned, and at two A. M., on the 15th we took passage on board a transport bound for Alexandria, Va., where we arrived about sunrise.

"On the 16th, I was on duty day and night, guarding the hospital supplies. The next day we were busy unloading the cargo from the vessel upon which we came, which consisted principally of supplies to be distributed among the various hospitals in the city. On the 20th we were still on guard over the supplies on the wharves and vessels at Alexandria.

"On the 21st, owing to the uncertainty as to where the different regiments were, to which our detail of guards and nurses belonged, it was proposed to send us to Camp Distribution, there to stay until we could be safely sent to our various commands. We numbered about forty men, and the majority were anxious to rejoin their regiments without delay, and hearing that the army was at Leesburg, we decided to try to find them. Filling our haversacks with provisions, which the ladies of our hospital gave us, we were placed in charge of a commissioned officer, who formed one of our number, and at three P M. Saturday we got on the cars at Alexandria and rode fifteen miles over a very poor railroad, which was as far as they could run, the bridges beyond being destroyed and the country unsafe, owing to bushwhackers and guerillas. Leaving the cars behind us we struck out through the country and marched to Johnson farm, where we bivouacked for the night.

"Sunday morning found us again on the tramp, and after marching through Drainesville, we crossed Broad run, and at seven P M. we arrived at Goose Creek, a small hamlet of about half a dozen dwellings, where we camped for the night near a house occupied by a widow lady, Mrs. Miller, son and a daughter named Virginia. I did not see a single able-bodied man, all being in the rebel army. But the ladies were very pleasant, and none of our party was allowed to forage any, and paid a fair price for everything they bought. In the evening a number of our boys called upon Mrs. Miller and her family, and she expressed a desire to hear some good Union songs. Elias Blanchard and several others complied with her request, and in return Miss Virginia favored us with some Confederate songs. We had no alarms during the night, and on Monday morning several of us lightened our knapsacks by giving Mrs. Miller what we could spare.

"The next thing was to provide some way to cross Goose creek, which was quite a large stream of water. Finally we found a scow, and a boy who ferried us across, six at a time. After all had crossed over we fell in line and marched on until ten A. M., when we reached Leesburg, which was quite a large town, with fine, pleasantly shaded streets. We had expected to find the Third Corps there, and were very much disappointed when told that they were at Gum Springs, fifteen miles away. We procured three days' rations of hard-tack, coffee and sugar, and at four P M. we left there and marched a few miles and encamped for the night. The early morning found us on the move. We again crossed Goose creek, at a place where a bridge had recently been built by the Eleventh Corps, and marching on through a fine section of country, the fields of which were covered with corn and wheat, we found our corps at noon, and I re-joined my regiment, glad to be once more with my comrades."

At ten A. M., on June 25th, the corps was again set in motion. The march led to the Potomac at Edwards Ferry, near the mouth of Goose creek, where a pontoon bridge had been constructed. After a brief halt upon the Maryland shore, the march was continued by way of the towpath of the Ohio and Chesapeake canal. Rain was falling heavily, and soon the tramping of many feet made the towpath very insecure footing. Darkness fell; still the tramp continued hour after hour, slipping, sliding—sometimes cursing when a misstep caused some one to measure his length in the mud—the canal on one side, the steep river-bank upon the other—no place for halting, nothing to do but worry on through the darkness and dampness, hoping that the canal would soon be crossed and a halt ordered. The division was stretched out like a skirmish-line. At last the Monocacy was reached, the canal crossed, and at two o'clock in the morning, after a march of twenty-five miles, those who were with their commands had an opportunity to lie down and rest upon the sodden ground. But the division was well scattered, and up to eleven o'clock, the time that the march was resumed, stragglers kept coming in.

The night of the 26th the bivouac was upon the Catoctin mountain.

June 27th, the Eleventh Regiment was rear-guard to the wagon-train, and were early on the move. We soon met evidence that the old flag was still loved and cherished by many of the inhabitants of Maryland. As we passed a farm-house standing some distance back from the road, a group of ladies standing upon the porch greeted us by waving the Stars and Stripes. This evidence of loyalty and friendship, a thing to which we had been strangers for some time, put new life into each lagging footstep, and, dressing-up the ranks, we passed as on review, saluting the ladies with colors, music and three hearty cheers. Later in the day we passed through the town of Jefferson, and there received a very enthusiastic welcome. Flags were waving across the streets, and from many windows white handkerchiefs held by fair hands fluttered welcomes from porches, windows and doorways. But with a steady tramp we passed through and left the town behind, and at nine P. M. reached Burkettsville, where we bivouacked for the night. Burkettsville was a pleasant village, beautifully situated at the foot of the South mountains. It contained quite a number of dwellings and two churches, and as we marched through it, Sunday morning, June 28th, bells were calling the worshipers to assemble. The sweet tones, vibrating upon the calm morning air, redolent with all the odors of queenly June, and re-echoing from the green mountain-sides, seemed sadly at variance with the marching columns, the glittering rifles and frowning cannons around. They brought to our mental vision scenes that we had left far behind us in our own loved Northland—scenes that many were to look upon never again. For a while we were oblivious to the instruments of death around us. We heard not the tramping of horses, the rumble of guns and the clanking of sabers. We saw not the dusty roadway filled with a winding column of blue. No! We were again wending our way toward where the village spire peeped above the trees. We saw from every road and footpath friends and loved ones hastening, and we heard the pastor's opening prayer and the sweet tones of the choir as they carried aloft the music of some old familiar hymn. We saw the gray-haired father's reverent bow and the mother's time-wrinkled yet tender hands closed in silent devotion. We were awakened from our reverie by the command,

"Close up! Close up!" The vision had passed; home was far away and war's stern realities around us.

Later in the day we marched through Middletown, beyond which we halted for dinner, then past a hamlet called Jerusalem, and soon in the distance we saw the spires of Frederick. Before reaching the town the ranks were closed up and flags unfurled, and with bands playing and colors flying we marched through the city that gave birth to the author of the "Star Spangled Banner." The inhabitants greeted us with every demonstration of delight, but they seemed to be surprised at our numbers. One old gentleman who from an upper window was busily engaged in waving a flag, as he gazed down the long street and saw the blue-coated column come pouring steadily on, kept exclaiming, as if in wonder, "Still they come! still they come!" As the boys passed beneath his window they greeted him with hearty cheers. We marched through the city without a halt and on beyond the Monocacy river, where a halt was made for the night, after a march of nineteen miles.

The transition from the pine forests and desolated fields of Virginia, from contact with a disloyal people, who meet you with open defiance or ill-concealed dislike, to the fruitful fields and overflowing loyalty of western Maryland was especially grateful to the army. It gave new courage to the heart and life to the lagging footstep.

Colonel Schoonover, writing of the march through Maryland, says: "There was enthusiasm in the towns and hospitality in the farm-houses. Cup after cup of water was passed to the thirsty soldiers from the many springs bursting out along the roadside. Up through the beautiful valleys and cozy towns we were welcomed with bright smiles and waving handkerchiefs. At one point on the roadside a number of big-hearted women had provided a large quantity of sandwiches and handed them to the men as they passed by. This act of generosity and kindness brought forth repeated and hearty cheers from the ranks. I do not know how far down the line the lunch reached, but I am prepared to give my individual testimony in favor of Maryland sandwiches."

The beat of drums roused us from slumber at early dawn on the morning of June 29th, and before we had time to prepare any breakfast, the order came to fall in. So, with empty stomachs, we started in the direction of Taneytown, once the residence of Chief Justice Taney, whose "Dred Scott" decision was one of the brands that helped to kindle the flame of rebellion. We crossed Pipe creek on the way, and at five P M. bivouacked for the night one mile beyond Taneytown. During the day General Daniel E. Sickles, commander of the Third Corps, who had been absent on leave, re-joined it, and the wild cheering that followed his passage through the ranks showed the great esteem in which he was held by the men under him. And here let me say that I do not believe any General of the war possessed in a greater degree the love and confidence of his men.

The long marches had been hard upon the men, and doubly hard upon their clothing. Shoes, especially, were in a very dilapidated condition, some of the men being entirely barefoot. The supply-trains being within reach, a rest was therefore taken until noon of the 30th, and the much-needed shoes and stockings issued. The halt gave the country people around an opportunity to indulge their curiosity. They came trooping from every direction to see the soldiers, never having seen such an aggregation of men before. One old lady was overheard saying, "Uriah, I must run right home and get the children, for they will never get a chance to see such a sight again." The field-pieces, especially, were objects of wonder and awe, such instruments of death having perhaps been heard of, but never before seen. No doubt in years to come, around many a winter fireside the aged will tell to eager-listening children how they saw the grand Army of the Potomac sweeping up to the bloody yet decisive battle of Gettysburg.

About one P M. the command was again under way. The march was back to Taneytown, and then headed toward Emmettsburg. After a march of about four miles a halt was made for the night in a wheat-field. The grain had been cut and bound, and the sheaves made luxurious beds for the soldiers.

Hooker, finding himself hampered, and his plans thwarted by Halleck, had, on the 28th of June, tendered his resignation, which was quickly accepted, and General George G. Meade, the commander of the Fifth Corps, was given command of the army The immediate cause of Hooker's resignation was the refusal of Halleck to permit him to withdraw the ten thousand men, held as a useless garrison, at Harper's Ferry. With them he wished to strengthen Slocum, who had been instructed to act directly against Lee's communications (a movement countermanded by Meade). That Halleck's refusal was the result of dislike for Hooker was shown by the fact that Meade was permitted to break up the post at Harper's Ferry, notwithstanding Hooker had been refused permission to do so. The army knew Meade only as the commander of the Fifth Corps, but it had become accustomed to sudden changes, and it excited but little comment.

On the morning of July 1st, after the regiment was formed for the march, the following order was read by Adjutant Schoonover:

"HEADQUARTERS ARMY OF THE POTOMAC,
"June 30th, 1863.

"The commanding General requests that previous to the engagement soon expected with the enemy, corps and all other commanding officers will address their troops, explaining to them briefly the immense issues involved in this struggle. The enemy are on our soil, the whole country now looks anxiously to the army to deliver it from the presence of the foe. Our failure to do so will leave us no such welcome as the swelling of millions of hearts with pride and joy at our success would give to every soldier in the army. Homes, friends and domestic altars are involved. The army has fought well heretofore, it is believed that it will fight more desperately and bravely than ever if it is addressed in fitting terms. Corps and other commanders are authorized to order the instant death of any soldier who fails in his duty at this hour.

"By command of   MAJOR-GENERAL MEADE.
"S. WILLIAMS, *A. A. G.*"

After the reading of the order from General Meade, Colonel McAllister addressed the Eleventh Regiment as follows:

"Sons of New Jersey, the hour of battle is at hand. The soil of Pennsylvania is the contested field. We must stand shoulder-to-shoulder with her sons and drive the enemy from

Captain A. H. Ackerman.

her borders, cost what it may. Your past bright record is a guarantee to me that you will not falter. In the dark days of the revolution, when the gallant Jersey Blues were fighting for liberty upon their own soil, their Pennsylvania brothers rushed to their assistance and helped them triumph. We are now called upon to do for Pennsylvania what she did for us. Now with hearts filled with love of country and a firm reliance on God, let us go forward. Are you ready for the march and the fight?"

"Yes, yes," was the answer, with three hearty cheers. It was a scene never to be forgotten. The less than three hundred that remained of the old regiment, formed in hollow square, although footsore and weary from days of toilsome marching, listened, eager to catch the words of the leader who always said, "Come." And as his ringing words fell upon their ears, guns were grasped tighter and faces, bronzed by a year's sun and storms, lit up with the glow of the patriotic fires that glowed within their hearts, revealing a stern determination to do all that men and patriots could do to wipe away the stain that the contaminating touch of treason's footsteps had placed upon the free soil of the loyal Keystone State.

With hearts warmed and weariness almost forgotten, the regiment again pressed forward. Emmettsburg, a town that had been partly destroyed by fire—the work, it was said, of a Southern sympathizer—was reached about noon. Just beyond the town the troops were halted, and as the impression prevailed that they would remain there through the balance of the day and night, and as provisions had become scarce, many of the men scattered among the surrounding farmers in search of food. Here Hand, of Company B, again became separated from his command. He had gone out in search of something to eat, and visited house after house only to find that some one had been before him. At last, when about two miles from camp, he struck a house, near the mountain, that had not been visited. He purchased a pan of milk, two pies and a loaf of bread. While settling for his purchases the farmer asked him if he had heard firing in the direction of Gettysburg. Hand replied that he had not. The farmer told him to listen and he would hear it. He did hear it then, and on looking back toward Emmettsburg he saw that the troops were in motion. Hastily filling his canteen, and drinking as much of the milk as he could, he put the bread in his haversack and the pies on a cabbage-leaf, which he took in his hands. Starting back upon a run, soon the pies began to break and their contents to ooze out between his fingers. To save them he was compelled to stop and eat them. On reaching the place where the regiment had been he found that all had left except Joseph Decker of his company, who had remained to take care of his things. Hand divided the bread and milk, and then they started after the regiment, which they overtook near morning.

Not far from Emmettsburg we crossed Mason and Dixon's line, and once more trod the soil of a Northern State. Just as we crossed the line a German woman came out of a house with a pail of water, saying: "Here's Pennsylvania water for you, boys." The boys responded by giving three cheers for the old Keystone State.

News had been received that the First Corps had met the enemy at Gettysburg, and that General Reynolds, its commander, had been killed. We had not gone far before we heard the dull boom of cannon, and we knew that all haste would be made to reach the scene of the conflict. Evening came, but there was no time for eating. Darkness closed around us, but there was no time for rest. Trains were left behind in the hurry, for we must be in the enemy's front by the morning.

About midnight we took the wrong road, and only the fortunate capture of the enemy's videttes, without giving an alarm, saved us from marching into their lines. A farmer said they had a battery planted commanding the road only a short distance ahead. The order was passed down the line to about-face and retrace our steps as quietly as possible. Soon we struck the right road, and about two A. M. on the morning of July 2d we halted near what was to become one of the most famous battle-fields of modern times. Worn-out with rapid marching, we soon were slumbering peacefully; nor did we dream that ere another sun should set many of our number would be lying pulseless and still but a short distance from where we were then resting.

Before entering into an account of the battle, it would be well, perhaps, to give the reader a faint idea of the general features of the battle-field.

Gettysburg, the county seat of Adams, is situated near the center of the county, and about ten miles south and east of the range of hills known as the South Mountains. The surrounding country is rough, being broken by ridges of granite that in some early geological period the internal fires had forced up through the softer shale.

The town, previous to its rude awakening in 1863, was a quiet, sleepy one, nestling peacefully in a pleasant hollow formed by two ridges. The ridges are not continuous, but here and there fall away to almost level stretches, but without, however, entirely losing their outlines. Frequent rounded knolls also mark their general course. Looking westward from the town, at the distance of half a mile the eye rested upon a long wooded crest, the center of which was crowned by the buildings of the Lutheran Theological Seminary, from which fact the western ridge took the name of Seminary Ridge. The eastern ridge—which was occupied by the Union troops—was shaped somewhat like a fish-hook, and began on the western side of Rock creek, at a wooded knoll called Culp's hill, circling around to Cemetery Hill—the site of the village burying-ground—and then bore nearly due south and terminated at Big Roundtop, nearly three miles away. Little Roundtop, a lower and less precipitous eminence, lay to the north of Big Roundtop, and separated from it by a rocky, wooded valley. Some distance north of Little Roundtop the ridge almost entirely disappeared, leaving a stretch of comparatively low ground.

A short distance to the west of Roundtop was a triangular-shaped ridge, a portion of which was known as the Devil's Den. The Devil's Den was a vast pile of irregular-shaped granite blocks, separated here and there by deep fissures. Its face was precipitous, and from beneath it flowed a spring of clear cold water. The land between Roundtop and the Devil's Den was low and marshy, and was traversed by a sluggish stream.

Two roads ran from the town to the southward, the Taneytown road on the west, and the Baltimore pike to the eastward. The Emmettsburg road, however, entered the Baltimore pike a short distance from the town, near the base of Cemetery Hill. It bore west of south, following a minor ridge. South of the junction of the Emmettsburg and Baltimore roads, the Taneytown road crossed the Emmettsburg road and Cemetery Ridge diagonally, and then took a course southward between the two, keeping to the eastward of the Ridge and the Little Roundtop. The principal cross-road was one connecting the Baltimore and Taneytown roads, just south of Powers Hill, and another connecting the three ran just north of Little Roundtop and crossed the Emmettsburg road at the Peach Orchard, one mile from Roundtop. Another left the Emmettsburg road still further south and followed the valley between the Roundtops. These were the roads that traversed the field, or were in the immediate vicinity of the field of operations of the regiment. But various other roads centered upon the village from the east, north and westward—ten in all, I believe, entered the town. This alone would make it a point of great strategic importance. The Hanover road entered from the east; from the northeast came the road to York. Almost due north a road led to Carlisle, in the Cumberland Valley, but between it and the York road was one leading to Hunterstown and other points. To the northwest ran the road to Chambersburg, but north of it, to join it again at Cashtown, ran the road to Mummasburg. A road leaving further south and running southwest led to Fairfield and Mouterey.

The many roads centering at the village and the open farmland surrounding it afforded excellent facilities for moving and manœuvring troops.

The morning of July 2d dawned close and foggy, but with no indication to those in the ranks that a tremendous struggle was to take place within a few hours.

About ten o'clock we were moved forward and placed *en masse*. We remained in position until nearly three, when the line was advanced and deployed along the Emmettsburg road. The position of the Eleventh New Jersey was to the left of what was known as the Smith house. In the rear of the buildings was an apple orchard, and south of that a young peach orchard. This fact has led some to believe that our position was in the historic peach orchard, which was still further to the left and beyond a cross-road, or rather at the junction of the cross-road with the Emmettsburg road. Our first position was with the right of the regiment, resting near the buildings, and the regiment extending down and nearly parallel with the road, but some twenty paces to the east of it. The First Brigade occupied the right of the division and corps. The Eleventh New Jersey was upon the left of the brigade, the Second New Hampshire, Twenty-sixth Pennsylvania, Sixteenth and Eleventh Massachusetts extending to the right. The First Massachusetts occupied an advanced position across the road, near a house occupied by a family by the name of Miller, the house, however, being known as the Rogers house. The enemy had posted a long line of batteries on the ridge to our left in a position to command Birney's front and enfilade Graham's and Humphries' divisions. Scarcely had the line taken position when they opened upon us a terrific fire. Our batteries responding, for half an hour the earth trembled beneath the jar of guns. Seeley's Battery (K), Fourth United States, which had been posted on our right, was ordered to our left, and its place was taken by Turnbull's Battery, from the artillery reserve. The air seemed thick with flying missiles. Tons of metal hurtled over and fell around us, and it was only by hugging the ground closely that we escaped serious loss. Fortunately but few men in the regiment were struck, but there were many narrow escapes.

There is nothing more trying to the nerves of soldiers than lying unprotected under a galling artillery fire, and we were not sorry when its cessation told us that the enemy were advancing to the charge. We had not long to wait. On our right and front, Wright, Perry and Wilcox, of R. H. Anderson's Division, A. P Hill's Corps, led their veteran brigades; and to the left, through the peach orchard, Barksdale led his Mississippians; Kershaw's Brigade was next on the enemy's right, and his brigade, with Barksdale's left advancing at a right angle with our line of battle, completely enfiladed Carr's Brigade and rendered its position untenable.

Barksdale, as he led his brigade, riding a white horse and wearing upon his head a red fez, was perhaps the most conspicuous figure in the charge; his example and enthusiasm were equal to a brigade of men.

General Carr, our brigade commander, seeing that the most effectual way of checking the charge of the enemy was by bringing down their leader, sent Captain Benedict to the commander of the Eleventh New Jersey with orders to bring down the officer on the white horse. Captain Cory, whose company was on the extreme left of the regiment, was instructed to direct the entire fire of his Company (H) at this officer. He did so, with the result that the officer fell. After the fighting for the day had ceased his rank was ascertained, and he was carried to General Carr's headquarters, where it was found that he was fatally wounded, being pierced with five balls.

As has been seen, Barksdale's charge pushing back everything from his front, struck our left flank, necessitating a change of front. The movement successfully executed (though a difficult one under fire), placed our regiment at an angle with the Emmettsburg road and nearly parallel with the cross-roads belows It also threw us back from the ridge along the Emmettsburg road and placed us on the low ground in rear of the orchard. We were then facing towards the peach orchard, but the position placed us under a cross-fire from Anderson's troops. Our batteries ploughed lanes through the living masses in front of them, yet they pressed on. Here occurred our most desperate fighting and our greatest loss. In a little less than half an hour we lost four officers killed and ten wounded, and three-fifths of our enlisted men. Quoting from Schoonover:

"As the enemy's line appeared in splendid order on the high ground in our front, Major Kearney, overflowing with excitement, exclaimed 'I tell you we are going to have a fight!' The words were hardly uttered when a ball crashed through his knee. His hand dropped from my shoulder, where it was resting, and he spun like a top to the rear, landing at least ten feet from me. Having sent two men to carry him to a place of safety, I hurried to the right of the regiment to notify the Colonel of the Major's absence and there learned that *he* had been severly wounded and taken to the rear. I informed Captain Martin, the senior officer present, that he was in command of the regiment. Returning to the left, an order was received from General Carr to change front by bringing our left to the rear, to meet General Barksdale's charge. During the execution of this movement Captains Logan and Martin were wounded, and both were killed before reaching a place of safety. A moment later Captain Ackerman, the next senior, fell dead by my side. This was the third commanding officer killed and the second wounded in the space of ten or twelve minutes. After maintaining this position for about half an hour, with ranks sadly thinned and somewhat disorganized, the line fell back."

During the earlier part of the engagement Adjutant Schoonover was struck in the breast by a piece of shell, but not seriously injured. Being again struck with a buckshot, he was forced to go temporarily to the rear.

Some distance to the rear of our second position there grew a hedge-row, or fringe of chaparral, near which the brigade finally took position, and from which it made a charge and re-occupied the ground held during the hottest part of the battle. During this movement the remnant of the regiment was commanded by Captain Loyd. This line was maintained during the greater part of the night. Adjutant Schoonover's absence was a brief one, as he re-joined the regiment during the early part of the evening and, by request of Captain Sleeper, the senior officer present, took command. Captain Loyd, being disabled, had been compelled to seek surgical aid.

During the desperate fighting of the afternoon the regiment had become somewhat disorganized and scattered, so that, perhaps, not more than one-half of the survivors were present with the colors during the forward movement in the evening. But little sleep was obtained by those who remained on the front during the night, and, added to the want of sleep and that exhaustion and feeling of depression which follow a desperate struggle, were the pangs of hunger, as for two days past the rations had been meager. The forced march of the 1st of July, lasting well into the morning of the 2d, had taken us away from our trains,

Captain S. M. Layton.

and the movements and fighting of the 2d had prevented any opportunity for drawing rations. So that the morning of the 3d found the survivors of the Eleventh weak for the want of food. Men were seen turning their haversacks inside out, hoping to find a few crumbs remaining, or wandering over the fields where other troops had been, picking up the crumbs that had fallen.

The position of the Third Corps on the morning of July 3d was to the left of the First Corps, and the Eleventh Regiment found itself in a rocky woodland. Here a ration of hard bread and coffee was issued in the morning, and somewhat later in the day a ration of fresh meat was brought up, but before it could be issued, orders came to fall in. Leaving a guard over the meat—for that was too precious to lose—we started on a double-quick to the right and front. After proceeding nearly a mile, a halt was made in rear of a line of batteries, which occupied the crest in front. This position was held during the heavy cannonading that preceded Pickett's charge, and until the charge had been repulsed. Then we marched back to our former position in the wood. Pickett's charge had proved a failure, and the battle of Gettysburg was practically ended.

During the heavy cannonading, when supporting the batteries, the Adjutant had his horse shot from under him. Sergeant Egan, of Company E, was struck on the leg by a glancing piece of shell. Jumping to his feet and clapping his hand upon the injured spot, he declared, very emphatically, that it would take more than that to send him to the rear.

In all bodies of troops there are men to be found who, to put it mildly, deem "discretion the better part of valor." We do not claim that there was none such in the Eleventh, but the number was few, and the reputation for bravery won by it in the bloody woods of Chancellorsville was ably maintained at Gettysburg. There were many individual acts of bravery performed upon the battle-field, but the majority of them will have to go unrecorded, because of the forgetfulness or reticence of the survivors.

In concluding his report of the engagement of the 2d, Adjutant Schoonover thus refers to the conduct of both officers and men: "To mention some may seem to do gross injustice to others, but I cannot pass by the untiring efforts of Lieutenant Buckley to rally the men. Captains Loyd and Cory also deserve special mention for their coolness and bravery. As an act of individual bravery I desire to mention that of Corporal Thomas Johnson, of Company I. When two color-bearers had been shot down I ordered him to take the colors and advance twenty yards to the front, as the regiment was wavering. He did so, and did not leave his position until ordered to the rear. The services of Lieutenant Joseph C. Baldwin, on the 3d, as Acting Adjutant, were invaluable."

Corporal Thomas Johnson, of Company I, spoken of as taking the colors at Gettysburg, was one of the most fearless of the many brave men of the regiment, but unfortunately he was wofully lacking in education, which unfitted him for the higher positions that he otherwise might have attained and that his courage deserved. He was promoted to Sergeant, September 1st, '63, and received the complimentary commission of Second Lieutenant of Company A June 13th, '65. Such commissions were issued to a number of non-commissioned officers about the time of the regiment's discharge, but it was a very empty honor, as none of the recipients were mustered into the positions to which they were supposed to have been promoted.

Among the many brave men who fell on the afternoon of the 2d there was none whose loss was more deeply felt by his comrades than Sergeant Eliphalet Sturdevant, of Company E. He was a man who had reached middle life with stainless character, unostentatious in manner, of a retiring yet kindly disposition, having a pleasant word and a helping hand for all; yet he was firm and decided in duty, and, above all, a sincere Christian, who became a soldier from pure love of country and deep sense of duty. He was a good singer, and his musical voice was often heard leading in some patriotic song to cheer the men on their long and weary marches. He fell severely wounded and was taken to the field hospital, where his left leg and right arm were amputated, from the effects of which he died on July 13th.

Captain Luther Martin, who, at the time of his death, was the senior Captain with the regiment, was a printer, and for a long time was engaged in the "Fredonian" office, New Brunswick. He afterward became proprietor of the "Plainfield Gazette." He first joined the army June 7th, '61, as Second

Lieutenant of Company A, First New Jersey Volunteers. His health becoming impaired, he was compelled to resign. November 28th, '61, when the Eleventh was being organized, having thoroughly recovered, he accepted a commission as Captain, and recruited Company D. He was a brave and conscientious officer.

Captain Dorastus B. Logan was first wounded in the foot. Edward Kinney, from E, and a man from C, went to assist him to the rear, but they had not gone far when the Company C man was killed. Kinney then endeavored, unassisted, to get the captain to a place of safety, but was himself knocked down by a piece of shell and forced to abandon the Captain, who was killed before he could be taken off the field.

In the death of Captain Andrew Ackerman the regiment lost a gallent and promising officer.

Major Kearney, as before mentioned, was wounded in the knee. He was taken from the field and sent to St. Luke's Hospital, New York, where he died August 9th. Of him the "Paterson Guardian," of August 12th, '63, says:

"We regret to learn of the death of Major Philip J. Kearney, of the Eleventh Regiment, which occurred on Sunday night. Major Kearney, who was but twenty-two years old, was a cousin and namesake of General Phil. Kearney, and, like him, has given his life for the cause of his country. He was brave, cool, and daring, and greatly beloved by the regiment. He was on engineering service in Mexico when the rebellion broke out, but returned to this country, and, being commissioned Captain, recruited in this city Company A, of the Eleventh. He was subsequently promoted Major."

General Joseph B. Carr, Commander of the First Brigade, in his report to General A. A. Humphries, Division Commander, calls attention to the meritorious conduct of Colonel Robert McAllister, Major Kearney and Adjutant John Schoonover, and to Lieutenant John Oldershaw, of the Eleventh, acting Aid-de-camp. He tenders his sincere thanks for valuable services rendered during the battle. Lieutenant—

afterward Captain—Oldershaw seems to have been eminently fitted for the position of staff officer. He served on the staff of General Slough at Alexandria, afterward upon that of General Berry at Chancellorsville, and again upon Carr's at Gettysburg, and from each chief under whom he served he received the highest commendation.

As an instance of how a man may sometimes pass through the most imminent danger, and yet escape serious injury, we will take the case of Adjutant Schoonover. After the battle of Gettysburg was over, in taking an inventory of his clothing six bullet-holes were found, and one rent made by a piece of shell. Add to this the fact that his horse was shot from under him on the 3d, and we have a chapter of miraculous escapes.

Company F, I think, had in its ranks the tallest man in the regiment. He measured six feet four inches and wore a No. 14 shoe. The Government had made no provisions for feet of that size, and it was necessary to send to Philadelphia for shoes to fit them. During the battle this man was struck on the top of the head—a mere scalp-wound, but sufficient to produce temporary insensibility. He was left for dead upon the field, but a few days afterward, much to the surprise of all, he came walking into the regiment. Adjutant Schoonover meeting him, remarked, "Why, I thought you were killed." He replied, "So I was; but only on top of the head." The Adjutant dryly remarked, "You ought to be thankful that you are not six-foot-five."

In this connection, as an evidence of rather more than ordinary endurance, may be mentioned the case of Private Thomas D. Marbecker, of Company E. At the battle of Chancellorsville he received a severe wound and was taken to Potomac Creek hospital, when it was ascertained that Lee was moving northward. The hospital was broken up and the patients sent to Washington and Alexandria. Marbecker was sent to the Mansion House, Alexandria. Not liking hospital life, he resolved to rejoin his regiment at the first opportunity. The next morning, after reaching the Mansion House, some baggage-wagons were brought to the hospital to take a squad of convalescents to the convalescent-camp. Watching his opportunity, he climbed into one of the wagons with them, reaching the camp at noon. Soon afterward the examining surgeon came along, and Marbecker, without displaying his wound—though it was in an unhealed condition—reported himself fit for duty. He started for the regiment the next morning by way of the Ohio and Chesapeake canal, and rejoined it at Gum Springs, Va., June 24th. All that he possessed in the way of equipment was a haversack, canteen and woolen blanket. But that night a member of his company, Charles Kinney, who was on guard over the horses, received a kick that rendered him unfit for duty. Marbecker took *his* gun and equipments and next morning started with the boys for Gettysburg, though compelled to go limping along with one hand holding his clothing away from his unhealed wound. Adjutant Schoonover, seeing his condition, wanted him placed in an ambulance; but he asked to be permitted to stay with his company. Like many others, he became nearly barefoot before reaching Taneytown, where shoes were issued. He stayed with the company, however, and fought with it through the battle of Gettysburg; but it was not until the rest afforded by the encampment at Beverly Ford that the wound entirely healed.

The battle of Gettysburg was a terribly destructive one to the Eleventh Regiment. Few regiments engaged in it suffered as great a percentage of loss. It went into the engagement with 255 muskets. Its losses aggregated 157; of these, 3 officers and 18 enlisted men were killed and 9 officers and 115 enlisted men were wounded, and 12 missing. Of the wounded, Major Kearney and nine enlisted men died of their wounds soon afterward.

The killed were: Captains Andrew Ackerman, of Company C; Luther Martin, of Company D, and Dorastus B. Logan, of Company H. Sergeant Corum Richter, Privates Joseph Cheston and John Clark, of Company C; Corporal Isaac Hendershot and Private Randolph Merriman, of Company D; Private Thomas Tinney, of Company E; Private John L. Cozzins, of Company F; Privates George S. Bird, George H. Bunting,

Henry Elbertson, Michael Goff, Stewart Parent and Peter Robbins, of Company G ; Private Edward Barber, of Company H ; Corporals W H. Morgan and Jeremiah O'Brien, and Privates Henry Kring and Martin Bekie, of Company K.

The wounded were :

Field and Staff—Colonel Robert McAllister, severely; Major Philip J. Kearney, severely ; Adjutant John Schoonover, slightly.

Company A—First Sergeant Joseph Burns, severely ; Corporal Tyler L. Haring, died July 4th, 1863, at field hospital ; Corporal Emilie Wappenstein, Privates Emmet Burk, Christopher Snyder, George H. Johnson and Isaac Harlow, slightly ; Henry McMahon, Robert E. Mayo (arm amputated), William H. Weaver, Archibald Patton, Daniel Snyder and Hiram Martin, severely.

Company B—First Lieutenant William S. Provost, severely ; First Sergeant William Hand, slightly ; Corporals Charles A. Vorhees and Thaddeus O'Doane, severely ; Privates John H. Rue (died July 19th), James A. Louther, Albert Oss, William Smith, Fidelle Hasse, Samuel Stacker, severely ; Benjamin F Jackson, died July 7th ; Jacob Van Pelt, died at Baltimore, July 9th ; John Vorhees and Andrew Webster, slightly.

Company C—Second Lieutenant John B. Faussett, severely ; Sergeant David Schaffer, slightly ; Corporal Amos Rockhill and Privates John Linsey, Franklin Armstrong, James K. Webb, John Crane, Charles Stevenson and Peter Cougle, severely, and Richard V Howell, slightly.

Company D—Corporal Emanuel Runyon, Privates Richard Burtrone, Edward Spellman and Theodore Beatty.

Company E—Sergeant Eliphalet Sturdevant, died July 13th ; Sergeant William Egan, slightly ; Corporals Benjamin Joiner and Absalom Talmadge, severely ; Elise F Rose, slightly ; Privates Charles Bowman, Samuel Morse, severely ; James F Gibson, Edward J. Kinney, James King, Thomas Scattergood, John Wilson and Joseph Walton, slightly.

Company F—Captain William H. Lloyd, slightly; First Lieutenant Edwin R. Good, severely; First Sergeant Benjamin F Moorehouse, Sergeant Thomas S. White and James C. White, slightly; Corporals John F Bartine, Edward White, Charles Dilks and George Morton, severely; Privates Edward Powers, William H. Calhoun, Ephraim Robbins, severely; James Thomson, William Collins and Miller H. Lewis, slightly.

Company G—Sergeant F W King, severely; O. F Holloway, slightly; Corporals George Halloway and Israel Nixon, severely; Privates Charles Kœnig, Smith H. Eldridge, Thomas Lowry, George A. McGuire, George F. Seaver, William Emmons, Abijah Thomson and John W Lloyd, severely; Chapman Marcellus, Thomas Foutch, Thomas Kelly and Joseph Fowler, slightly.

Company H—Second Lieutenant William E. Axtell, severely; Sergeant John V Lanterman, Privates William Halsey, Patrick King, John J Sites, John C. Nutt, Bartley Owen, Joseph L. Decker, severely; Joshua Barber, Timothy K. Pruden, slightly.

Company I—Sergeant Thomas J. Thompson, slightly; Corporals Richard J. Merrill and John W Joline, severely; Corporals E. W Robinson and Michael Coony, slightly; Privates George Chamberlain, Jacob L. Chevalier, James Finnons, Francis Wassimer, William H. Luce, John M. Errickson, Alfred Barcalow, Henry L. Mollison and Daniel J. Buckley, severely; Stacy Babcock, slightly. Silas D. Clark died July 2d.

Company K—First Sergeant Charles C. Reilly, slightly; Corporal Edward Appleton, severely; Privates Amnon J. Foote, John Ardner, Gershom J. Forate, Frederick Soldner, William Carson (leg amputated), severely; John Labort, slightly.

I cannot vouch for the absolute correctness of the names in the list of wounded herein given. It has been gleaned from various sources, but principally from the reports on file at the Adjutant-General's office. As these reports were generally made soon after a battle, it was possible for mistakes to occur. Men have been reported wounded—and even killed—who in a few days turned up uninjured, having for one cause or another wandered from their commands. But from the comparisons that I have been enabled to make, I think the aggregate loss will be found correct.

Adjutant Schoonover, in his report to Le Grand Benedict, Assistant Adjutant-General of the brigade (a copy of which I

Adjutant Alexander Beach, Jr.

have before me), gives the loss as 18 killed, 130 wounded, and 6 missing, a total of 154. But as there were 18 enlisted men and 3 commissioned officers killed, it seems evident that he has failed to include the officers, which would make the killed 21 and the aggregate the same as that which I have given. The only difference in the two estimates would then be that six of those whom I have given as missing are included in the Adjutant's list of wounded.

General Carr's report, dated August 1st, '63, gives the losses as 3 officers and 14 enlisted men killed, 9 officers and 115 enlisted men wounded (he gives no missing), or an aggregate of only 141. The official roster gives 3 officers and 18 men killed, a total of 21. If that is correct, there must be a deficiency of 4 in General Carr's report of the killed. These, with the 12 missing added, would make the loss as I have given it—157

With the exception of a reconnoissance sent out by General Birney, and an attack upon a battery by Crawford—who were both cautioned by Meade not to bring on a battle—the army lay inactive during the 4th. Lee showed no disposition to renew the conflict, and Meade did not care to jeopardize the laurels already won.

It was not until the morning of the 5th that it was definitely ascertained that Lee's army was retreating.

Burial parties were sent out, and those who could get away from their commands went out to view the scene of carnage, and surely it was a scene never to be forgotten. Upon the open fields, like sheaves bound by the reaper, in crevices of the rocks, behind fences, trees and buildings; in thickets, where they had crept for safety only to die in agony; by stream or wall or hedge, wherever the battle had raged or their weakening steps could carry them, lay the dead. Some, with faces bloated and blackened beyond recognition, lay with glassy eyes staring up at the blazing summer sun; others, with faces downward and clenched hands filled with grass or earth, which told of the agony of the last moments. Here a headless trunk, there a severed limb; in all the grotesque positions that unbearable pain and intense suffering contorts the human form, they lay. Upon the faces of some death had frozen a smile; some showed the trembling shadow of fear, while upon others was indelibly set the grim stamp of determination. All around was the wreck the battle-storm leaves in its wake—broken caissons, dismounted guns, small arms bent and twisted by the storm or dropped and scattered by disabled hands; dead and bloated horses, torn and ragged equipments, and all the sorrowful wreck that the waves of battle leave at their ebb; and over all, hugging the earth like a fog, poisoning every breath, the pestilential stench of decaying humanity.

Chapter VII.

Wapping Heights—March to Beverly Ford—Rappahannock.

THE 4th, 5th and 6th of July passed without any change in the position of the regiment or any incident to mar the quietness of the bivouac. Toward evening on the 4th, however, there began one of those severe storms of rain that seemed to follow nearly every heavy battle. Shelter-tents were pitched, but they were soon found insufficient for protection, for the rain poured through and under them so that the boys obtained but little rest during the night.

It will be well to take a look backward. Less than a year had passed since the regiment left the State, 979 strong; yet here at the end of its third battle it mustered less than a company. To be sure, all its losses were not battle-losses. Many had died of disease; some had been discharged for disability; some were on detached service; many had either grown tired of the service or fearful of its dangers, and had "Folded their tents like the Arabs and had silently stolen away"; and a few, whose patriotism when at home had flamed with the heat of a Vesuvian eruption, finding that their stomachs were too weak to digest hard bread when seasoned with burning powder, or their nerves too delicate to stand the sight of bloodshed, were trying to live a quiet and unostentatious life in the shadow of some hospital or convalescent camp until discharge should come. However, the proportion of desertions from the Eleventh up to this time was not greater than that of many other regiments during their first year's service, and no regiment was without its quota of the second class—the weak-kneed and faint-hearted.

We left the field of Gettysburg at daylight on the 7th and reached Emmettsburg at noon. The afternoon's march led through Franklinville to Mechanicsville, where we halted for the night, having marched a distance of eighteen miles.

It rained continuously the night of the 7th, and rain was still falling when we took up the line of march at six o'clock the morning of the 8th. It cleared, however, during the day, but the muddy roads made the march a very tiresome one. At Lewistown we halted for about two hours and then resumed the march for Frederick City, the vicinity of which was reached about five o'clock. After resting an hour we marched through the town, and halted for the night about two miles beyond.

In Frederick City the famous Seventh New York were doing guard duty, and their handsome suits, white collars, shining boots and equipments, natty little cartridge-boxes and generally neat appearance contrasted strangely with the mud-splattered, smoke-grimed and generally tattered troops who marched by them. Among the members of the Seventh we saw our old Drum-Major, George F Durant, who had been discharged by order from the War Department which directed the discharge of all chief musicians and superfluous bands. As his old comrades filed by him they made him the subject of many good-natured gibes, and jokingly invited him to share their muddy march, but he laughingly declined.

July 9th, General Carr took command of the division, General Humphries having been appointed Chief of Staff to General Meade. Lieutenant-Colonel Tripp, of the Sixteenth Massachusetts, being the senior regimental commander present, took command of the brigade. The casualties among the staff officers of the brigade had been heavy, so that the majority of the regiments were under the command of line officers, Captain Dunning, of Company K, being in command of the Eleventh. General French's division, formerly stationed at Harper's Ferry, here joined us, and General French took command of the Third Corps.

The march was resumed at six A. M. on the morning of the 9th, and as we left the valley of the Monocacy and climbed the slopes of the mountains the backward view was a magnificent one. In the distance Frederick City, with its spires and houses glorified by the morning's golden sunlight; in the far and middle distance, well-kept farm-buildings seemingly peeping from groves of fruit or forest trees, and all around green pastures, fields of moving corn and shocks of golden grain, and, through it all, twisting here and there like a silver thread through a rich arabesque, dividing the near from the far, flowed the quiet, limpid stream. At noon we reached Middletown, peacefully snuggled in the lap of the hills, and rested two hours. We then marched to Turner's Gap and bivouacked for the night.

July 10th General Prince took command of the Second Division and Carr resumed command of the brigade. We marched to Keedysville, where we thought to remain for the night, but after a rest of a couple of hours the march was resumed and kept up until midnight, when a halt was made near Boonsboro. There had been a cavalry brush at Boonsboro the day previous, and the vicinity showed signs of the encounter.

We took an early start on the morning of the 11th, marching a mile before breakfast to get up an appetite. After breakfast we took the road to Funkstown, beyond which we halted and remained for the night. Our bivouac was in a wheat-field, and the sheaves made very comfortable beds.

Sunday, July 12th, was a beautiful summer day, but everything seemed to indicate that its peacefulness would be broken by the boom of cannon and the rattle of musketry. Orders had been issued to be ready to move at a moment's notice, and couriers riding to and fro seemed to point to an approaching conflict. Yet notwithstanding these indications of battle a well-attended religious service was held in a field near by.

About noon orders came to move, and the men obeyed with alacrity. They believed that at last Meade had determined to attack, and so enthusiastic were they, so anxious for the fight, that they had no doubt the result would be the capture of Lee's army. That had been the prevailing spirit from the time that victory was declared at Gettysburg. Major-General David B. Birney, when asked by the Committee on the Conduct of the War as to the condition of the army after the battle, answered, "I have never seen the army so confident of success, in more admirable spirits, and so anxious for a fight." But a quiet march of about two miles, and then we again went into bivouac. It soon came to be understood by the men that another grand opportunity was to pass unimproved; that when the Potomac should be fit to cross, Lee was to be permitted to retire unmolested.

No move was made on the 13th, but before we had time to cook coffee on the morning of the 14th we were moving forward. We soon came to a double line of breastworks, but their former occupants were safe upon the Virginia shore. Sunrise of the 15th found us packed up and on the way. We passed through the villages of Fairplay and Sharpsburg, and, crossing the Antietam creek, bivouacked for the night.

On the 16th we marched through Rohrersville and Brownsville and halted for the night, in the midst of a heavy rain, near Burnsides' old camp in Pleasant Valley.

The rain was still falling on the morning of the 17th. We lay in camp until 4 P M., when we marched to the Potomac, and, crossing a pontoon bridge, entered historic Harper's Ferry. The town seemed to be entirely deserted. The stores were empty and the houses desolate; no fires sent their curling wreaths of smoke from the chimneys; no curious faces peered from windows or doorways; the tramp of passing troops, the rumble of baggage-wagons and artillery were the only sounds that echoed through the silent streets. Crossing the Shenandoah bridge, we wound beneath the overhanging cliffs of Bolivar Heights and entered Loudon Valley. After marching about two miles on the Leesburgh road, we bivouacked for the night.

Four o'clock A. M. of the 18th found us *en route*, and at 8.30 we reached the village of Hillsboro, whose inhabitants were bitterly disloyal. The country through which we were passing had been greatly favored by nature, and was one of much natural beauty. Park-like forests of hardwood occurred at intervals, while the fields were naturally fertile, but disfigured by squalid negro-cabins or the more squalid cabins of the poorer whites, while even the more pretentious mansions of the richer class showed the blighting touch of the indolence that is one of the concomitants of slavery. The surface of the country was rolling and watered by frequent streams, while along the northwest horizon stretched nature's eternal windbreak, the rugged Blue Ridge mountains.

Eight o'clock A. M. of the 19th found us again on the way, but after a march of four miles we encamped in a delightful piece of woodland near Woodford's grove. In that part of Virginia, and on down to Warrenton, the blackberry seemed to grow in wild luxuriance; roadsides and hedges and fallow-fields were thick with the brambles drooping with their loads of the black, luscious fruit. As soon as a halt was ordered and arms were stacked, the men would scatter to fill their stomachs and caps with the rich, juicy berry. Nowhere in my wanderings have I seen the *Rubus fruticosus* grow in greater luxuriance or possess a richer flavor. Or is it only a memory? Mutton, too, seemed to thrive near Woodford, for some of the boys declared that mutton and blackberry sauce was really an epicurean dish. Notwithstanding the transient pleasures gathered by the wayside, the men were out of spirits, and went about their duties in a listless, uninterested manner. They recognized the fact that the opportunity to deal a vital blow to the Confederacy had been neglected, and that Lee, upon his own ground, would be able to hold the army at bay for months, perhaps years. As one of the men tersely wrote from this point, we were out of clothing, and *very* tired.

On July 20th we were called up at three A. M., and at sunrise marched to Upperville, where an attack was expected. The Eleventh was posted on a hill as support to the First New Jersey battery. We remained in position during the 21st, but no enemy appeared.

At two P M. of the 22d we were again on the way, and at night bivouacked near Piedmont.

At half-past four the following morning the march was resumed in the direction of Manassas Gap, which was reached about nine o'clock. The corps was immediately formed for action, with battalions closed in mass. Keeping this formation, it advanced up the mountain, the Excelsior Brigade in front. It was a beautiful sight, the entire corps being in view as it advanced up the steep hillside, a line of skirmishers leading. The enemy was encountered near the summit, and for awhile the firing was pretty sharp, but soon the rebels retreated down the farther side,

Captain Charles A. Oliver.

keeping up a severe shell-fire, however, from a battery posted on a hill beyond. In this encounter the division lost about two hundred men; there were no casualties in the Eleventh. It was the intention of Meade to intercept the march of Lee's army by pushing through Manassas Gap, and for that purpose the Third Corps was advanced. The other corps was to follow. General

Lee, leaving a small body to delay the Union advance, had already crossed the Shenandoah and was pushing on up the Valley.

On the morning of the 24th the advance was continued to Front Royal. Finding no enemy, with the exception of about one hundred wounded, we returned to Markham and encamped for the night.

In connection with the battle of Manassas Gap, an incident occurred which resulted in the dishonorable dismissal from the service, without trial, of a lieutenant who was in command of his company.

When the firing of the skirmishers had become quite brisk, and the line of battle was about to advance to their support, it was discovered that the commanding officer of the regiment was nowhere to be found, and by request of Captain Sleeper, the only captain present, the adjutant took command. At this juncture of affairs the lieutenant spoken of above declared positively that he would " not go into the fight." When asked for his reason he replied that if he did he would " disgrace himself and his company." An appeal was made to his honor, as an officer in command, with a warning of the result of such action. As the line moved forward he went to the rear, and did not make his appearance until the regiment returned and all danger for the present had passed. Schoonover, who had no patience with cowardice in any form, resolved to try an experiment and make an example of this officer. He at once addressed a letter to the commanding officer of the army, through the proper channels, requesting that Lieutenant —— be dishonorably dismissed from the service of the United States, for cowardice in the face of the enemy. The next day he was so dismissed, by command of Major-General Meade.

At five A. M. the next morning the march was resumed, and Piedmont reached about nine, when a halt was made until noon. The footsore and lame were then placed in ambulances, and the march continued three miles beyond the village of Salem. The village of Salem showed traces of former prosperity, but in the absence of its able-bodied inhabitants, decay was creeping upon it.

The march of the day had been a hot and dusty one, and partly through a flat and uninteresting country. Springs and running streams were few and the men suffered very much with thirst. A well along the roadside, in the village, offered a cooling draught, but so great was the crush around it that we marched by without making an effort to obtain water. The clear running stream, near the banks of which we bivouaced, was therefore hailed with grateful delight. The Eleventh, however, spent the night on picket.

The march of the 26th led us through Warrenton and to the wooded banks of a running stream about three miles beyond. There new clothing was issued, and the men enjoyed a luxury they had been deprived of for weeks. With the exception of the few days the regiment lay at Gum Springs, from the time it had broken camp in front of Fredericksburg, on June 11th, to its halt beyond Warrenton, on July 26th, the men had had no opportunity to thoroughly cleanse their persons or clothing. With the exception of shoes, no clothing had been issued since before the opening of the campaign, and a majority of those who had started with a change in their knapsacks had been compelled to throw them away, to lighten loads, during the hot and dusty marches northward. Consequently, the majority of the men literally carried their wardrobes on their backs.

A suit of clothing worn for six weeks without proper washing is not only apt to become slightly soiled, but to furnish happy hunting-grounds for the *pediculus*, a species of insect that is very prolific in warm weather—and one that causes untold annoyance to the person so unfortunate as to make its acquaintance. It was not an uncommon thing, during the halts on the march to and from Gettysburg, to see whole regiments with their under-garments off, intently examining the seams, as if they were inspectors of clothing, concerned in the material and making. Even field and staff officers might have been seen skirmishing desperately with the common enemy. It was therefore with feelings of great satisfaction that we received a new outfit of clothing while lying along the swift-running stream beyond Warrenton.

The next problem was to make a transfer of clothing without making a transfer of inhabitants. A happy idea suggested itself. The new clothing was taken down to the stream and laid on the bank. The men then waded across to the other side, where they divested themselves of their old garments, and, after a thorough wash, re-crossed to where the new clothing was left. Once in their new habilaments they felt like new men. It may be an exaggeration, but some of the men said that the cast-off clothing made desperate efforts to re-cross the stream and follow them back to camp.

A. B. Searing, of Company E, writing from this place, says: "Both clothing and men are about worn-out. The Fifth Corporal is acting Lieutenant, and one of the privates acting First Sergeant. There are about nine well men in the company; the rest are worn-out with overmarching—this making the forty-seventh day since breaking camp below Falmouth."

On the 27th, Lieutenant-Colonel Moore and two other officers re-joined the regiment.

On the 31st the First Massachusetts left the brigade, having been ordered to New York to assist in quelling the draft riots. And let me say here that with the exception of a few demagogues, whose sympathies were with slavery and disunion, those who engaged in the riots were principally foreigners—men who had come to this country to escape the tyranny of European governments. Ignorant of, or careless of, the fact that the issue was one of slavery or freedom, they lent themselves as willing instruments to rivet such fetters upon the limbs of others as they had for ages been trying to break from their own, and notwithstanding the fact that thousands of their own countrymen were laying down their lives for the cause of freedom in their adopted country, they committed the most atrocious acts through prejudice of race and color. But such are the inconsistencies of human nature.

The 31st being the day set apart as a day of national thanksgiving for the success of the Union armies, religious services were held near General Carr's headquarters. In the evening the band of the Eighty-fourth Pennsylvania serenaded the regimental officers, and Mr. Gridley, our regimental sutler, related his experience as a runner from Mosby's Guerillas. He came very near being captured. In his efforts to escape he killed two horses by overdriving.

August 1st we moved to within two miles of Beverly ford and laid out a new camp. Seventy men were detailed from the regiment for picket. They marched to Fox's ford and from there to Beverly ford, on the Rappahannock, and established a picket-line along the river. The day was excessively warm and some of the detail were sunstruck. Any survivor of the old regiment who did picket duty along this line, especially near the mouth of the stream that emptied into the river near the old dam or lock, will not have forgotten the Rappahannock mosquitoes. Jersey has the reputation of being pre-eminent in the cultivation of this agile little songster, but it is the experience of the writer that for size, pertinacity, audacity and general cussedness, the "critter" that has its habitat along the banks of the beautiful Rappahannock may well challenge the world. The boys insisted that the enemy had them trained, not only to annoy the Union pickets, but to commit depredations on the supplies of the Union army. I will not vouch for the truth of the statement, but I have it from the lips of an alleged eye-witness that two of them were seen trying to carry a Union beef over to the enemy's lines.

We remained in camp near Beverly ford until September 15th, undergoing the usual routine of camp and picket duty. The weather was very warm, many cases of sunstroke occurred, and bowel troubles were prevalent. But notwithstanding, the regiment grew slowly in numbers by the return of those who had been absent because of sickness or wounds.

There was a review of the division by General Prince on August 12th, and one of the corps by General Meade on September 7th.

On the 21st of August Adjutant Schoonover received his commission as Lieutenant-Colonel, an honor that he had gallantly earned.

On the 29th of August quite a number of the Eleventh went over to the Fifth Corps to witness the execution of five deserters from the One Hundred and Eighteenth Pennsylvania. It was a sad sight, yet the true soldier can feel but little sympathy for men like these, who were guilty of repeated desertions. One of them was said to have deserted twelve times and had taken the thirteenth bounty when caught. Of the number, two were Catholics, two Hebrews, and one a Protestant.

On September 15th we received orders to move at four P.M., but darkness came before we got under way for the Rappahannock. The march led through dense woods and miry swamps, but at last, near morning, we struck an open field and lay down to rest. Much to our surprise and disgust, when daylight came we found ourselves within five hundred yards of our old camp. Nearly all night long we had been circling around through the woods, scarcely more than a mile from our starting-point at any time. However, we made a new start on the morning of the 16th, the First Brigade in front, and, marching to Freeman's ford, waded the river. After crossing we again lost our direction, but upon reaching the McDown house a native was pressed into service as guide, and without any further mishaps we reached the road to Culpepper. On our route we also forded the Aestham river, a swift and moderately deep stream, and toward night encamped near Culpepper, after a wearisome march of twenty miles. The march, however, had its compensations, for the country was not quite so barren as the region we had left, and apples, peaches, chickens and corn were gathered in on the way.

On the morning of the 17th we took our position about one mile to the right of the town, the First Brigade on our right, the Second in our rear.

The morning of the 18th was very stormy, but about noon it cleared and we moved to a new position on a hill beyond the wood. Captain Halsey here received his commission as Major.

On the 19th we again changed position, company streets were laid out, and everything seemed to indicate a permanent encampment.

We remained quietly in camp until October 8th, when the division was ordered to James City to support Kilpatrick's cavalry. Leaving our knapsacks stored in the depot at Culpepper, we started under light marching orders at 4:30. General Carr having been assigned to the Third Division, McAllister commanded the brigade. It will be remembered that Colonel McAllister had been severely wounded at Gettysburg. His wounds having healed, he re-joined the regiment on October 2d. The night of his return he was serenaded by the band of the Eleventh Massachusetts, and speeches were made by himself, Halsey and others. We marched through Culpepper and at 11 A. M. went into position near James City. Notwithstanding this section of the country had been visited frequently by detachments from both armies, there seemed to be plenty of forageable material remaining, which the men were not backward in appropriating.

On the 10th, despatches received from the Signal Corps indicated that Lee was again moving northward. A detachment of his army had crossed the Rapidan in our front, capturing seventy of our division pickets. At twelve o'clock we fell back to a new position, and at 3 P M. retired about three miles and took position on the Culpepper road. The enemy, having crossed in force, were pressing hard upon the cavalry in front. About nine P M. we were ordered to return to Culpepper. One of our men having sprained his ankle, Chaplain Cline (but recently joined, Knighton having resigned) placed him upon his horse, and, taking the soldier's rifle, marched alongside. This little incident, trifling as it may appear, served to indicate the character of the man who henceforth was to be our moral and spiritual teacher. It showed the unselfishness, the thoughtfulness for others, the kindliness of heart, that characterized Chaplain Cline throughout his entire connection with the regiment, and won for him the love and esteem of both officers and men. We did not reach Culpepper until after midnight. After getting our knapsacks and drawing eight days' rations, we lay down to rest until morning.

Sunrise of the 11th found us again on the way, fairly entered upon the race for Centerville, the enemy following closely We crossed the Aestham river on pontoons, and at midnight forded the Rappahannock at Freeman's ford. Once over the river a rapid pace was kept up until about three o'clock in the morning, when we halted in the roadway. There were good rail-fences along each side of the road when we halted, but they quickly disappeared, and soon rows of camp-fires glowed along each side. The genial warmth was welcome, for the night was chilly and our clothing being wet from fording the river added to our discomfort.

On the 12th the Second Division of the Third Corps, to which we belonged, picketed the river from Beverly to Freeman's ford. As we were marching along on the following morning the writer picked from the dust of the road a dried and shriveled human hand, a relic, no doubt, of some former battle or skirmish.

At eight o'clock the pickets re-joined the division at the De Long house. The Eighty-fourth and Twenty-sixth Pennsylvanias were thrown out as flankers, and the march resumed by way of Warrenton Junction and Auburn to Greenwich, which was reached at three o'clock on the morning of the 14th, marching all night. During this march—as it was afterward ascertained—we passed so close to two brigades of Stuart's cavalry that they could hear the conversation of our men.

During the 13th the First Division of the Third Corps (Birney's) had encountered Stuart's troopers near Auburn, and after a sharp fight of half an hour, and a loss of about fifty men, repulsed them. The Union troops engaged in this fight were principally Collis' Brigade and the Tenth Massachusetts Battery. Stuart, finding himself cut off, was obliged to bivouac within the Union lines, and while the Second Division was passing, his troops lay concealed in a thick growth of pines between the lines of march of the Second Corps and the Second Division of the Third Corps.

As has been stated, the Second Division reached Greenwich at 8 A. M. on the morning of the 14th. After a rest of an hour the column pushed on, the Eleventh Regiment acting as

Captain William H. Meeker.

flankers. Heavy firing was heard in the direction of Bristow, but the march was continued across the historic plains of Manassas until half-past three, when we halted in columns of regiments for an hour and a half's rest, upon the old battle-field of Bull Run. At five P M., after fording Bull Run creek, the march was continued to near Centerville, when we again formed in columns of regiments and lay down to the rest so much needed, for the men were nearly exhausted by the long marches and loss of sleep. The firing heard during the day was occasioned by an attack of the enemy upon the Second and Fifth Corps, near Bristow. They were repulsed, however, with the loss of eleven pieces of artillery and five hundred prisoners.

Meade succeeded in concentrating his army around Centerville, and Lee, seeing that an attack would be folly, began to fall back, tearing up the railroad as he went.

On the 15th we marched to Union Mills. During the day the enemy attempted to force a passage over Bull Run, at McLean's ford, two miles above, but were handsomely repulsed by the Second New Jersey Brigade, with a loss of sixty killed and wounded. During this attack we were momentarily expecting to be called into action, and at one time were formed in line and ordered to load, but the attack being repulsed, our services were not needed.

The "race," as this retreat was familiarly called, was about ended, but the prestige remained with Lee. With an inferior force he had compelled the retreat of the Union army, caused the destruction of considerable material, wrecked the railroad to beyond the Rappahannock, and captured about two thousand prisoners, the majority of whom, however, were stragglers.

On the 16th, the First Massachusetts, which had been to New York to assist in quelling the draft riots, re-joined the brigade. We also received a visit from General Daniel E. Sickles, our old corps commander, who had lost a leg at Gettysburg. He was received with every demonstration of joy. So great was the enthusiasm, and so eager were the men to get near him, that it was with the greatest difficulty that he could make his way through the crowds that collected around him. At one point he was completely surrounded, and the boys good-naturedly told him that he could not go any further until he had given them a speech. He laughingly replied that it should never be the fate of a good general to get surrounded, but if such fate befell him, the first thing he should do was to try to cut his way out. He had become surrounded (fortunately by friends), and the only way he saw to cut his way out was by a short speech; and the speech was given. Sickles, by his gallantry and soldierly qualities, had endeared himself to nearly every man in the old Third Corps, and especially was he the idol of the Second Division.

We remained at Union Mills until the morning of the 19th, when, in the midst of a heavy rain, we again started toward the Rappahannock. We halted for the night at Bristow Station. The enemy had completely destroyed the railroad, bridges were burned, the road torn up, sleepers burned, and rails heated and bent so as to be entirely useless.

We moved at six A. M. on the 20th, and encamped for the night three miles beyond Greenwich. At Greenwich was a very handsome property, owned by an alleged British subject. Men from the Eleventh were detailed to guard it. The owner complained very bitterly to Colonel Schoonover of his treatment by the soldiers. His lawn, he said, had been destroyed by the cavalry and artillery; the soldiers had killed and eaten his Southdowns; and, worst of all, he had no wine to offer to his friends, as the government would not permit him to bring it through the lines. Poor fellow! we sympathized with him even while greasing our jaws with a chop from his imported mutton; and I know that the chops tasted as good as if they had been cut from dyed-in-the-wool American sheep. As for his wine—I do not suppose we would have been classed as his friends; but good, straight, forty-rod commissary would touch a spot, in the average soldier, that the richest of imported wines could not reach.

The position of safe-guard, though often a sinecure, was not eagerly sought after by the men. If they did their duty they were very apt to get the ill-will of their comrades. Especially was that the case if guarding anything edible. The soldier considered food, in any of its varieties, legitimate spoil of war, and vigilant indeed would be the guard that could keep it from being confiscated. Dry wood was also considered contraband. If an encampment was near or a bivouac made for the night, a pile of rails or line of fence offered temptation not to be resisted. How often, when orders were given not to disturb a fence and guards were put on to protect it, have we seen it steal away, rail by rail, until, to the despair of the guard, he had no fence to protect! The guard's sympathies were with his comrades, and, if possible, he would shut his eyes to their depredations. This was illustrated by a case related by Colonel Schoonover. On one occasion a guard was placed over a pile of dry rails near the house of the proprietor. A coffee-cooler approached and asked for a rail. "Can't have it," replied the guard, but added, "of course, if a big crowd of you came I could not protect them." The big crowd did come, and the pile soon disappeared.

October 21st we left Greenwich early in the morning and marched to Catlett's Station, where it was rumored that we were to make a permanent encampment. Three days' rations were issued and company streets marked out, but the rumor proved to be unfounded. The nights had begun to grow quite cold, and the men, being destitute of blankets and overcoats—none having been issued since the burning at Chancellorsville—suffered considerably, the nights being passed in alternate freezing and thawing. They would lie down until thoroughly chilled, then, by walking around or standing by the camp-fires, get thawed out sufficiently to try another nap.

On the 26th the regiment moved about one mile, and located another camp. Some of the men began stockading their tents and finished them in time to enjoy their shelter for one night before another move was ordered. The few days that the troops remained in this location the regimental pickets did duty in the vicinity of Weaversville and along Cedar creek. The surrounding woodland seemed to be the favorite haunt of squirrels, both gray and black often being seen upon the same tree. It was hard for those in whose veins coursed sportsman blood to resist the temptation to shoot, but they were compelled to refrain from so doing by fear of alarming the army, and the tempting game gamboled unmolested. The surrounding inhabitants professed to be pure and unadulterated Unionists. They said that they had helped to destroy the railroad, but under duress. However, I think their Unionism lasted only so long as the boys in blue remained with them.

On the 29th the much-longed-for and badly-needed woolen blankets arrived.

At seven o'clock on the morning of the 30th we again broke camp and marched three miles beyond Warrenton Junction, where we remained until November 7th, doing guard and picket duty, and sometimes taking a hand at railroad-building.

On the morning of the 7th we again advanced, and as we approached the river the boom of guns told us that a battle was in progress. We reached Kelly's ford about two o'clock. The First Division being in the lead, it encountered the enemy at that point, and, crossing the river, after some severe fighting drove them from their position, capturing one battle-flag and a number of prisoners. The loss to McAllister's brigade was twelve men. The pontoons being laid, about sundown the Second Division crossed the river and took position on the high ground beyond. The few houses constituting the hamlet of Kellysville, or Kelly's ford, showed marks of the engagement, and one standing on the bluff near our position, which had been deserted, had been well riddled by shells. The Sixth Corps, which had crossed some miles to our right, at Rappahannock Station, had been more successful, capturing sixteen hundred prisoners, six pieces of artillery, four battle-flags and a pontoon bridge.

On the morning of the 8th a colored servant—supposed to be General Ewell's—ignorantly rode into our lines with a breakfast neatly packed in a basket. He rode a splendid animal, which, with the negro and breakfast, was confiscated.

Early in the morning we again advanced, seeing troops in the distance. Preparations for battle were made, but they proved to be the Sixth Corps. Near the railroad we halted for a couple of hours, and, being Sunday, Chaplain Cline took advantage of the occasion to hold religious service. He spoke of how our friends at home were worshiping in peace and quietness, and contrasted our surroundings—armies marshaled in battle array, the glitter of guns, the rattle of equipments, horsemen hurrying to and fro, and now and then the dull boom of cannon; one condition safety, the other imminent danger. After a rest of a couple of hours we took to the march again, and about half past three reached Brandy Station, where we halted for the night. Near Brandy Station we found that the enemy had made every preparation for a winter encampment. Their log-cabins were commodious and well built, roofed principally with boards. They were far superior to any we had occupied, and I think we learned from them something of the art of making ourselves comfortable for the winter. There was also evidence of a hasty departure. In some places officers' swords were found hanging in their quarters, fires were still burning, and in some instances the meat was cooking for supper and the dough ready-mixed for baking. No doubt the "Yankees" were heartily anathematized for so summarily dispossessing them.

November 9th we lay at Brandy Station, closed in mass, until just as night was approaching we deployed in line of battle and lay down to rest. We held the same position until the morning of the 11th, when we moved about one mile and took possession of one of the enemy's deserted camps. The weather had become cold enough to make some other shelter than simple tents desirable, and as soon as possible we set about preparing winter quarters. As the position of the rebels' camp did not suit our alignment, new streets were laid out, and the work of building begun. As the enemy's camp furnished material, ready prepared, it was not long before we had comfortable quarters erected. The situation was all that could be desired. In front of us was rolling farm-land, and but a few yards from camp a fine stream of running water. To the rear, as far as the eye could reach, an unbroken forest seemed to offer an inexhaustible supply of firewood.

On the 12th we received a welcome visit from Major Webb, the paymaster, and drew two months' pay.

On the 16th, General Sedgwick, accompanied by some Russian officers, reviewed the Corps, and on the 18th brigade inspection was held.

On the 20th, on behalf of the State, General Torbert presented the Eleventh with a new stand of colors, to take the place of the battle-worn ones that had been returned.

On November 23d, orders were received to be ready to march in the morning.

Reveille was beaten at four A. M. on the 24th. We got our breakfasts, packed up, and fell into line, but it was raining heavily, and the order to march was countermanded.

Chapter VIII.

Locust Grove—Mine Run.

EARLY morning of the 26th found us on the march. About noon we halted in a wood near Jacob's ford, on the Rapidan. Between the wood and the river was an open field about three hundred yards wide. Not knowing what force of the enemy might be concealed in the thickets beyond the river, some precaution was necessary. A section of artillery was placed in position at the edge of the wood to cover the advance of the pontoons. The wagons containing the boats were then hurried forward, the drivers lashing their teams to a run. The boats were quickly placed in the water, and a detachment of the Eleventh New Jersey, under Captain Loyd, soon ferried across, Colonel Schoonover going in the first boat and the first to jump ashore as it struck the opposite side. The bluff on the southern shore was so steep that a horseman could ascend only with difficulty. The men quickly dashed to the top, and forming a skirmish-line, advanced across the field. The rebel videttes fired a few shots and then fell back.

A. B. Searing says: "I was climbing over a high rail-fence when I saw, across the field, a rebel soldier rise out of a clump of bushes, take aim, and fire. The bullet whistled overhead, doing no harm, but the soldier's face, the sun glistening on his rifle, seems indelibly impressed upon my mind. Passing on, I examined the bushes where he had been, and found an empty cartridge-paper stamped "Richmond, Va." At a farm-house near by two rebel soldiers were captured who were home on furlough. After the retreat of the enemy's pickets, a detachment of cavalry crossed, and, forming in line, went forward at a gallop. After we had crossed the field we halted for a few minutes in front of a house occupied by an old widow lady. She complained very bitterly because our line was placed in front of her house, saying that her own men would shoot her.

The old lady was talked to in a consoling manner and her fears quieted, but she gave us to understand that she was a bitter secessionist, and denounced our cause as wicked. Leaving the old lady's house in the rear, we pressed forward through a narrow wood-road. We had advanced about four miles when, from a

Lieutenant Joseph C. Baldwin.

mill in front, our column was again fired upon. The firing resulted in the wounding of a dog. As it came yelping to the rear it was followed by the doctors and other non-combatants, who no doubt—like the dog—thought the rear the safest place. Darkness had fallen, and it being ascertained that we were upon the wrong road—one that would lead us in front of the enemy's works instead of upon the flank—we fell back two or three miles and bivouacked for the night."

We moved early on the morning of the 27th, taking the road to Robertson's Tavern. The enemy formed across the road and disputed our passage, but skirmishers were thrown forward and we continued to advance. Colonel Blaisdell, commanding the brigade, ordered the Eleventh New Jersey to relieve the First Massachusetts, who were on the skirmish-line. We did so, and continued to advance until we struck the enemy in strong line of battle, posted along the edge of a clearing in which was a house and other farm-buildings. Around these buildings the enemy was strongly posted. Our skirmishers advanced under the personal command of Colonel Schoonover to a line of fence running along the edge of the field. Our line of battle was formed just in the rear, near the edge of the wood. Soon the firing became brisk, and the enemy advanced to the attack. The Twenty-sixth Pennsylvania, on our left, at first gave way, carrying a portion of the Eleventh with them, but our men soon rallied, and the Twenty-sixth rallying again, took position on the line and fought splendidly. After awhile the Fifth Excelsior, on our right, gave way, and soon the troops upon our left fell back, leaving both flanks of the Eleventh exposed, notwithstanding which it held its ground. Just at this critical moment an aid from Colonel Blaisdell came forward with orders for the Eleventh New Jersey to advance. He did not come near enough to deliver the order in person, but sent it forward with one of our men. McAllister called back for him to deliver the order in person, but the situation being uncomfortably warm just then, he failed to do so. The smoke of battle lifting, revealed the enemy overlaping each flank—a few minutes more and the line of retreat would be closed and the regiment captured. The order was given to fall back, which we did slowly. Keeping our faces to the enemy, we fought our way back to where our artillery was posted and lay down in the edge of the wood. Our guns fired over us, and sent such a shower of canister in the advancing ranks of the enemy that they soon fell back. As we were falling back, and just as we reached the clearing at the edge of the wood, Johnson, our color-bearer, unfurled the colors and waved them defiantly in the face of the enemy.

The following graphic description was written by Captain Hand, formerly Sergeant of Company B:

"At the battle of Locust Grove, November 27th, '63, most of our regiment was armed with Harper's Ferry muskets, but some of us had *lost* our muskets and *found* Springfield rifles. Mine had been lost and I found a splendid rifle, which came very near being the cause of my being lost. Colonel Schoonover went up to the picket-line while we were in line of battle and discovered the enemy's pickets just across an open field in the edge of the wood about easy rifle range, but too far away for the muskets to be effective. He called back for some one with a good rifle to come up. I responded, leaving my knapsack and haversack, expecting to return soon, but almost as soon as I had taken position on the picket-line and had commenced firing the enemy began to advance, and when they showed themselves in the open field our line arose and began firing over our heads, so that if we attempted to fall back we were in as much danger from friends as foes. I was lying next to a man by the name of Valentine Greer. We had no protection whatever, so we lay as close as we could and kept firing as fast as possible. On the ground between us we had a package of cartridges open from which we loaded. The enemy kept advancing, but our men held their ground, and there seemed nothing for us skirmishers to do except to continue firing. I was all the while hoping that our men would advance to where we were, but the enemy did the advancing. Finally, when they were very near, a shot struck poor Greer in the head. He gave a short, quick groan and turned on his back, and I thought he was dead, but I learned afterward that he lived until the next morning. When the enemy were almost near enough to reach me with their hands I discovered that our line was retreating. I looked over my shoulder and saw a ravine running in the direction our men were going. I started for the same, taking Greer's gun with me as well as my own. Springfield rifles were scarce in those days, and I was not willing to leave it for the enemy to use. I spent the greater part of the night in looking over the battle-field for the body of my friend Joe Frazee, who was killed there, but it had been taken away and properly cared for by Sergeant Hewson, of our company, who was in charge of an ambulance train."

On some parts of the skirmish-line the enemy actually did reach our skirmishers. Joshua Beach, of Company E, was literally pulled over the fence by them. Some time during the early part of the night, Colonel McAllister asked for men to go out over the field to see if any of our wounded remained there. Sergeant William Hand, of Company B, Edward Kinney and the writer, of Company E, and several others whose names I have forgotten, volunteered for the service. The duty was not a pleasant one, owing to the uncertainty as to where the enemy's pickets were posted.

Our party started down the road leading through the wood, but had not gone far when we heard groans and calls from the right. Advancing in that direction, we found a wounded rebel lying behind a log. He had been struck below the knee and his leg was completely shattered. Finding that we were Yankees, he said he did not expect us to do much for him, but would be glad if we would fix him so that he could rest a little more comfortably. He told us he belonged to Johnson's division and was from North Carolina, and had been only two weeks in the service, leaving a wife and eight children at home. He said that he had escaped conscription for a long while, but they caught him at last, and this was the result. That he was speaking truthfully was evidenced by his knapsack, which contained such articles as only a new recruit would carry. We assured him that we would take him to the rear, where his wound would be cared for, and he seemed very grateful when we left him in charge of some stretcher-bearers whom we met at the edge of the wood. Poor fellow! we heard he died next day, after undergoing amputation.

Returning to the wood after taking out the North Carolinian, we soon found the body of James M. Woodruff, of Company H. Woodruff was only a boy and had a great penchant for boots, and just before breaking camp had bought a new pair of cavalry boots. These were a tempting prize to the "Johnnies," and in order to get them off they had pulled his body astride a tree. Further to the left we found Rinaldo Stevens, of Company A, who was severely wounded. He was taken to the rear and succeeded in reaching Alexandria, where he died at the Mansion House hospital on December 8th. While some of the party was taking Stevens to the rear, the others moved forward to where the skirmish-line had been posted. The members of Company E were looking for their comrade, Charles Mann. Mann was a soldier who never shirked a duty, and had volunteered to go forward as a skirmisher. We knew that, if not a prisoner, he was either dead or too badly wounded to get off the field. We found him lying on his back, dead, near where he had been fighting. He made the last of three brothers, all of whom gave their lives for the preservation of the Union. When Charles Mann went into the battle he had upon his person quite a sum of money, besides a good watch. When found, he had been stripped of everything of value. He was left lying where found and buried next morning. Adam, of Company A, Fifth New Jersey, died on board a hospital-ship at Fortress Monroe from wounds received in one of the battles of the Peninsula. John, of Company E, Eleventh, was mortally wounded at Chancellorsville, and died in the hands of the enemy.

To illustrate how indifferent to danger or thoughtless of peril a soldier may sometimes become, I will mention an incident that occurred during this battle. A member of Company E, who at that time was an inveterate smoker, took out his pipe, filled and lit it, and resumed firing as coolly as if nothing unusual was occurring. Another member of the same company, Ed. Kinney, his Hibernian blood being pretty well warmed up, took a position on a stump, and after exhausting the cartridges in the top part of his cartridge-box, endeavored to draw the magazines so as to get at the lower boxes, but he tugged and pulled in vain, the damp weather having rusted them fast. Colonel Schoonover and the writer both went to his assistance, but with a like result. I have heard profanity in many forms, and in various languages, but never any to exceed that uttered by Kinney on this occasion.

War has its humors, as well as pathos, and things sometimes occur upon a battle-field, amidst the most imminent dangers that excite the laughter of the spectators. On one occasion, at Locust Grove, a wounded man, belonging to Company C, was being carried out upon a stretcher. Before a place of safety was reached, a solid shot came whizzing pretty close to the party. The stretcher-bearers dropped the stretcher and ran for shelter, but imagine their surprise when the wounded man, who previously could not walk, hastily jumped up and outstripped them in the race.

Colonel McAllister, in a letter dated December 14th, '63, thus refers to some of the incidents of this engagement: "The dying message of Corporal Joseph Frazee, of Company B, to his mother, was: 'I die for my country.' He was a noble and brave man. Sergeant Smith, who died on the field, shot through the head, was no less brave, and was moreover a true Christian."

The battle of Locust Grove lasted but a few hours, but it was fiercely fought, and the Eleventh New Jersey proved anew that they were entitled to the name that by common consent had been given them, "The fighting Eleventh." The aggregate loss of the regiment was 31—7 killed, 16 wounded, 7 prisoners and 1 missing. To give a correct idea of the percentage of loss it will be well to state that at the commencement of the battle of Locust Grove the regiment numbered less than two hundred men. The exact figures are not available. A. B. Searing, of Company E, who was a close observer and who made it a point to write down everything of importance that came to his notice, says that at the close of the battle we had only 105 men remaining with the regiment.

The killed were Sergeant Alfred Smith, of Company A; Corporal Joseph H. Frazee and Valentine Greer, of Company B; Corporal Peter Burk and Private Jeremiah Dunham, of Company D; Privates Charles Mann, of Company E, and James Woodruff, of Company H.

The wounded were Sergeant-Major William S. Rockhill, Sergeant Joseph Burns, Corporal William Colfer, and Private Rinaldo Stevens (who died December 8th), of Company A; Corporal Thomas Blackwood and Private Ephraim Britton, of Company C; Albert E. Lyons and George Zindle, of Company E; William S. Pitman, of Company G; Sergeant Henry C. Woodruff and Corporal John Fleming, of Company H; Sergeant Thomas Johnson, Privates Christian Quod and Steven G. Cronk, of Company I; Sergeants Charles Repp and Ebenezer Kennedy, of Company K.

The prisoners were Henry Hoffman and Patrick Brennan, of Company D; Joshua Beech, Cyrus L. Talmadge and William Hoffman, of Company E; Daniel Smires, of Company G, and Jacob Menner, of Company K. John Ardner, of Company K, marked missing, was no doubt killed. Of the prisoners only two, Daniel Smires and Patrick Brennan, lived to return from the rebel prisons.

Among the seemingly miraculous escapes was that of Corporal Thomas Blackwood, of Company C. He was what Colonel McAllister denominated "one of the praying members," a man to be found in attendance at any of the religious services held in the regiment and prominent in all efforts tending to the moral welfare of the men. It was his invariable custom to carry a copy of the New Testament in his blouse-pocket, and to that habit he owed his preservation at Locust Grove. A bullet striking him on the breast, penetrated the Testament and was held by it, thereby saving him from what no doubt would have been a severe, if not mortal, wound.

As letters written at any time during the regiment's service relative to comrades who fell upon the field of battle may well be considered a part of the regiment's history, I will here insert a letter from Chaplain Cline to Mrs. Elizabeth Dunham, who was made a widow by the death of Jeremiah Dunham, at Locust Grove. He says:

"MADAM—The sad news of the death of your husband has already been borne to you. Our Hospital Steward, Mr. Titsworth, told me he would write to his father and request *him* to break to you the sorrowful intelligence. Your husband fell a martyr in his country's cause in the battle near Jacob's mill-ford, Rapidan river, Friday afternoon, November 27th. He was buried and his grave marked. I know this is sorrowful tidings to tell you—that he whom you dearly loved can see you no more on earth; that he can come to his home no more. Oh, this terrible war is breaking so many hearts, and making desolate so many happy homes! But what a glorious death it is to die for one's country! The graves of such patriots as your husband are honored graves. Is not this a consolation? He rests now; a Christian soldier, and, thanks be to God, your husband not only fought the battles of his country, but that better fight—the good fight of faith. He had enlisted under the banner of Jesus Christ and was fighting the battle of the Lord. But he has fought his last fight for his country and his God, and hath conquered, and has gone to receive his reward. He will be remembered by his countrymen as one who gave his life for their welfare, and, we humbly trust and believe, will wear the victor's crown in heaven. As you are aware, I have been in the regiment only since last September, but in my little acquaintance with Mr. Dunham, I learned to love him. I have had many seasons of pleasant conversation with him in his tent, and in my own, and have enjoyed his presence and his assistance at our religious meetings. He was a frequent attendant at our prayer-meetings, our Sabbath service, and our Bible-class, and seemed deeply interested in the study of the Scriptures, and by his remarks rendered the lessons more interesting and instructive to us all. I already miss him—I, too, am mourning, and would not have you cease to weep over his sad and sudden death. Oh, no! Jesus wept at the grave of his friend Lazarus, but when you weep, mourn not as those who have no hope; remember who has afflicted you. God is too wise to err and too good to afflict us for our harm. He does all things well, all things work together for good to them that love God. 'Whom the Lord loveth he chasteneth, and scourgeth every one whom he receiveth.' God says concerning you and your children, 'A father of the fatherless, and a judge of the widow is God in his holy habita-

Lieutenant William Hand.

tion.'—Psalm 68:5. Again, 'Leave thy fatherless children; I will preserve them, and let thy widows trust in me.' 'Trust in the Lord, he will sustain thee.' 'He will never leave thee nor forsake thee.' We all sympathize with you in your affliction, and you are remembered at our prayer-meetings. If I can do anything for you, I shall take great pleasure in doing it. Please write me. I believe nothing was found on the person of your husband. If he had anything, it was taken by the enemy, as they had possession of the field for a time. May God bless you and yours.

"Respectfully, &c.,
"E. CLARK CLINE,
"*Chaplain Eleventh New Jersey Volunteers.*"

Colonel Schoonover, who was something of an expert with the rifle, took delight in acting as a sharpshooter upon the advance line whenever occasion offered. He therefore could not resist the temptation presented by the skirmish-line at Locust Grove. It will be remembered that our skirmishers had been posted along a fence at the edge of the wood. The enemy's line was posted along a fence on the opposite side of the narrow field which intervened. Some of them, however, had crept forward and were hidden in the high grass. A constant fire was kept up between the two lines. Schoonover crept forward to the fence where our skirmishers were posted—to have advanced in an erect position would have been to court death—and borrowing a gun from one of the men, awaited a shot. He made two shots, but without effect. The third shot was at a rebel who had been lying in the grass a short distance from the fence. An occasional puff of smoke revealed the positions of those who had had the temerity to conceal themselves in the grass some distance beyond their picket-line. He directed some of the men near him to fire at the spot where the smoke was seen to rise, while others were to hold their fire and take the game on the wing. He had a fair open shot at one as he was scaling the fence. The shot must have taken effect, for the man required assistance to reach a place of safety. But the sharpshooting from that part of our line elicited a sharp return, during which Valentine Greer, of Company B, was shot through the head.

Before daylight on the morning of November 28th we were again on the move to join General Warren. Through torrents of rain, and mud ankle-deep, we pushed forward. Late in the afternoon we halted about three miles beyond Robertson's tavern.

Supposing that we were to remain all night, tents were put up and preparations made to pass the night as comfortably as circumstances would permit; but at dark orders came to move forward. The intense darkness, combined with the almost impassable condition of the roads, made marching very difficult. After struggling along for four hours, making only that many miles, we halted for the remainder of the night. It was bitterly cold, but soon large fires were built, and the chilled and weary men lay down to catch a few hours' rest.

Early on Sunday morning, the 29th, we were again on the move, but seemingly in a purposeless manner. We would move and halt, move on again and wait. It was very cold, a genuine winter's day, and, as no fire was allowed, it was only by constant walking or stamping that we could keep our feet from freezing. We bivouacked for the night in a pine wood, and though it was bitterly cold, ice forming an inch in thickness, no fires could be built, owing to the proximity of the enemy; so the best we could do was to wrap our overcoats and blankets around us and shiver and stamp the night away. Some of the men were even destitute of overcoats, having only a single blanket to protect them.

On the morning of the 30th we marched up the plank-road and massed just to the left of it. The Second and Third Divisions of the Third Corps had been ordered to report to General Warren, to join in a contemplated charge upon the enemy, who were posted in strong works beyond Mine Run. As we lay in position, with their works in plain view, there was not a man, officer or private, who did not fully realize the danger of the undertaking. I cannot better describe the position and feelings of the men than by quoting the words of Colonel Schoonover:

"At six o'clock in the morning Colonel McAllister, commanding the brigade, sent for the regimental commanders and gave them, under the circumstances, this remarkable information: At seven o'clock our artillery would open on the right and continue firing without cessation for one hour, when a simultaneous charge of thirty thousand men, under General

Warren, would be made upon the enemy's works. He wished us to communicate these facts to the line officers, and they in turn to their men, so that all, both officers and men, could fully understand the importance and magnitude of the work before them, and make whatever preparations they might desire. Upon my return I called the officers together and repeated the information given me, and endeavored to impress upon their minds their duties as officers, and gave such general instructions as I deemed proper. The officers seemed silent and thoughtful. It was admitted that one-half, at least, would fall in the assault, while to hold the works would cost many lives.

"Perhaps there never was an hour in the regiment's history when both officers and men so thoroughly realized the great danger of an undertaking as they did upon this occasion. The scene was an unusual one. Many things combined to make it so. The enemy's works, with their guns glistening in the sunlight, three lines of abatis, and a swampy, difficult approach, were all in plain sight. The morning was intensely cold. To be wounded on a day like this was not a pleasant thing to contemplate. It is doubtful if the survivors of well-fought fields anticipated the opening of such a tragedy as this bid fair to be with any emotions of pleasure. And the eagerness which is sometimes manifested by those who have never experienced the realities of battle, has more of seriousness about it to the veteran soldier. I doubt that if on any similar occasion in the experience of the regiment so many valuables, addresses and messages to friends were given to the chaplain as there were on that cold winter morning at Mine Run. It was a strange, sad spectacle. But as the morning wore on the rumor came that the charge had been abandoned. It was reported that it did not meet the approval of General Warren.* The cloud was lifted, and a

---

* Colonel Schoonover states that he was recently informed by Colonel Washington A. Roebling, of Trenton, who was on Warren's staff, that the General and himself made a careful inspection of the enemy's works from our picket-line — creeping out for that purpose. General Warren believed the works were too formidable to make a successful charge upon them.

marked change was soon manifested along the line. Officers and men breathed freely once more, and many were the expressions of admiration for General Warren and his wise decision."

It was said that Warren, when asked if he could take the position in his front, answered yes, but that he would lose twenty thousand men in doing it.

I well remember the morning of the contemplated charge. I had been in charge of a picket detail on the flank during the night, with orders to assemble and follow at daylight. As I came up to the regiment I was met by Bishop W. Mains, who said, "Tom, you should have stayed back; we are to make a charge at eight o'clock." Together we went out beyond the lines to view the position, and if I ever regretted being prompt in the performance of duty it was that morning after viewing the slashed timber which covered the slope up which our charge would lead. We remained in position until night and then fell back about three miles and bivouacked.

About ten A. M. on December 1st the brigade received orders to report to General Gregg, commanding the cavalry, at Parker's Store. We reached our position about three P. M., and were formed in line of battle along the road, and remained until daylight the next morning. There was no rest during the night, as an attack was momentarily expected. Soon after daylight orders came to move. The Eleventh New Jersey brought up the rear of the brigade, only a troop of cavalry being in its rear. We marched down the plank-road toward Chancellorsville until we came to the road leading to Germania ford, and, turning to the left, we followed it until the ford was reached, where we crossed the river. After crossing the river we marched about four miles, then encamped in a wood. A day's rations were issued, and for the first time in several days we enjoyed a square meal.

On the evening of the 3d we reached our old camp at Brandy Station.

The campaign had been a short but very severe one. Not only had the men been compelled to undergo the hardship incident to cold and storm, but owing to the bad condition of the roads it had been impossible to forward sufficient supplies, and many of the men suffered the pangs of hunger. Some, being two or three days without rations, tried to quiet the gnawings of hunger by chewing hard corn. Just before re-crossing the Rapidan, a field was passed in which a few small turnips remained. They were eagerly seized and greedily devoured. How welcome, then, was the day's ration received after reaching the north side of the river! I know of one case, at least, where it made only one square meal.

On this campaign Chaplain Cline won the entire confidence of the men by his active sympathy and many acts of kindness. He could often be seen tramping through the mud while some tired soldier was having a lift upon his horse. Soldiers were skeptical of professions. It took a practical demonstration to win their belief and confidence. The Chaplain, by these practical demonstrations of sympathy for the men, won their confidence and thereby opened the way for the good work that the winter brought forth.

It will be remembered that when Sergeant William Hand went forward to the skirmish-line at Locust Grove, he left his knapsack, with blanket and overcoat, on the main line of battle. When the rapid advance of the enemy in strong force pushed the regiment back, Hand was compelled to get out as best he could, with no time to recover his knapsack. This left him with no protection but a thin blouse, and during the bitter cold that followed he suffered very much. The night that we left the position beyond Robertson's tavern, a horseman came along and inquired if there were any Plainfield men in the regiment. Hand recognized him as Thomson Thorn, an old friend and neighbor. While talking together, Thorn observed that Hand was very cold and thinly clad, and asked him where his overcoat and blanket were. The details of his loss were told. Thorn turned and rode away, saying, "I have something for you." He soon returned with a blanket, a half-side of fresh pork and a haversack of potatoes. As large fires were permitted that night, Company B at least enjoyed a comfortable supper, for there was enough to supply them all.

The Mine Run campaign ended the active operations for the year 1863, and the army settled down to the quiet and rest of winter quarters at Brandy Station.

Before entering into a description of our life at Brandy Station, it might be well to take a glance backward and summarize the losses, and note the changes that had occurred in the regiment since the beginning of its career.

The roster gives the total strength of the regiment when mustered at Trenton as 979 officers and men.

The losses, up to January 1st, '64, were as follows: Officers killed, 6; died of wound, 1; enlisted men killed, 22; died of wounds, 23; died from other causes, 57; missing in action, 13. Discharged for disability and other causes—officers, 3; enlisted men, 162. Deserted, 122; transferred, 60; officers resigned, 14; officers promoted to another regiment, 1. Making a total loss of 484. In addition there had been 21 officers and 288 men wounded, making an apparent loss of 793, and a remaining strength of 186. To be sure, many of the wounded had returned to their commands, but it is a question if the absent, sick and on detached service, would not counterbalance the accretions made from that source. In the absence of the Adjutant's morning report I think it would be safe to say that the effective strength of the regiment on January 1st, '64, did not exceed 200. Searing, who was a close observer, places the strength of the regiment, after the battle of Locust Grove, at 105. I do not know from what source his information was obtained, but from the figures I have been able to obtain, I must consider his estimate too low. Of the 122 deserters, 82 had deserted before the regiment left Trenton, and 19 more before its first battle; making 101 in all before the regiment had fired a shot. Of the sick, left behind at Trenton, one had died and 11 been discharged before leaving the State. Deducting the deserters and those left behind, sick, instead of the regiment leaving the State 979 strong, as the rolls would seem to indicate, it numbered 860 officers and men.

As has been previously stated, when the regiment marched from Alexandria 4 commissioned officers and 215 men were left behind sick. So that it will be seen that the regiment never had a fighting strength of more than 600. Of those left behind at Alexandria a large proportion never reported back to the regiment, being either transferred to the Veteran Reserve Corps or numbered with the discharged.

Following is the official report, by Colonel McAllister, of the part taken by the Eleventh New Jersey Volunteers in the campaign and battle of Mine Run, November 26th to December 3d, 1863:

"HEADQUARTERS 11TH REG., N. J. V.,
"NEAR BRANDY STATION, VA.,
"Dec. 4th, 1863.

"SIR—I have the honor, in accordance with orders from Corps Headquarters, to report, relative to the part my regiment took in the late campaign and battle beyond the Rapidan river, as follows:

"Thursday morning, Nov. 26th, broke camp and moved toward the river. 1 P. M., arrived at Jacobs' Ford; Colonel Blaisdell, commanding Brigade, ordered me to march down to the river, close by the pontoons, and as soon as a boat was launched in the water, man it with twenty-five (25) men and cross without delay. We soon reached the opposite shore, deployed as skirmishers, and marched up to the crest of the hill, when we discovered a few rebel cavalrymen, who fired a few shots and disappeared. I then advanced the line until ordered to halt for further orders. In about 1½ hours the column moved forward, the rebels firing occasionally and retreating. On arriving at a creek and mill, we halted, countermarched, and bivouacked for the night in the woods.

"Sep. 27th. Up early, and moved on a road leading towards Robertson's tavern. The enemy crossed our road and disputed our passage. Skirmishers were thrown out, and we continued our advance for a short time, when the enemy showed himself in force. I was then ordered to support the skirmishers, which I did for 1½ hrs., as circumstances required, when I was ordered to relieve Col. McLaughlin, which order I obeyed, with my right resting on the road and advanced my pickets to the fence and the regiment close in their rear. The enemy fired rapidly. Lt. Col. Schoonover went in person on the picket-line, directing operations, increasing our fire and driving the enemy back. The fire now slackened, everything seemed to be working favorable. The enemy now advanced in force. The 26th Penn. Reg. on my left

Lieutenant John B. Faussett.

gave way, carrying with it some of our men. Major Halsey and myself soon brought them back, the 26th Penn. Reg. rallied, and all fought splendidly. In a short time the 5th Excelsior Regiment broke, afterwards the line on my left gave way. My regiment stood firm holding the enemy in check until the ground on my flanks was occupied by the enemy in force; three minutes more and we would have been taken prisoners. I then ordered my men to fall back. In doing so, Johnson, the color-bearer, on reaching the open space at the cross-roads stopped, unfurled the National flag and waved it in the face of the enemy. On arriving at the battery, we re-formed and joined the brigade at Division Headquarters, formed in line of battle and lay down to rest. Our loss in this battle was (6) six killed, twenty (20) wounded, (2) two missing, (2) two taken prisoner, in all (30) thirty. With but few exceptions our officers and men did well. I cannot refrain from mentioning the names of Lt. Col. Schoonover, Maj. Halsey and Adjt. Beach. They acquitted themselves with honor.

"Nov. 28th, 1 A. M. Ordered to advance on the picket-line, where we remained until early dawn, then moved with the column toward and past Robertson's Tavern, bivouacked for the night between the turnpike and plank-road toward Orange Court House.

"Nov. 29th. Moved forward toward the plank-road, to support Gen. Warren. Bivouacked in the woods for the night.

"Nov. 30th. Ordered to report to Gen. Warren. Moved up the plank-road, filed off to the left in line of battle—in front of the enemy's works—preparatory to a charge, lay there until evening, returned (3) three miles and bivouacked for the night.

"Dec. 1st, 12 A. M. Ordered with the Brigade to report to Gen. Gregg, down the plank-road, at Parker's Store. Arrived at 3 P M., formed line of battle along the road and remained there until daylight next morning.

"December 2d. Early dawn, moved with and in rear of the brigade. Nothing in rear of us but one regiment of cavalry. Came down the plank-road towards Chancellorsville, then struck off in the direction of Culpepper Ford. Crossed on pontoons, then moved to Ely's Ford, turned in direction of the camp and bivouacked for the night.

"December 3d, 8 A. M. Started at the head of our brigade and reached camp early in the evening.

"Very respectfully,
"Your obdt. servant,
"ROBERT MCALLISTER,
"*Col. Comdg. Regt.*"

Chapter IX.

Camp at Brandy Station.

THE five months spent in quarters at Brandy Station, though not a period of unalloyed pleasure, was yet perhaps the most pleasant period in our army experience. Easy communication with the North enabled us to receive many testimonials of love from the friends left behind. Many boxes of delicacies, and packages of books and papers found their way to the front. Although drills, inspections, etc., were kept up, we found leisure for reading, writing, and practicing the social amenities in a manner peculiar to army life. Frequent reviews were held, not so much to test the discipline and proficiency of the troops as to exhibit them to the admiring eyes of the female friends and relatives of the officers in command. Access to the army being easy, and comparatively safe, and there being no indications of another campaign during the winter, the wives of general and staff officers took advantage of the opportunity offered to visit the army. The boys learned to know them by sight and to read the indications pretty closely. If a strange lady was seen issuing from headquarters, a review of some kind was sure to follow within a few days; and though they became somewhat irksome, from their frequency, the men were gallant enough to submit without much grumbling.

The long rows of log cabins, with wide streets between, had few claims to architectural beauty. Outwardly they presented pretty much the same appearance—rough surfaces of logs, chinked between and daubed plentifully with Virginia mud, and roofed with canvas more or less weather-stained, according to its age of service. At one end an uncouth projection, something like a bay-window in its first stage of evolution, continued some feet above the roof, and in some instances terminating in a headless pork or sugar-barrel, constituted a fire-place and chimney. A low opening, closed with a rubber blanket, or rough door made of cracker-boxes, hung with leather hinges, served for an entrance, and all around an embankment of dirt to keep the water from entering. Inside, the general arrangements were alike; across one end, bunks, one above another, to accommodate four persons, made of poles and filled with aromatic pine boughs known as Virginia feathers; hooks on each side, where the guns and equipments were hung; a floor of split logs, boards or hardened earth, dependent upon opportunity or the energy of the inmates. At one side a rude table, made of pieces of boxes or any odd bits of board that could be obtained, and hung with pieces of leather so as to be lowered when not in use; above the fire-place, perhaps a rude shelf. These were the general features, but in the minor details there was as much difference as there was diversity of tastes of the inmates. Some were so neat and orderly that one would almost think that a woman's hand had arranged them. The table would be covered with paper or a piece of muslin, and in the center piled whatever reading-matter the mess might possess, accompanied by the almost universal package of Killikinnick, for it was a hard matter to get four soldiers together without one or more smokers being of the party. All had to be kept reasonably clean, as frequent inspections were made and a few hours' extra drill or some other punishment awaited the negligent.

The ordinary routine of camp duty was the same, day after day—reveille and roll-call, sick-call, guard-mount, two hours' drill, either company, battalion, or brigade—then dinner. Afternoon, two hours' drill, dress-parade, roll-call at retreat, tattoo at nine, and taps a quarter of an hour later, when all lights were supposed to be extinguished. In many tents convivial parties would frequently gather, who paid but little attention to taps. The officer of the day, passing around, would call out, "Lights out in there." "All right, Lieutenant," would be the answer, and the lights would disappear, only to spring up again brightly as soon as the sound of his footsteps had died away.

Some one has said, "Turn a sailor adrift upon a log in mid-ocean and he will get whiskey." It might almost as well be said, "Put a soldier in the center of an arid desert, and if he has a love for the ardent he will manage some way to get it." Certain it is that though every effort was made to prevent the private soldier getting intoxicating liquors, he could at any time during the winter encampment get as much as he had money with which to pay. Sutlers and commissaries were under orders not to sell it to enlisted men, but soldiers were full of strategy, and if a forged order or pair of shoulder-straps assumed for the occasion would not bring it, they would find some other way.

About this time a question of seniority arose between Colonel McAllister, of the Eleventh New Jersey, and Colonel Blaisdell, of the Eleventh Massachusetts. Pending the settlement of the question McAllister was in command of the brigade. He was known as a sincere Christian, but of rather a puritanical bent, and strongly opposed to the use of intoxicants in any form. It was very rarely, and only upon extraordinary occasions, that he would allow it to be issued to the men. And this recalls a little incident of which he was the hero. At Gettysburg, after he was wounded and taken to the rear, he was being cared for by Dr. Welling. The doctor urged him to take a little whiskey to stimulate his waning strength, but McAllister steadily refused. Welling then, without his knowledge, prepared an appetizing milk punch, which McAllister readily drank. He was heard afterward speaking in terms of praise of the milk given by the Gettysburg cows.

But to return: Blaisdell, on the other hand, was not particularly known as a teetotaler, and did not object to the men having their regular ration of stimulants. Though both colonels were brave and gallant soldiers, they could not, because of disparity of tastes and dispositions, become very warm friends. It was a current rumor in the camp at the time that Blaisdell had said if he regained command of the brigade by the holidays, he would have the entire brigade drunk. I cannot vouch for the truth of the rumor, but it is a matter of history that such an occurrence transpired, and shortly after Blaisdell took command an unusual quantity of "commissary" was issued, and the drinking men, on one night at least, were pretty thoroughly intoxicated. The over-indulgence came near bringing about a serious riot. The camp of the Excelsior Brigade adjoined ours, and visits back and forth were frequent. On the night in question some of the members of the Fourth Excelsior were visiting friends in Company K, of the Eleventh. Cards were brought out and drink flowed freely. As a result a dispute arose, ending in a fight. The visitors, getting the worst of it, ran to their camp for assistance. A crowd came pouring over and the battle spread. Other companies became involved, and even the Twenty-sixth Pennsylvania, or rather members of it, who were always our warmest friends, came with offers of assistance. It was not until Colonel McAllister armed a part of the regiment and charged the crowd that the trouble was ended.

It is almost impossible to collect a body of men without having some who are inclined to cast off moral restraint. The Eleventh contained some such men, but I think the moral tone of the regiment was equal to, if not above, the average. That it was so was owing to the earnest efforts of its colonel, and above all to its chaplain, E. Clark Cline, who possessed in an eminent degree those qualities that win the love of the thoughtful and command the respect of the most reckless. Allied to a winning kindliness of manner was an earnest Christianity that none could question. He was ever ready to give aid to even the humblest, and no circumstances, no matter how trying, were ever known to extort from him any but the gentlest words. All who were with the regiment while he was connected with it know how earnestly he worked for the moral and spiritual welfare of its members. As soon as we became settled in camp, therefore, a chapel was erected and meetings were held regularly through the winter, which resulted in a number of conversions. In addition, a temperance society was organized and many induced to sign the pledge.

On the evening of February 29th the Hon. John Hill, of Boonton, addressed the temperance organization, and it also received visits from Mr. Fay and Miss Helen L. Gilson, of Chelsea, Mass. There is a great deal of truth in the old couplet:

> "Wherever God erects a house of prayer,
> The devil always builds a chapel there."

For no sooner had the temperance society been organized than the liquor element organized an anti-temperance society, pledging themselves to destroy (by drinking) all the liquor they could get. The badge that distinguished the members of this society was a cent cut in two, and one-half suspended from the button-hole by a narrow ribbon. This society consisted of enlisted men. Another one, of like character, existed among the line officers, whose badge consisted of a grain of corn, typical of the source of commissary whiskey.

Among the amusements of the winter were balls and minstrel performances. A large hall, 40 by 70 feet, had been built for the use of the brigade. The season was opened by a grand ball held by the officers, and as there were many ladies visiting the army, of course it was a very enjoyable affair. Afterward the room was turned over to the use of enlisted men, and the regiments would take turns in giving entertainments. But as the enlisted men had no wives nor daughters visiting them, and a dance without something resembling femininity not being very attractive, the want was filled by dressing in female garb the youngest and most effeminate of the soldiers. Some sent North for female apparel, but as that was not always practicable, many ways were resorted to and many varieties of material used to get up costumes. Colonel McAllister, no doubt, would have been very indignant had he known that one of his table-covers sometimes figured as a skirt upon George W Lindley, the writer's "steady company." Said cover was procured through Charles Abers, of Company E, employed at regimental headquarters. Hoops were fashionable in those days, and grapevines being plenty in Virginia forests, a little ingenuity produced a passable article of crinoline. Woolen mufflers and handkerchiefs formed an important part of the dress-goods, but the crowning mark of the whole costume was the head-dress, glittering with crescents and silver stars, made of pasteboard and tin-foil. Some of the boys developed a great talent for dressing, and the correctness of their costumes, with their slender forms and almost girlish features, would have deceived any but the most critical observer. When all were gathered beneath the brilliant glow of the hundreds of penny-dips that shone from bayonet-formed candelabra, the many-colored costumes and sparkling jewels formed an *ensemble* that was immense. Excellent music was furnished, both string and brass, by the musicians of the brigade, and at midnight an excellent supper was given. It cost something, for sutlers' charges were high; but oh! the fun we had!

Moralists might say, "You could have put your time to better use." Perhaps! But I do not think any who participated in these diversions lost any of their soldierly qualities. They fought just as desperately and died just as bravely as if they had spent the time shivering in the shadows and brooding over possible death. I do not think a man is any better or braver because he wears an elongated countenance and continually mutters, "*Memento mori.*"

Tiring of dances the hall was given up to a troupe of minstrels who gave really good performances, for the members were nearly all professionals. What profession or calling could you not find represented in the army?

The season closed with a grand conflagration. Some incendiary fired the building, and in spite of the heroic efforts of the New York firemen, from the Excelsior Brigade, who quickly had their machines on the spot—said machines consisting of the running-gears of baggage-wagons with ropes attached—the building was entirely consumed. No insurance.

Several snow-storms occurred during the winter. At one time snow fell to the depth of a foot. The camp was quickly cleared of it by shoveling it into rubber blankets and carrying it away.

On the night of February 3d there was a very heavy hailstorm, hail-stones as large as walnuts falling.

On the morning of February 6th we were aroused long before daylight by the beating of drums. Orders were received to pack knapsacks, put three days' rations in our haversacks, and be ready to move at seven o'clock, but it was not until five P M. that the bugle sounded for us to fall in. Cannonading had been heard all day in the direction of the Rapidan, and though the roads were in a miserable condition from the rain of

Captain John Oldershaw.

the previous night we pressed rapidly forward. About ten P M. we crossed Robertson's river and encamped for the balance of the night in the woods beyond. Large fires were quickly kindled, and spreading our rubber blankets on the ground and our woolen ones over us, we were soon sleeping as only tired soldiers can.

The 7th was Sunday, and Chaplain Cline, as was his custom, distributed papers and tracts. At one o'clock we gathered around a large stump, which served as a pulpit, and listened to an excellent sermon. The meeting was an impressive one and many hearts were touched by the chaplain's earnest words. The circumstances by which we were surrounded lent solemnity to the occasion. The ground we were occupying had been the scene of a conflict the day before, and while we were listening the occasional boom of cannon could be heard not far away. We did not know how soon we should be called into action. I have no doubt many serious thoughts were evoked, for they will at times come to the most thoughtless. At four P. M. we were ordered to return to camp, which was reached a little after dark.

Near where our regiment did picket-duty lived two families. One, by the name of Stuart, were bitter secessionists; the name of the other family was Jackson, and consisted of an old man—who called himself Hickory Jackson—wife and two daughters. They were all profoundly loyal to the Union. At the time of the retreat from Culpepper, General Buford's cavalry was engaged in a skirmish on Jackson's farm, a number of men being wounded on both sides. After the fighting was over, Jackson and his daughters carried in and cared for the Union wounded, which so enraged the Confederates, who shortly afterward occupied the ground, that they threatened to hang him, and even went so far as to put the rope around his neck. That his life was spared was no doubt due to consideration of his age.

On February 15th the division was reviewed by about thirty of the wives and daughters of field and staff officers. General Prince was ostensibly in command, but I think our real commanders in those days were the visiting ladies. The balance of the month of February passed without anything of note occurring. We went through the ordinary round of duties, and having plenty to eat and comfortable quarters we really enjoyed the passing hours.

The Sixth Corps having been advanced to Madison Court House on the 28th to aid a cavalry movement under Custer, the Third Corps occupied their picket-line during their absence.

On March 1st the Eleventh occupied a part of the Sixth Corps' old picket-line, near the residence of a Mr. Farner.

By an act of Congress, approved February 29th, '64, the grade of Lieutenant-General had been revived. The act carried with it the command of all the armies of the United States. On March 9th, General U. S. Grant received his commission as Lieutenant-General, and on the 10th visited the headquarters of the Army of the Potomac, then at Brandy Station. Soon the sounds of preparation for the opening of the spring campaign were heard.

On March 4th General Meade had recommended to the War Department the consolidation of the five infantry corps of the army into three corps. An order from the War Department, on March 25th, authorized the carrying-out of Meade's suggestion. The Second, Fifth and Sixth were to be retained, but consolidated into two divisions. The old First Corps, consolidated into two divisions, made the Third and Fourth Divisions of the Fifth Corps. French's Division, which had joined the Third Corps after Gettysburg, was sent to the Sixth Corps, making its Third Division. The old Third, that had won the proud name of "Old Guard of the Potomac," made the Third and Fourth Divisions of the Second Corps. The new arrangement caused a great deal of dissatisfaction, especially among the members of the old Second Division. They were proud of the glorious record that the old White Diamonds had made. But when it became known that it was to retain its distinctive badge, and, though merged with other troops, would still be known as the White Diamonds, the voice of complaint ceased, and the day came when they were just as proud to be known as "Hancock's Foot Cavalry" as they had been of the title "Old Guard."

On April 8th, the regiment was detailed to do picket-duty along the Rappahannock, below Kelly's Ford. Five of the picket-posts were on a narrow strip of land between the river and a creek (or mill-race), the strip terminating at the upper end in a swamp. The creek was crossed by a rude bridge of logs. It had been raining more or less for several days, and after the posts had been relieved on the 9th the rain came down again in torrents, the river and creek began to rise, and before the men between the creek and river were aware of any danger their fires were drowned out and the bridge swept away. They started for higher ground, but the creek was too deep and swift to ford. The only alternative lay through the swamp. After floundering about in it until eleven o'clock, sometimes in water up to the armpits, they succeeded in reaching high ground near the ruins of an old building. Here they built a large fire and remained until morning, drying their clothing. When daylight came they found that a man by the name of Smith, belonging to the Twenty-sixth Pennsylvania, was missing, no doubt having been carried away by the torrent while trying to ford the creek.

About the middle of April suttlers and civilians were ordered to the rear, and the order was a warning to us that we had not much longer to remain idle.

On the 22d the Second Corps, numbering about 25,000 men, was reviewed by General Grant, and for the first time we saw the man who was to lead us to ultimate victory.

On the 25th the division was consolidated into two brigades. The First Brigade, consisting of the First and Sixteenth Massachusetts, Twenty-sixth and One Hundred and Fifteenth Pennsylvania, the Fifth, Sixth, Seventh, Eighth and Eleventh New Jersey, was placed under the command of Colonel Robert McAllister, of the Eleventh New Jersey. The Second Brigade, consisting of the Eleventh Massachusetts, Seventieth, Seventy-first, Seventy-second, Seventy-third, Seventy-fourth and One Hundred and Twentieth New York and Eighty-fourth Pennsylvania, was placed under command of Colonel William R. Brewster, of the Seventy-third New York or Fourth Excelsior. General Gersham Mott was assigned to the command of the division.

It was evident to every man in the army that active operations were soon to begin. From the fact that General Grant was to make his headquarters with the Army of the Potomac, and from what we had heard of him as a fighter, we were satisfied that the indecision that had marked previous campaigns would no longer exist.

L

CHAPTER X.

Across the Rapidan and Southward—Wilderness—Spottsylvania—Cold Harbor.

ON THE morning of May 4th, '64, between twelve and one o'clock, came the long-expected order to move. It was after daylight, however, when we bid farewell to the old encampment that for five months had been our home, and where we had enjoyed more pleasures and more real comfort than during any other period in our army-life. It was well that we could not pierce the future and see the dreadful carnage through which we were to pass; that we could not know the hardships and terrible losses that we were to meet. Could we have seen before us our course from the Rapidan to the James, strewn as it became with the bodies of dead men; could we have heard the groans of the thousands of mangled comrades that were to echo along that bloody march, I doubt not but our hearts would have

NOTE.—At the battle of Chancellorsville Lieutenant John B. Faussett was reported as slightly wounded. The injury was more serious than at first supposed, and proved to be permanent. He had on at the time a private's overcoat. The bullet, passing through it, struck a buckle on his shoulder-belt, twisting that out of shape; it struck a stud in his shirt-front, crushed the stone, and, stopping against his breast, caused a severe contusion. At the battle of Gettysburg he was wounded in the head, and the New York papers reported him among the killed, but he recovered and re-joined his regiment. On the march to the Wilderness he was sun-struck; he endeavored to keep up with his command, but he could not, and fell unconscious on the top of the bluff on the south side of the Rapidan, where he lay until evening, in imminent peril of rolling into the swift-flowing stream. Regaining consciousness he endeavored, in a staggering, uncertain way, to follow the line of march. While in this condition he was seen by Colonel Gilkyson and others, who at first thought that he was intoxicated, but an examination showed that he was suffering from sun-stroke and scarcely conscious of what he was doing. He was cared for and to sent to the hospital.

become faint. About noon we reached the Rapidan and crossed upon pontoons at Ely's ford, and about five P M. reached the old battle-field of Chancellorsville. We were escorting the trains and consequently did not reach the appointed stopping-place until several hours after the main body of the corps. The head of the corps had reached Chancellorsville at ten A. M., and the entire corps, with the exception of the trains and the troops guarding them, was up by one P M. We had marched about twenty-five miles, the day had been unusually warm and many officers and men were overcome with the heat, those showing the least endurance who had indulged the most freely in commissary whiskey during the winter. Thousands of blankets and overcoats were left on the roadside. It was a veritable harvest for the darkies living along the line of march. One sable female was observed " toting " off seven overcoats and two pairs of boots. We bivouacked not far from the scene of our desperate fighting of the year before, and many of the men took the opportunity to visit our old battle-line to the right of the plank-road, where we had first met the enemy's onslaught. The scarred trees gave evidence of the fight, and all around lay the wreckage of the battle. But saddest of all were the bleached bones of the comrades who had fallen there. They had been hastily buried in shallow graves and the winter's storms had in places washed away the light soil and laid bare the fleshless bones. Here an arm was seen protruding from the earth, and there the whitened skeleton of a foot peeped above the dead leaves. Skulls lay around, and among those picked up was that of Sergeant Daniel Bender, of Company H, with the cap still upon it. He had been shot through the head, the bullet piercing the visor of his cap. Upon the under side of the visor of his cap was stamped " D. Bender, Co. H, 11th N. J. V " A. B. Searing, of Company E, cut out the inscription and brought it home.

Early on the 5th we were on the move, our destination being Shady Grove church, on the Catharpin road. The head of the column had reached a point two miles beyond Todd's tavern, which is situated near the junction of the Brock and Catharpin roads, when General Hancock received orders to halt the corps at Todd's tavern and await developments, as the enemy had been discovered in force on the pike. It soon became apparent that the enemy were moving in force down the Orange plank-road and pike. General Hancock was ordered to move up the Brock road to its junction with the Orange plank-road, preparations to be made to move forward to Parker's store.

No sooner had we taken position along the Brock road than we began to throw up breastworks along the western side of the road. We had no entrenching tools. Hastily throwing together what rails and fallen timber we could find, we covered them as best we could with dirt, using our bayonets to loosen the earth, and cups, tin-plates and hands to throw it up. Quite a respectable line of defense against infantry was soon constructed, but it would have been useless had it been possible for the enemy to have brought artillery against it.

The corps was formed along the Brock road, Birney's division to the right, Mott's division continuing the line to the south of the road. Both divisions were under the command of General Birney. At 4:15 the order was given to advance. We moved forward by columns of companies to the front. Our front was covered with a dense growth of bushes, matted and locked together by green runners commonly called "cat briars." After great difficulty we found our way through and formed line of battle in the more open wood beyond. Firing began almost immediately and raged with fury. General Hancock says: "The fight became very fierce at once, the lines of battle were exceedingly close, the musketry continuous and deadly along the entire line." After advancing a distance, pressing the enemy back, the Excelsior Brigade, on our left, gave way, the enemy having got upon their flank. The First Brigade, however, held its position until the enemy got upon its flank, when it, too, was compelled to fall back to the line of works along the road, where it re-formed.

The fighting on the right by Birney's and Getty's divisions continued until eight o'clock. Hill's lines were shattered, and had there been an hour more of daylight, he would have been driven from the field. General Alexander Hays, commanding the Second Brigade of Birney's division, was killed at the head of his command. Owing to the dense forests, little artillery could be used. A section of Dow's battery, on the Orange plankroad, did good service, this and the remainder of Dow's battery, in the second line, on the left of Mott's division, being the only artillery in position on that part of the field or along our division front.

Daylight of the 6th found us under arms and ready to advance. The line moved forward at 4:30, Mott's and Birney's divisions being in the front line. The enemy was attacked with vigor, and after a severe contest his lines were broken and pushed back in confusion through the woods, with severe loss in killed, wounded and prisoners. Mott's division had pushed beyond the rest of Birney's line. So far in advance was it that its shots fell in the rear of the enemy's batteries. We were now about one mile in advance of our works upon the Brock road, but in fighting our way forward through the thick undergrowth, our lines had become broken and confused. While in this condition, Longstreet made an attack upon our left, striking Frank's Brigade, of Gibbons' Division—which had fought its way to a junction with McAllister—on the left and rear, and quickly swept it out of the way. McAllister, who, at the first fire upon Frank's Brigade, had in person ascertained the position of the flanking force, changed the front of his brigade to meet the attack, but the enemy overlapping and getting in its rear, it too was forced back. The confusion extending to the right, the line was ordered to withdraw to the breastworks on the Brock road.

Longstreet made preparations to follow up his success, and at four o'clock pushed forward to the attack. McAllister's Brigade occupied the second line of works that had been built east of the road, the Excelsiors occupying the line in front. As Longstreet's men came yelling through the woods the Excelsiors wavered and seemed on the point of breaking, but the confusion was only momentary. Settling down to their work they fought gallantly until their ammunition was exhausted. Just as their fire slackened the enemy planted a flag upon the works and were about to leap over when the word "Charge" was given to the Eleventh New Jersey and Sixteenth Massachusetts. The men

Lieutenant Titus Berry

rushed impetuously forward and quickly swept the enemy back from the works. The Eleventh New Jersey, whose colors were the first to be planted upon the front line, were eager to pursue; they swept over and beyond the line, but were ordered to return. The musketry-fire maintained during this attack has seldom been equaled. "It was like one continuous roll of thunder, long, deep and heavy, grand, yet fearful to listen to. It was the music to enliven and electrify a soldier, and cheer after cheer went up from the Union lines, while out in the tangled jungle was heard the peculiar 'ki yi' of Longstreet's men."

During this attack Dow's battery, the Sixth Maine—one section on the plank-road and one on the left of the division—did effective service. During the fight of the morning the first line of works, composed almost entirely of dry logs, took fire. They were still burning when Longstreet made the attack in the afternoon. The smoke and heat compelling the abandonment of some parts of the line, Hancock's men being nearly out of ammunition and the trains too far to the rear to replenish quickly, all thought of following up Longstreet's repulse was abandoned, and the day's fighting was ended. Our loss was comparatively small, the heaviest loss falling upon Birney's and Getty's men, to our right. Lieutenant Kennedy and a number of enlisted men were wounded. David Alpaugh, of Company E, a recruit who had joined the regiment on February 12th, received a bullet and three buckshot in his thigh. George W Lindley, of Company K, one of the color-guard, had a very narrow escape. A bullet, striking a daguerreotype that he carried in his breast-pocket, was thereby deflected; the daguerreotype was broken into pieces, but his life was saved. I will say, in passing, that it was the picture of a young lady who afterward became his wife.

Colonel McAllister, as usual, was in the thickest of the fray Two horses were shot from under him, one a new black that he had bought during the winter, and Old Charlie, known to every old member of the regiment. Charlie was a great favorite with the Colonel, having accompanied him through nearly all of his campaigns.

The night of the 6th we lay on our arms in rear of the second line of works.

On the morning of the 7th we were early under arms, and though we were moved from point to point, the day passed without any engagement. During the afternoon Colonel Schoonover was detailed as division officer of the day, and directed to take the Eleventh New Jersey and Twenty-sixth Pennsylvania and establish a picket-line through the battle-ground of the previous day. Schoonover says: "The establishment of this line in the darkness, the men stumbling over the dead bodies of friends and foes, was a duty not altogether pleasant."

Though little that was startling occurred during this night's picket-duty, the surroundings were such as to make a vivid and lasting impression upon the minds of all who participated in it. The stillness of the night, the gloom of the forest, so deep as to be almost shadowless, making the forms of comrades only a pace or two distant look like dim silhouettes against a darker background; clumps of bushes, stumps and fallen limbs took weird and threatening shapes; imagination played fantastic tricks, and fallen logs became lurking foes and the harmless murmur of each gentle breeze the voice of waiting enemies, and as we moved slowly forward through the gloom our feet would come in contact with some yielding substance, and, reaching down, our hands perhaps would fall upon the clammy face of a corpse, for the woods was filled with death's ghastly trophies. Everything seemed shadowy and unreal. A volley from the enemy would have given relief to the strained nerves. But hark! A cheer breaks from the right of the Union lines. Oh! what a relief. The strained nerves relax, the silence is broken; down the line it sweeps; regiment after regiment takes it up and carries it along until it dies away on the extreme left. The rebels, though ignorant of the cause, send back yells of defiance, from left to right. Keeping pace with the Union cheer sweeps the southern yell. And what has caused this burst of enthusiasm from Union throats? Grant is riding along the lines.

Sunday morning, May 8th, we pushed our picket-line further to the front, passing over portions of the battle-field thickly strewn with the dead of both armies. In some places feeble attempts had been made toward burying the dead; no graves were dug, only a little dirt thrown over the faces and bodies, leaving the limbs exposed. But many were lying just as they fell. A. B. Searing, says: "In one place I counted twenty-four

Confederates and twenty Union soldiers lying close together. In another place I noticed a dead Confederate upon his knees, with his face buried in the dirt. Still another I saw hanging dead upon the top rail of a fence, his feet on one side and his head on the other." In places the positions of the opposing forces were marked by two lines of dead, lying almost as thickly as lines of battle, and not over twenty yards apart.

During the night of the 7th, and morning of the 8th, the army moved toward Spottsylvania Court House. The Eleventh New Jersey was the last body of infantry to leave the field of the Wilderness. The picket-line was withdrawn about ten o'clock A. M. without interruption from the enemy. They fired a few shots as we left the plank-road, upon a small body of cavalry that was in our rear, but they gave us no further trouble.

During the morning of the 8th, while yet on the picket-line, Sergeant Hand and Andrew Webster captured a rebel who had two Union prisoners in charge, who were from an Ohio regiment. He had started with them to the rear, but lost his bearings, and came too close to the Union lines. The Ohio men were very happy to find themselves again within the Union lines, and willingly assumed the duty of taking their former guard to Union headquarters. Soon afterward a man was seen running swiftly toward our lines. He was ordered to halt, but was too much excited to heed the command. As he was unarmed, and wore a blue coat, he was not fired upon. Reaching our lines he fell, completely exhausted. It was some minutes before he could tell his story. He was a very young Ohio boy, and had been captured and sent under guard to the rear; the guards becoming careless, he made a break for liberty—two shots were fired after him, but fortunately were badly aimed. He was very glad to find himself again among friends.

"The impression among officers and men no doubt was pretty general that a retreat of the army across the Rapidan would be ordered, as it had been the custom in the past to fight a battle and then retreat, and it was not unreasonable to suppose this would be repeated. When the order came from General Grant to move on toward Spottsylvania Court House, the boys made up their minds that 'Meade's and Lee's express route,' as they called it, was to be abandoned, and that Grant proposed to establish an office nearer Richmond."

The march to Todd's Tavern, though not a long one, was a very warm one, two officers and a number of men falling from sunstroke. We reached the brigade in the afternoon and at once went to work building a strong line of earthworks, many of the men using their plates for want of shovels. The night the regiment lay at Todd's Tavern its commanding officer, Colonel Schoonover, enjoyed the luxury of a cellar-door for a resting-place, being quite sick during the afternoon, and suffering with a burning thirst and showing other symptoms of fever. Dr. Welling prescribed for him "Commissary thick with ginger." I do not know whether the whiskey and ginger or the cellar-door was the more efficacious, but the symptoms abated and the colonel was ready for duty in the morning.

On the morning of the 9th we moved to a position on the Catharpin road, where we remained until three o'clock in the morning, getting but little rest, however, for twice during the night we were called to arms by heavy picket-firing.

We marched at three A. M. the morning of the 10th, the division having been ordered to report to General Wright, commanding the Sixth Corps. About nine o'clock we took position to the left of the Sixth Corps, the left of the division resting near the Brown house. We immediately threw up works and remained in position until five P M., when the division was formed and ordered to advance. It went forward through the woods, pressing the enemy's pickets back until near their breastworks, when it was met by an enfilading fire from their batteries, which caused it to fall back in some confusion. The Eleventh was on the left of the division, and when Colonel Schoonover observed the line breaking away from the right, he ordered the regiment to lie down, and with the exception of a small portion of his command, which was broken from the right and carried back with the rest of the division, it was held in this advanced position. After remaining there quietly for some time, word was sent to General Mott that the Eleventh was still at the front and awaiting orders. Instructions were soon received from the commanding officer of the division to establish a picket line, which was done, the regiment remaining in this position during the night and until dark the next day.

During the advance on the 5th, Lieutenant-Colonel Schoonover was slightly wounded; Sergeant Iliff, Company E, was taken prisoner, and Ellis F Rose, of the same company, was missing—no doubt killed, as he was not heard from afterward. Sergeant Marbacher was struck on the haversack, which was swinging on his hip, by a partially-spent canister, which did no harm, however, further than to damage his rations and cause him to fall into a ditch over which he was about to jump.

There was no apparent cause why the division should have fallen back in confusion on this occasion, as the losses do not indicate that the enemy's fire was very destructive. Grant in his Memoirs says the movement failed because of the "feeble action of Mott." Certainly it will be admitted that the Eleventh Regiment is entitled to marked credit for remaining in this advanced position after the entire division, with this exception, had gone in confusion to the rear.

During the forenoon of the 11th, the picket-line was much annoyed by sharpshooters who fired from the protection of the Landron house, about one-fourth of a mile in front. In the afternoon an order was received from General Mott to take what men of the Eleventh were on the skirmish-line and the Twenty-sixth Regiment and charge upon this house. The advance was made under a galling fire from the enemy, with considerable loss until the fire of the enemy's artillery was drawn, when the line was ordered to withdraw. This movement was under the command of Lieutenant Colonel Schoonover. Sergeant-Major John Lanterman, one of the bravest and coolest soldiers, under all circumstances, that we had in the regiment, was killed by a sharpshooter from this house, and his loss was very much felt. His name was soon to have been forwarded to the Governor for a captain's commission. Lieutenant Savidge was also badly wounded. It was supposed at the time that this movement was merely intended to dislodge the enemy's sharpshooters, but it was afterwards learned that it was for the more important purpose of developing the enemy's position.

On page 225, volume second, "Grant's Memoirs," may be found this statement:

"On the 11th there was no battle and but little firing; none except by Mott, who made a reconnoissance to ascertain if there was a weak point in the enemy's line."

At dark the regiment was ordered to re-join the brigade, which was in position about one mile to the right, in rear of the Sixth Corps; but hardly had it reported when the division was ordered to its old position near the Brown house. It will be remembered that on the morning of the 10th Mott's Division, the Fourth of the Second Corps, had been detached from the corps and ordered to report to General Wright, commanding the Sixth Corps—the position of the balance of the corps being on the right of the Fifth Corps, holding the extreme right of the Union line. But on the afternoon of the 11th General Meade received an order from General Grant directing him to move the three divisions of the Second Corps by the rear of the Fifth and Sixth, under cover of the night, and place the entire Second Corps in position between the Sixth and Ninth Corps, so as to join the Ninth in a vigorous attack upon the enemy at four o'clock on the morning of the 12th. Mott's Division was therefore moved to its old position near the Brown house, where the remainder of the corps joined it, and all took position between the Sixth and Ninth Corps, ready for the assault as soon as there was sufficient light to enable the troops to keep their direction. The formation for attack was: Barlow's and Birney's Divisions in front, Birney on the right, Mott in Birney's rear in one line; Gibbon's Division in reserve in rear of Barlow and Birney. At 4:35 the order was given to advance. In moving forward a gap was formed to the right of Birney, and McAllister's brigade was deflected to the right to fill this gap, thereby becoming a part of the first line.

In order to understand the battle of May 12th it is necessary to have some idea of the formation of the enemy's lines, at least that part involved in the assault. I will make no attempt to describe the entire course of the enemy's works, but, starting at a point on the Brock road—that is, the road running from Germania ford to Spottsylvania Court House—the line ran a a little east of north for about two hundred yards, then east for a short distance, then northeast for about a fourth of a mile. That part of the line was held by Kershaw, whose left extended beyond the right of the Fifth Corps. Then the line ran east of north for about one-fourth of a mile through slashed timber to a point where a re-entrant connected a short inner parallel with the main line. Rhodes' Division of Ewell's Corps held this part of the line, Dale's Brigade resting on the Bloody Angle. Here a short angle looked southwest from this angle; for about half a mile the general course was northeast, with two or three eastward-deflecting angles, until it reached the high cleared ground of Landron's farm. Here it turned sharply and ran southeastward for a fourth of a mile, having fairly open ground in front and woods about the McCool house in the rear. This part of the line was occupied by Johnson's Division, of Ewell's Corps. Then the line looked east and northeast for another fourth of a mile, and then bore a little west of south until it reached a small stream, an affluent of the Ny, which ran from the direction of the McCool house. Another small stream, coming from the westward, passed through their lines about two hundred yards to the south, and the two met just outside the Union works. Between these streams their line was broken, but the gap was protected by a detached work on the high ground. A little to the rear from these detached works a line extended about two-thirds of the way across to the westward line of defense. From this second stream the line ran southeast until it struck a third stream, which ran northeasterly and nearly due east from the point where we took up the line on the Brock road. About an eighth of a mile north of this point a line ran across in rear of the Harrison house, and connected with the western salient a short distance north of the Brock road. We will follow it no further, though the line was continued southward for nearly three miles, to a point near Snell's bridge on the river Po. The general contour of this portion of the enemy's lines resembled a horse-shoe with the toe sharply bent. The por-

Sergeant T. O'Donne.

tion of the line running east and west from the toe or apex was known as the east and west salients. Down the west salient, in front of the inner parallel mentioned, was the part of the line known as the "death, or bloody angle."

We said that in moving forward McAllister's brigade was pushed to the right and thereby became a part of the first line, but the troops, converging toward one common center, the apex of the enemy's works became densely massed, which necessitated further movements to the right and left. Barlow, therefore, struck the enemy's line on the eastern salient and McAllister well down on the western, just in front of the "death angle."

Stewart's Brigade, of Johnson's Division, held the east salient. Captain McHenry Howard, of Stewart's staff, says: "Stewart's Brigade broke first on the left at the angle; the brigade was taken flank and rear." This would indicate that Birney's and McAllister's troops must have entered the works before Barlow and Gibbons, whose troops had rushed forward and formed on Barlow's left, they being in Stewart's front. Birney, entering at the apex, would have struck Stewart on the flank, and McAllister, being further down the west salient, the fire from his troops would have struck Stewart's rear—the distance at this point from the east to the west salients being not more than five hundred yards.

But to return: As we moved forward orders were given to make as little noise as possible. The ground inclined up to the enemy's works and in our front was wooded; but to the left, Barlow soon struck the open ground of the Landron farm. As soon as they struck this open ground they gave voice to a cheer, which was answered by a volley of musketry and two cannon shots. The line now moved rapidly forward, and, before the enemy could recover, had swept over the works, capturing four thousand prisoners, twenty pieces of artillery, with their caissons and horses, thirty colors, a quantity of small arms, together with Major-General Edward Johnson and Brigadier-General George H. Stewart. But the battle was not to be so easily won as this initial success would seem to indicate. We pressed forward to the second line of works, but they had been strongly manned, and the advance was checked.

The position captured was of the utmost importance to Lee, and he rapidly threw forward reinforcements. Gordon's troops, who had been held to support both Johnson and Rhodes', and Ramsecure's Brigade from the left of Rhodes', were soon on the ground, and then ensued one of the most desperate struggles of the war. The Union forces were pushed back and the enemy again occupied the interior of the works, but the Union troops clung desperately to their face and could not be dislodged. "At the point occupied by the Eleventh Regiment, the reverse side of the salient, offered but little protection from the fire of the enemy's works on the hill, consequently our men moved a little to the left where a sharp descent in the ground running from and forming an acute angle with the salient offered some protection. For some distance to the left of where our line joined the works the enemy occupied one side and we the other. Our line under the brow of the hill opened fire over the top of the works so soon as formed. This was our only safety, for when our fire slackened for a moment the enemy would rise from behind the works and pour a destructive fire into our ranks along the foot of the hill. Our forces at this point was not less than ten ranks in depth. The enemy brought up their re-inforcements under cover of the woods in the rear. Many of them, either ignorant of our position or over-anxious to single out an officer, would raise their heads above the works and fall back dead. Our fire was mainly kept up by those in the rear loading their pieces and passing them up to the front ranks. A great portion of the enemy's fire was of a random character, although many of our men were hit by shots fired through the crevices of the logs and holes in the earth-works. Frequently their muskets could be seen with the barrels resting on top of the logs and the stock in a forked stick, the gun was then fired without exposing the hand. No doubt many of our men were struck by these shots, and invariably in the head. Lieutenant-Colonel Schoonover was slightly wounded under the ear by one of these shots. Occasionally during the day the enemy would display a regimental flag above the works, but the staff would be almost instantly cut off by our bullets. Their works at this point were constructed with traverses a few yards apart. Several times a white flag was shown above the works, and as soon as our fire would slacken, the men, evidently between two of these traverses, would jump over and surrender. At one time the men to the left of where the white flag was displayed discovered the movement too soon for us, and for our own safety we were compelled to open fire before all of them were safely over, and a number fell back into their own lines pierced by the bullets of friends and foes. The fire was kept up until nearly midnight, when it ceased, and the entire line fell into our hands after fourteen hours of constant fighting."

Colonel Schoonover says: "I went over the works at daylight the next morning, and the sight was one not easily forgotten. In the ditches between the traverses I counted two hundred and fifty dead, mostly shot in the head, and in some places they lay three and four deep. I only recollect finding one wounded man there. He was sitting erect, his eyes completely closed, and seemed in great agony. A short distance in the rear of the rebel works I noticed two rebel colonels lying side by side, while their horses lay near them. The evidence of the continued fire at this point during the day and part of the night was everywhere apparent. The trees near the works were stripped of their foliage, and looked as though an army of locusts had passed during the night. The brush between the lines was cut and torn into shreds, and the fallen bodies of men and horses lay there with the flesh shot and torn from the bones. The peculiar whirring sound of a flying ramrod was frequently heard during the day. I noticed two of these that had fastened themselves in the oak trees near by. While the great number of the enemy's dead and the terrible effects of our fire upon the logs composing the breastworks attested the general accuracy of our fire, the absence of the foliage from the top of the tallest trees made it evident that during a battle there is much random firing. There is a large percentage of men in actual battle who load carefully, aim deliberately and shoot to kill. On the other hand, it is not an uncommon thing for a soldier, amidst the excitement of battle, to load his gun, shut his eyes and fire in the air straight over his head."

General McGowan, of Wilcox's Division, Hill's Corps, says: "Our men lay on one side of the breastworks, the enemy on the other, and in many instances men were pulled over. The trenches on the right of the 'bloody angle' had to be cleared more than once. An oak tree, twenty-two inches in diameter, in the rear of the brigade, was cut down by musket-balls, and fell about twelve o'clock Thursday night, injuring several men in the First South Carolina Regiment."

Brigadier-General Lewis A. Grant, of the Sixth Corps, whose brigade took position on our left during the forenoon, says: "I was at the angle the next day. The sight was terrible and shocking—much worse than at 'bloody lane,' Antietam. There a great many men were lying in the road and across the rails of torn-down fences and out in the corn-field, but they were not piled several deep and their flesh was not so torn and mangled as at the 'angle.'"

Among the many acts of heroism performed during the terrible struggle of the 12th of May there is one that came under the observation of members of the Eleventh that is particularly worthy of note. A youthful soldier, belonging to one of the Vermont regiments that had taken position on our left, leaped upon the works, and, running a short distance along them, discharged his gun into the ranks of the enemy, not more than a foot away. This act he repeated several times, his comrades passing loaded guns up to him. It was a splendid exhibition of courage, and he paid for it with his life, for he soon fell back among his comrades, shot through the neck.

The loss to the Eleventh was about 70 in killed and wounded. That it was not greater was owing to its fortunate position at the ravine before mentioned, and to the fact that such an incessant fire was kept up that it was impossible for the enemy to fire with any accuracy.

The officers killed were Captain Samuel T. Sleeper, of Company I, and Lieutenant William Egan, of Company E. Egan was killed at the opening of the battle. As the regiment was moving forward through the wood, Egan and the writer were marching side by side, almost touching elbows, when a shot, coming from an oblique direction, passed through the ranks of Company I, killing Nathaniel Cole, then striking Egan in the lower part of the breast it passed entirely through his body. He fell without a groan.

Toward morning on the 13th Lee withdrew his troops from the salient and took position in the line across its base in rear of the Harrison house. Owing to the expiration of the terms of service of several of the regiments belonging to Mott's Division, and the losses in battle, its numbers had become so reduced that on the 13th it was consolidated into one brigade under General Mott and assigned to Birney's Division—the Third. McAllister, therefore, resumed command of the regiment. But little change occurred in the position of the regiment on the 13th other than was necessary to rectify the alignments and man the works along our front. A brisk picket-fire, however, was kept up throughout the day. In the evening orders were issued to be ready to attack at four o'clock on the morning of the 14th, but not to attack until further orders. The Fifth and Sixth Corps had been ordered to move to the left and attack the enemy's right on the morning of the 14th, and our attack was to be made in connection with theirs. But, owing to the bad condition of the roads and the intense darkness, they did not reach their positions until too late to make the attack a successful one. Consequently the day was a comparatively quiet one along the main line. The pickets, however, kept up a brisk fire and sharpshooters indulged in their usual diversion of trying to pick off any exposed officer. Though the day was a quiet one it was far from being a comfortable one to the army, for the rain fell steadily.

At four A. M. on the 15th the Second Corps was moved to the rear of the Ninth Corps. Our brigade, however, took position in the front line of works to the right of the Ninth Corps. This move of the brigade had been made necessary by an attack upon the picket-line, and, as usual, the White Diamonds were rushed to the point of danger, but the attack proved to be of little force, and as the day wore on it promised to be undisturbed except by the usual fire of pickets and sharpshooters. About noon the rebels ran out a battery and began throwing shells, more, I presume, as a matter of annoyance than with the expectation of any great havoc, yet it resulted in a great loss to the Eleventh Regiment by the killing of Lieutenant Joseph C. Baldwin, one of our best and most promising officers.

Colonel Schoonover says: "He had been serving on the staff of General McAllister, and had that morning joined the regiment, bringing with him a presentiment that his death was very near at hand. He was a general favorite, and his presence always brought with it sunshine and cheer; but on that day he was unusually depressed, and it seemed as if the shadow of his coming doom preceded the fatal shot. There was quiet along the lines, and not even a probability of danger that day. But Baldwin could not relieve his mind of the belief that he was to die soon. At this time the regiment, with the brigade, occupied the outer line of works, the corps being massed in rear, preparatory to an onward move. We were sitting side by side, leaning against one of the traverses, which had been placed in the works as a protection against a flank fire. His conversation was of home, of the church he used to attend, and especially of the coming marriage of his sister—cards having been received by him that very day. In the midst of all this quiet, the rebel General Rosser brought up a battery of artillery and commenced an enfilade of our lines. Few shots had been fired when one forced its way through between two of the logs composing the traverse, crushed the head of poor Baldwin, causing instant death. He had given his life for his country, and the blood which flowed from his wound sealed the cards which had brought an invitation to the marriage festivities of an only sister."

Baldwin was buried on the field, and his grave marked with a board bearing his name, rank and command. His body was recovered in January, 1866, and his funeral attended from St. Paul's church, Newark, January 29th, 1866. His remains were buried at Fairfield, N. J., by the side of his wife, who had died just six months previous to his death. When killed he was writing to his sister, and the last sentence was, "The rebs keep throwing shells, but they are well spent, and from my position

I can't see that they do any harm." He was a ready writer and corresponded for several papers, his best *nom de plumes* being "Ned Carroll" and "Frank Greenwood." In one fictitious dispatch from the seat of war he graphically described the death of Comrade Ned Carroll, and signed it "Frank Greenwood." It was a strange coincidence that it proved a faithful description of the manner of his own death a few weeks later.

The 16th and 17th were passed in comparative quiet, but on the night of the 17th, just as we had fallen asleep, orders came to be ready to move at a moment's notice. We moved about half a mile, stacked arms and lay down again. Meade, thinking the concentration of our forces upon the enemy's right had induced them to so weaken their left that a successful attack might be made there, ordered the Sixth and Second Corps to move under cover of the night to the position of May 12th, and attack on the morning of the 18th. The assault was made at four A. M., by Barlow's and Gibbons' Divisions of the Second Corp, with the Sixth Corp on their right. Birney's Division, being held in reserve, took position in the works under a severe fire of shells. The assault was without result, the enemy being found on the alert and their works strongly manned.

On the evening of the 17th a strong picket detail was sent out from the brigade to relieve those already posted. The picket-line ran northward from the main line until it reached two negro cabins connected with the Landron estate and within sight of the line of works that we had thrown up near the Brown house. Then it turned eastward. Late in the afternoon of the 17th, Sergeant Marbaker, of Company E, with six men from various companies, relieved a lieutenant and six men at the angle-post, situated at one of the cabins. Explicit orders were given not to fire unless the enemy made an attack, and not to disturb them if they attempted to form a picket-line. Just before dark it was noticed that they were collecting behind our abandoned works near the Brown house. Thinking they were only forming a few picket-posts no shots were fired at them. Suddenly an attack was made upon our picket-line to the left, which attracted our attention. Upon turning again toward the Brown house a heavy skirmish-line was found advancing from behind the line of works. The pickets to the left were driven in, and those in the vicinity of the cabins, seeing a strong force advancing, fell back to the main line. Only Marbaker remained, sheltered by the chimney. It was either the risk of being shot or certain capture. To escape he must necessarily run up hill, exposed to the fire of a hundred guns. Several times he stepped out preparatory to a run, but the whizzing bullets would quickly send him to cover again. At last, when the enemy had advanced to within less than a hundred yards of him, the dread of rebel prisons prevailed and he made a dash for liberty. Immediately the rebel skirmish-line opened upon him, and though the bullets whistled pretty lively, providentially, he escaped injury. I will not say that he out ran the bullets, but I do know that it would have taken a pretty fast horse to have beaten him up the hill. Fortunately the ascent was not a very long one, and the descent on the other side quite steep, so that cover was soon reached. The enemy advanced to within easy musket-shot of the main line, but soon withdrew. The pickets that had fallen back were posted again that night in the open ground in front of the works, and on the morning of the 18th were advanced to the woods beyond and westward of the Brown house, where they remained until the morning of the 19th.

During the night of the 18th, or morning of the 19th, the Second Corps was withdrawn from the right and marched to Anderson's Mill, which point was reached a little after daylight. Whether intentionally or through neglect, the pickets belonging to Mott's brigade—about fifty men under command of a captain from the Eighth New Jersey—were not called in. Two shots from the left, just after daylight on the morning of the 19th, warned the captain in command to look about him. In doing so he found that his command was alone, no pickets being either to his right or left. He gave the command to assemble on the right, and started toward where the corps had been left on the

18th, but on reaching the open ground by the Brown house was confronted by a rebel skirmish-line. The direction of march was then changed for the Fredericksburg road, but it was only by the sharpest of marching that the detail escaped capture, and it was not until late in the afternoon that it re-joined the brigade at Anderson's Mill. The report had been spread that the entire detail had been made prisoners, and its appearance in camp made quite a sensation.

Of the guns captured on the morning of the 12th, eight pieces were brought into our lines by McAllister's men; two, however, were placed in position, when captured, and served with effect against their former owners, the gunners being volunteers from the infantry, among them being Sergeant William Hand, of Company B.

The loss of the regiment in the various conflicts around Spottsylvania was 70 in killed, wounded and missing. In view of the severity of the fighting that had occurred the loss does not seem to be great. But when it is remembered that at the opening of the campaign the regiment could have numbered but few over two hundred, it will be seen that, taken in connection with the loss at the Wilderness, it was relatively great.

The corps was withdrawn from the right on the morning of the 19th and marched to Anderson's Mill, where it went into bivouac. The men were informed that they would remain there until the following morning. After two weeks of almost continuous fighting the prospect of having twenty-four hours' rest was indeed a pleasant one. But rest is a very uncertain quantity in campaigning, and as we were taking our supper, preparatory, as we supposed, to a good night's sleep, the orders came to fall in and move with all possible despatch. "Ewell had been directed by General Lee to demonstrate on his front" to ascertain whether Grant was moving to the left. The attack fell upon Tyler's Division, which was composed of new troops, principally heavy artillery, that had never before been engaged.

General Hancock says they "acquitted themselves well." The firing becoming heavy, Hancock was directed to send a division to Tyler's assistance. Birney's Division was therefore doubled-quicked to the scene of action and into line of battle. Two of the brigades took position to the right of Tyler, but the force of the attack was nearly spent and by ten o'clock all was quiet again. Ewell, in this dash, captured a few wagons, but they were re-taken.

Sergeant Thomas D. Marbaker.

On the morning of the 20th we returned to our former position at Anderson's Mill. McAllister, writing from here, says: "Our losses in the brigade have been over 800. In the Eleventh New Jersey there is only one line officer on duty."

The loss to the army in the battles of the Wilderness and Spottsylvania Court House, including the Ninth Corps, had been—killed and wounded, 28,207; missing, 4,903; and there had been 4,225 sick sent to Washington. Making a total loss to the army in sixteen days of 37,335.

At midnight of the 20th the Second Corps left Anderson's Mill. This was a movement of the Second Corps alone, the object being to isolate it from the rest of the army, with the expectation that Lee would follow and strike it, thus giving the rest of the Army of the Potomac an opportunity to attack him before he had time to intrench. Our course for a while ran eastward until we struck the road leading to Guiney's Station. There the few survivors of the old First Massachusetts, whose time had expired, bid us good-bye. They turned their faces northward toward home, friends and safety; we ours southward, toward future battles and greater hardships. We reached Guiney's Station about daylight. Our route lay through a fertile, well cultivated country Coming as we did from a region where marching armies had tramped-out every sign of husbandry, or swamp and tangled thickets had impeded every footstep, these fields, garnished with the green of growing crops and dotted with well-kept homesteads, seemed an earthly paradise. We passed through the village of Bowling Green, forty-five miles from Richmond. Before the war it contained a free population of about 250; now not an able-bodied man remained, and the women, many of whom were clothed in mourning, took care to let us know that they were bitterly disloyal, and many were the prophecies of evil bestowed upon us. But the colored population, both male and female, was very much in evidence, and stood grouped along the roadway watching for every article that a soldier might find too heavy to carry One sable female was noticed carrying off a dozen coats and as many shirts—but *they* were self-propelling—and a pair or two of boots, and not forgetting to turn around and show her ivories whenever the boys would give her a "whoop."

About four P. M. we crossed the Mettapony river near Milford Station and halted about one mile beyond, having marched a distance of about twenty miles. The day had been very warm and several cases of sunstroke occurred.

On Sunday, the 22d, we worked all day throwing up earthworks which we were to occupy only one night, for seven A. M. Monday found us again on the march, headed for the North Anna river, which we reached at four P M. Colonel Schoonover was detailed to post the picket-line. Across the river the enemy could be seen busily at work. After dark our picket-line was relieved and the brigade moved four miles down the river and again threw up earthworks. It was nearly morning when they were completed, and the men got but little rest. We had now been nineteen days upon the campaign. They had been nineteen days of almost constant toil, marching, fighting or working, and all were nearly exhausted. Yet the men worked cheerfully, for they had learned by experience the value and added strength of an earthwork. Though we had learned the value of works and cheerfully built them, there were many whose strength gave way to the constant strain.

General McAllister, writing from here, says: "Work, work! fight, fight, takes all our time; we sleep only from two to four hours a day. It is the hardest campaign I have ever seen, and before its commencement would not have believed that I could have gone through it; but God has given me health and strength to bear up."

Soon after daylight on the 24th the enemy opened upon us with artillery from beyond the river. Just above where we were lying, at Chesterfield ford, the North Anna was spanned by a light wooden bridge. The enemy had a battery planted so as to command the bridge and its approaches; it seemed impossible for troops to cross without meeting with serious loss. About 7 A. M. our skirmishers pushed across, followed closely by the Sixth New Jersey, and they in turn by the brigade, led by McAllister, and though the rebels kept up a constant fire of shot and shell the crossing was effected without serious loss, which seemed miraculous, for one fair shot striking the bridge would have been sufficient to render it impassable. Though the rebel battery was posted less than half a mile away, and was served at short intervals throughout the day, not one shot struck the bridge. When the sound of a passing shot is heard men will often involuntarily dodge. The action does not detract from their courage, but it sometimes causes merriment. Several dodges had been made on the morning in question by the men behind the works, and Colonel Schoonover had laughingly chided the men. As we started to cross the bridge the enemy sent in their shots a little faster, and one, passing pretty close to the Colonel, he unthinkingly made obeisance to it. That was one for the boys, and they quickly called out, "Dodge the big ones, Colonel!" After crossing the river we took position in the enemy's abandoned works. All day they kept up a fire of shell without, however, doing much damage. After dark the line was advanced, and another night was spent with pick and shovel.

We remained comparatively quiet until midnight on the 26th, when we re-crossed the river, and, after marching about a mile, halted in an open field and obtained what we then considered a good rest. It continued until twelve o'clock on the 27th, when the march was resumed and kept up until one o'clock on the morning of the 28th, when we halted within a half mile of the Pamunkey river. A little rest was obtained there, but at ten A. M. we were again on the road, marching down the Pamunkey At five in the afternoon we crossed the river on pontoons at Huntley's, four miles above Hanovertown. During this march of more than thirty miles not more than one house to the mile could be seen. The Sixth Corps had crossed the river about noon and had taken position across the Hanover Court House, or River road, at Crump creek. The Second Corps formed line on the left of the Sixth, completing the cover of the road from Crump creek to Hawes' Shop. As usual, a good part of the night was spent in throwing up earthworks. When the regiment crossed at this place it went into line near a house occupied by a lady and her children. The formation of the line so near her house led her to believe that a battle was about to commence. She was wild from fright; reason seemed almost dethroned, and her frantic screaming made her an object of pity. She was finally pacified and persuaded to enter her house and remain there.

On the 29th General Hancock was directed to make a reconnoissance on the roads leading from Hawes' Shop to Atlees and Richmond, but it was not until late in the afternoon that we were put in motion. Barlow's Division was on the lead, and struck the enemy in force near where the Richmond road crosses the Totopotomy creek. The other two divisions of the corps coming up, Gibbons' took position on Barlow's left and Birney's on his right. This brought us near the road leading to Hanover Court House. There was no rest again that night, for morning was close at hand when our works were completed.

On the 30th the Eleventh New Jersey, Fifth New Jersey and First Massachusetts Heavy Artillery, under the command of Colonel McAllister, made a reconnoissance in connection with Colonel Egan. Skirmishers were thrown forward and to the left to connect with Colonel Egan. Egan's line soon encountered the enemy and were subjected to a heavy fire of musketry. At dark the division moved forward and threw up a new line of works.

Colonel Schoonover was division officer of the day, and as such it was his duty to establish the picket-line for the night. He says: "I had one of the toughest jobs I ever undertook— that of establishing a picket-line with a regiment of heavy artillery in a dense forest, through swamps and ravines, and momentarily in danger of running into the enemy's lines. The line was completed at half-past two in the morning. Once we drew the enemy's fire and had one man wounded; several were stuck in the mud. On the morning of the 31st fifty men reported to me with instructions that I should feel for the enemy. I did so, and, in conjunction with a party on the left, entered their works on the opposite side of the valley. We lost one man killed and took two prisoners. The enemy's flags and cannon were in plain view before us. I took a hasty sketch of their works and reported the situation to General Mott."

The brigade advanced at seven A. M., and, under a heavy fire of shell, took possession of a line of works that the enemy had abandoned. We soon moved forward again, and, under a fire from the rebel batteries, built a new line of works. One man was wounded in the regiment during the day. After dark we crossed the valley and began the construction of another line, but about midnight re-crossed and occupied the line previously built. We had become so accustomed to building works during the night only to abandon them in the morning that it was no surprise to us when the order came at seven o'clock on the following morning, June 1st, to fall in. We moved to the right and took position on the road leading to Hanover Court House. There we hoped to have a little rest, but soon an aid came riding up with orders for the Eleventh New Jersey to picket the roads at the Overton house. Two men, of Company K, who had been sent on a scout, were captured near the Butler house. In the afternoon we were joined by the Twentieth Indiana, and the picket-line was extended, the left resting at the Overtons and the right at Butler's. The Butler house was used as headquarters for the picket-line, and it was from Miss Butler that we obtained information of the capture of our two men. Miss Butler's father had been arrested by our cavalry and was held a prisoner within our lines. She seemed very much distressed, and shed tears profusely when making known her troubles. Schoonover says: "Visions of a good old-fashioned night's rest loomed up before me, but just as Miss Butler came in with a mattress and pillow, orders came to assemble the picket immediately."

We re-joined the brigade and lay down until daylight of the 2d, when we took up the march for Cold Harbor, which we reached about ten A. M. We rested until the afternoon, then moved about one mile, and were formed in columns of regiments, and bivouacked for the night. Late in the afternoon heavy firing was heard upon the right. It was occasioned by Early's attack upon Burnside. He succeeded in capturing a number of prisoners from the skirmish-lines of the Ninth and Fifth Corps, but the main object of the attack was not accomplished, which was to sweep down upon and turn our right flank. The night was a stormy and disagreeable one. Rations had become scarce, and it was necessary to send men back to carry up boxes of hard-tack, as the wagons could not get to us. I think the labor of carrying them was entirely superfluous, for, had they been unboxed, they were sufficiently animated to have been driven up. But a hungry soldier was seldom very fastidious in regard to food, in fact they could not afford to be—the only alternative being eat what was issued or go hungry; so the hard-tack was eaten and, in the absence of meat, served for both rations.

The men passed an uncomfortable night and were but little rested when, at four o'clock on the morning of the 3d, orders came to fall in. A general attack had been ordered. The formation of the Second Corps was Barlow's and Gibbons' Divisions in advance, Birney's supporting. As we moved into position across an open field, outside the works, we were exposed to a heavy fire of artillery and had four men wounded. The line was formed back of a hill which afforded some protection from a direct fire, but we were still exposed to an enfilading fire from the enemy's salients. Two men (John H. Gilbert, of Company E, and White, of Company F,) were wounded while lying in line of battle. "The line of the Fifth Corps being too much extended to permit of offensive operations," at noon Birney's Division was sent to strengthen it. We remained on the line of the Fifth Corps until the afternoon of the 4th, when, being relieved by Burnside's troops, we returned to the left and rejoined the Second Corps.

There was very heavy firing along the line on the morning of the 4th, and everything seemed to indicate a renewal of the effort to take the enemy's position. But the welcome orders to suspend offensive operations was given. After being relieved by Burnside's troops, and marched to the rear, we were massed in the woods and given an opportunity to wash and rest.

One month had passed since leaving our comfortable quarters at Brandy Station—a month of unprecedented hardships, of desperate fighting, weary marches and long nights of exhausting labor. We had had scarcely a night of unbroken slumber, our little rest having been caught here and there as the exigencies of the campaign permitted, going sometimes for days without cooking a meal, but snatching a bite upon the line of battle, eating as we marched along, and sometimes, perhaps in the short intervals of labor, stealing time to cook a cup of the much-wished-for and much-needed coffee. It had been a campaign scarcely paralleled in the history of warfare. The line of march was dotted with the graves of our best and bravest, the hospitals in the rear filled with mangled humanity. And notwithstanding all this, and nearly exhausted as we were, we did not lose heart but looked forward cheerfully and hopefully, thinking that the end could not be far.

It rained the night of the 4th, but in spite of the rain we enjoyed our respite from the dangers and toils of the front.

At 5 P M. on the 5th we moved a short distance to the left and halted in rear of the second line of works. Just after dark, as we were moving still further to the left and just as we had reached an exposed position, the rebels opened upon us a terrific fire of shot and shell, and notwithstanding it was intensely dark they seemed to know our exact position. So fierce was the fire for a few minutes that the men scattered for cover. No doubt some will remember this incident from the malodorous pits into which some of them tumbled when seeking shelter in the darkness from the enemy's flying missiles. During this cannonading a shell burst directly in front of the writer's eyes, which, for the time, completely blinded him. The cannonading lasted only a few minutes, then the column continued its movement to the left and halted at Barker's Mills. This placed our division upon the extreme left of the Union lines and about three-quarters of a mile from the Chickahominy river. The lines were formed and strongly intrenched. The position of the Eleventh Regiment was on a hillside sloping down to the mill-pond. The works ran along the crest of the hill. This pond afforded splendid facilities for bathing and washing clothing, and the men took advantage of this opportunity to scrub off the grime and dust that had been accumulating during the month, for it was about the first opportunity that had been afforded for making a thorough cleansing since breaking camp at Brandy Station. But our pleasure was not entirely unalloyed, for our friends on the other side, fearful that we would forget them, occasionally kept sending us their iron compliments.

About five o'clock on the afternoon of the 9th a number of officers, including General Mott and staff, were sitting near the headquarters of the regiment, when the enemy opened a vigorous fire of shell upon our line of works, which extended along the crest, some twenty or thirty feet above the place occupied by the officers. As they thought their position an entirely safe one, and as an occasional shell fell into the pond among the bathers, who did not seem at all disturbed by the intruders, the affair was very keenly enjoyed. But soon a change came over the scene. A conical ten-pound shell burst over the works, and a piece of the missile, of about three pounds weight, shot directly down the hill and struck Colonel Schoonover in the back. His first impression was that he had been hit with a solid shot. In the language of the lamented Baldwin, he was ready to exclaim, "Life is in a nutshell, and I am shelled out." For a moment or two he thought that he was fatally wounded, but it proved to be only a bruise, which kept him from duty a day or two.

One of the most pleasant features of our stay at Barker's Mill was the amicable relations that existed between the pickets of the opposing armies. Along our front a mutual truce was agreed upon, and many a friendly chat was held (paradoxical as it may sound) with the enemy's pickets. The usual barter of tobacco, papers, sugar and coffee was carried on, and they even permitted our pickets to get water from a spring just within their lines. This was one of the strange anomalies of the war between North and South—in action bitterly intent upon taking each other's lives, but, when opportunities like this occurred, meeting with the friendly feeling of neighbors. This truce had one condition, the ignorance of which led to the death of a member of the

Eleventh. The condition was, that either party should be permitted to fire upon mounted officers. On the 10th Colonel McAllister was division officer of the day, and, being ignorant of the agreement between the pickets, took his orderly, Wilson Snooks, of Company C, and rode directly to the front. He was fired upon by a sharpshooter. The ball missed the Colonel but struck and instantly killed the orderly. He was buried the same day, near our works on the hill.

Chapter XI.

Across the James—Petersburg.

But Sunday night, June 12th, brought an end to the rest and comparative quiet that we had been enjoying at Barker's Mill. After darkness had fallen we quietly withdrew from our works, and, following the Fifth Corps, crossed the Chickahominy river at Long's bridge. The Fifth Corps took position covering the roads to the north and westward, while the Second continued toward the James by way of St. Mary's church and Charles City Court-House. About ten, bivouac was made for the night, but march was resumed at five A. M. on the 13th. The James river was reached at Wilcox landing about dark. The corps began crossing on the morning of the 14th, but it was not until after noon that we embarked upon the "James Powell" and were ferried over to Windmill Point. As we steamed across the beautiful river our hearts were filled with new hope, for we had bidden farewell to the swamp and miasmata of the Chickahominy, to the long line of graves that stretched not only across the peninsula, but across the hills, and valleys, and streams, and through the fertile fields and tangled swamps of Virginia up to the Rapidan. We were bidding farewell to old battle-fields and entering upon a new field of operations. It was well that the future was to us as a "sealed book"—that we could not see the hot, deadly trenches of Petersburg, the fierce assaults along the line, the nine months of constant toil and danger that stretched out between us and the end. Had we possessed that gift of prescience our hearts would have been less buoyant. We disembarked at Windmill Point and bivouacked for the night, and remained there until 10.30 A. M. on the 15th. Hancock had been ordered to wait for 60,000 rations that Butler was to send him. But as the rations did not arrive, orders were given to move forward. Had we moved directly to Petersburg after disembarking at Windmill Point, we could have reached it early on the 15th, before Lee would have had time to reinforce Beauregard, and perhaps the history of the war would have been different and thousands of lives and long months of toil saved. For it was not until sunset on the 15th that the First Brigade (Hogood's, of Hoke's Division) of reinforcements reached Beauregard and took position south of the Appomattox. Humphries says: "Had General Hancock's instructions merely directed him to move his corps by the most direct route to the intrenchments of Petersburg it would have arrived there by four o'clock—certainly by six o'clock—and in time to attack with Smith's force. It would have found no infantry and but little artillery on Smith's left, and continuing to advance would have secured Petersburg." But the fatal delay was caused by the order to wait for rations, which in our case were not received, and we reached the defenses of Petersburg early on the morning of the 16th, half famished, and would have gone breakfastless had it not been that the colored troops whom we relieved generously shared their rations with us.

We were now near Petersburg, within sight of its church-spires, and in the enemy's outer line of defenses captured by Hinks' colored troop on the 15th. The day was spent in maneuvering subject to a fire from the enemy's batteries. At five P. M. the division was formed in three lines of battle, the right resting upon the Petersburg road, the New Jersey regiments of the Third Brigade being in the Second line, with the Eleventh upon the extreme left. Soon after five the line moved out in front of the works and advanced upon the enemy. The advance was met with a severe fire, before which our first line disappeared. The second line, under command of McAllister, however, remained intact and advanced close to the enemy's works. Finding them too strong to be carried by assault, efforts were put forth to hold what ground had been gained, and though subject to a deadly fire, the New Jersey troops held their position until near morning, enabling other troops to fortify the ridge in their rear. The position of the Eleventh was on a hillside, and without any covering to shield it from the fire from the enemy's works which were situated just across the ravine. During the night we ran out of ammunition, but were supplied by the First Maine Heavy Artillery, who were throwing up works on the ridge in our rear. We held this exposed position until two

Lieutenant C. H. Rossiter.

o'clock in the morning, when, the line in our rear being completed, we were ordered back.

The loss to the Eleventh was five killed and thirty-five wounded. The killed were Captain Sydney M. Layton, of Company D; Private Thomas Twigg, of Company D; Private James Freeman, of Company G; Corporal James Fleming, of

Company H, and Private Stacy Babcock, of Company I. Of the wounded their injuries proved fatal to five: Roderick B. Nelson, of Company D, died August 31st, at New York; Miller H. Lewis, of Company F, died June 24th; John Barry, of Company G, died June 19th; William Linsey, of Company I, died June 28th; Sergeant Daniel Adriance, of Company K, at the field hospital, June 20th. Three others were so badly injured as to be unfit for any further active service and were discharged.

To many readers the word "regiment" signifies a body of one thousand men. And to such the loss will not appear very large. But when we take into consideration the fact that up to this time we had received but few recruits, and the continued losses by disease and battle had reduced our numbers to less than two hundred, the proportion of loss will be fully realized.

Sergeant David McAllister, while lying on the hillside, was struck in the foot, the bullet entering the heel, passing through the entire length of the foot and coming out between the first and second toes. As he raised up to go to the rear he was again struck, the second time in the neck, disabling him for life. It is natural for men to lie down when holding a line of battle; in fact, the order was generally given to do so; but a recumbent position in such a place as that occupied by the regiment on the 16th of June was one of the worst that could be taken, for the enemy's shots, coming, as they did, from the opposite rise of ground, would be apt to pass diagonally through the person struck. The writer recognized that fact, and would not lie down, though repeatedly importuned to do so by members of his company. Repeatedly some one would say: "Tom, get down; you'll get hit." But "Tom" steadily refused to do so.

Along toward midnight Hand, the writer and another got possession of a shovel and began digging a pit. The enemy were comparatively quiet while we were digging, but just as we got it large enough to shelter the three they opened with a volley. The pit was speedily occupied, and remained occupied until the regiment fell back.

On the 17th Colonel McAllister was transferred to the command of the Second Brigade, its commander having been wounded. Lieutenant-Colonel Schoonover was therefore left in command of the regiment. Under the hill in rear of the line of works erected the night before we lay quietly until dusk, when, the enemy making an attack upon our line, we were moved to the right. Some of the boys will remember this movement to the right under fire, from the eagerness with which they took advantage of the protection of the ditch that ran nearly parallel with our line of march.

During the 17th the enemy abandoned the line of works on our front that they had held so stubbornly on the 16th and took position across a ravine, from five hundred to a thousand yards further back.

On the night of the 17th Meade issued orders for an assault to be made early on the morning of the 18th by the Second, Ninth and Fifth Corps. The corps were formed in the order named, with the Second on the right. In compliance with this order the advance was made about daybreak, McAllister, with the Second Brigade, leading. On advancing it was found that the works on our immediate front had been abandoned. The line pressed forward, however, until they encountered the enemy in a new line of works. For a while the fighting was terrific, but the enemy's works were found too strongly manned to be carried, and our troops, being subject to an enfilading fire, were forced to retire; not, however, until they had suffered severe loss. Later in the day the Third Brigade made an assault over the same ground, the First Maine Heavy Artillery leading. This was one of the regiments that had been garrisoning the fortifications at Washington, and joined the Army of the Potomac. After Spottsylvania it was about 1,800 strong. The First Maine charged with vigor, and reached a point closer to the rebel lines than had the troops which preceded them. They struggled manfully for a while to hold their ground, but so terrific was the fire to which they were exposed that they in turn were compelled to fall back. Their loss in killed and wounded in this assault was six hundred and thirty-two. Fortunately for the Eleventh, it was not called upon to participate in this charge. The regiment had two men wounded on the 17th and one on the 18th.

General McAllister, writing of the operations of the 18th, says: "This division lost in the battle of yesterday (the 18th) more than a thousand men, and the greatest loss was in the Second and Third Brigades during their charges. The conduct of both brigades in these charges was highly creditable, but owing to their repulse Victory will never record their heroic deeds—deeds worthy of the greatest victory of the war. After the heavy artillery retired the ground was strewn with wounded, dead and dying. The cry of the wounded is 'Water! water! water!' but no relief can be sent them. Hundreds of our wounded thus died in sight. It was perfectly heartrending to hear their cries and yet be unable to give them that relief which we would so gladly have furnished."

On the 19th we moved to the right near the Hare house and threw up works. This was the beginning of the work afterward known as Fort Steadman. It will be remembered that Colonel McAllister was in command of the Second Brigade. When lying near the Hare house he had his headquarters in a little earthwork just in rear of the main line, but within range of the enemy's sharpshooters. One afternoon a major, just fresh from the North, who had been appointed quartermaster, visited him on business. It was about time for the evening meal, and the Colonel invited him to share it. While they were enjoying their coffee and hard-tack the sharpshooters began to send over their leaden compliments. The major was noticed to look up inquisitively as they went singing by. When about half through their meal one came quite close. "What kind of birds are those that sing so strangely?" asked the major. "Minie birds," says McAllister. "What birds?" Before his question could be answered again one struck close by and gave him the desired information. The major hastily excused himself, saying that he was not hungry, and rode away. We remained in the vicinity of the Hare house until one o'clock on the morning of the 21st, when we were relieved by a brigade of colored troops from the Ninth Corps, and marched to the rear and bivouacked in a field.

Chapter XII.

Mahone's Attack—Major Halsey and Others Captured.

THE MOVEMENT of the Second and Sixth Corps to the left of the Jerusalem plank-road, to get possession of the Weldon railroad, began on the 21st of June. In this advance the Eleventh New Jersey constituted the skirmish-line of the brigade. About dark it established the line along the edge of a wood, the enemy's entrenched picket-line being about two hundred yards to the front in an open field. This line the regiment occupied during the night of the 21st and still held on the 22d. Some distance from the left of our picket-line there was a large cleared space, across which the rebel vidette were in plain view. Intersecting our line was a wood-road leading out to this opening and back to a cleared field in front of our main line. Frequently during the day Colonel Schoonover had gone up this road, more through motives of curiosity than anything else. The last trip he made in that direction he discovered a movement of the enemy that saved the regiment from being captured entire. It was late in the afternoon and he was approaching a point from which he had a number of times taken a view of the enemy's vidette line, when he was met with a volley from the very spot that he had visited not half an hour before. The Sixth Corps was upon our left, but by some mistake a gap had been left between it and Barlow's Division of the Second Corps. The rebel General Hill, who was moving down to check this movement upon the Weldon road, had discovered this gap, and, at the time Schoonover was making his reconnoissance, was swinging through upon Barlow's flank and rear. Fortunately the Colonel escaped and hastened back. As he was making his way back he met the mail-carrier of Barlow's Division with a mule and two well-filled pouches leisurely making his way to the front. The situation of affairs was explained to him and he changed his direction to the rear without any argument. Schoonover then hastened to inform Barlow of the situation of affairs and found him washing his feet in a stream near by. His division, which had just got into position, was taking things very coolly, the shade of the forest being very grateful after their hot and dusty march. Hill's troops soon struck Barlow's Division on the flank and rear, which, as it invariably does, produced great confusion. Barlow's Division was rolled back upon Mott's and both were compelled to retreat with heavy loss. This exposed the flank of Gibbons' Division, and the enemy swept quickly upon them. They, too, were thrown into disorder and fell back with the loss of four guns and several regiments with their colors. The position of the Eleventh, upon the extreme front, was a particularly dangerous one, and but for the timely discovery of the enemy's advance by Colonel Schoonover the entire regiment would have been captured. As it was it was compelled to run a gauntlet of fire from front, flank and rear, but it escaped with the loss of Major Halsey and forty men.

During the march on the 21st, Hand, Mulvey and Dixon, of Company B, somehow captured a big turkey. They took turns in carrying it, hoping to get a chance to cook it, but the regiment was out on the skirmish-line all night, so that they had no opportunity, and during the flank movement next day Dixon and the turkey were both captured.

After the fiasco of the 22d, we strengthened our works and encamped in their rear, where we lay undisturbed until July 12th. Though we had a respite from the dangers of the battle, our rest was not a very enjoyable one. The heat was intense, almost unbearable; the roads and fields were but beds of dust, that rose in clouds before every gentle breeze, and everything was covered with the hue of earth. We would long for a breeze to fan away the stifling heat, and, when the breeze came, for a calm, that eyes, ears and nostrils might be freed from the smothering cloud. Vegetation almost disappeared. And to add intensity to our discomfort, water was scarce and bad, and could only be obtained by digging deep wells in the clay soil, and dipping it from the bottom of these with cans tied to the end of long poles. No rain had fallen since the 4th of June, and the drought remained unbroken until the 21st of July, a period of forty-seven days. Even here, amid all these discomforts, our good chaplain had prepared a place for religious services. A soldier's place of worship was necessarily a rude one. Above him spring no graceful arches of carven stone; no stained and pictured windows tempered the sun's hot glare and turned the brightness of day to a dim religious twilight; no fluted columns of polished stone reared their graceful shapes around him. His eye saw no masterpiece of sculptor's art looking from veiled niches; no miracle pictures of saints in gorgeous robes fastened the eye to panels or spandrels; no richly-upholstered seats wooed to rest and forgetfulness; no deep diapason of organ to awaken the slumbering music of the soul; no extraneous aids. And yet, perhaps, the worship was as acceptable as that of those who meet in temples made rich and gorgeous by the toil of the artisan and the genius of the artist.

Often, like the fathers of old, we met beneath the emerald arches of the forest, where God's voice could be heard whispering in the passing breeze and the voices of feathered songsters mingled with the songs of praise, and even the squirrel would cease his chattering as if to listen. Sometimes we sat among the violets, upon the springy turf of the meadow, while the daisies nodded to and fro as if in approval. Again it might be, as at Spottsylvania, where the sod was stained with blood and the crack of the rifle and the boom of the cannon gave emphasis to every prayer. But here we gathered upon rude seats of logs, cushioned with bark and moss and lichen; did we look up, our eyes rested upon a vaulted arch made dazzling with frescoes from God's own hand—frescoes of clouds that pigments could not imitate, sunshine beyond the painter's art; or night's jewels peeping through the rifted branches; columns too, had we, of soldierly pines, whose branches were eternally sighing; of sturdy oaks, whose rounded boles climbed upward from gnarled and knotted roots—truly, a "temple not made with hands." And mingling with the tones of man's worship was the hum of insects worshiping in unison.

On June 25th Colonel McAllister resumed command of the Third Brigade, and on the 28th again took command of the regiment. On the 30th the regiment was paid, receiving four months' pay.

On July 12th we moved out of the trenches and were massed near the Jerusalem plank-road, and told to "fix up" camp, and yet but little time was allowed us to do so, for we were employed both day and night in tearing down old works and building covered ways to enable our artillery and supplies to reach the front line of works. The Sixth Corps had been withdrawn from our left and sent to Washington and the Shenandoah Valley. Therefore it became necessary to contract our lines. Many of the works that had been built on the left were torn down, so that, should the enemy make an advance, there would be no lines of empty works behind which they could find shelter.

On July 23d, General Birney having been assigned to the command of the Tenth Corps, General Mott took command of the division and Colonel McAllister was again placed in command of the brigade. We were kept at work on the covered ways and other works constituting our line of defense. We were on fatigue duty every other day, starting out as early as four in the morning and remaining until seven in the evening. We worked in reliefs, two hours at a time—still it made a long and tiresome day.

Chapter XIII.

Across the James—Mine Explosion—Ream's Station.

About the 25th of July, General Grant determined to send a body of troops secretly to the north bank of the James. The object was threefold: first, to destroy the railroads leading northward; secondly, if the chances seemed favorable, the cavalry was to make a dash upon Richmond, infantry being sent to support the cavalry if the movement should prove successful; thirdly, he thought this movement might induce Lee to weaken the force holding Petersburg, so that there would be a better promise of success in the assault attending the springing of Burnside's mine. Accordingly, on the evening of the 26th, the corps was put in motion. We broke camp at four P M., crossed the Appomattox at Point of Rocks, and continued the march by the light of fires that had been built to guide us. We crossed the James river at daylight, at Deep Bottom. Bailey's creek, which is twelve miles below Richmond, empties at Deep Bottom. Two pontoons had been laid here, one above and one below the mouth of the creek. They were held by General Foster, of the Tenth Corps. Hancock determined to cross by the lower bridge and attack the enemy's left flank, leaving General Foster to hold them in front.

After crossing the James, the line was formed with the cavalry on the right. The enemy was not in any strong force east of the creek, and were driven away by our skirmishers, Barlow's skirmishers capturing a battery of four twenty-pound Parrot guns on the New Market road. The entire corps was advanced through the woods, swinging on the left. The enemy could be seen in strong force, and working very busily, on a ridge west of Bailey's creek, about a mile distant. A strong column could also be seen marching to the left. A few shots from the gunboat "Saugus," dropped in the marching column, soon caused a scattering, Hancock's orders not permitting an assault in front.

We were withdrawn to the line of works previously captured, where we remained until the night of the 28th. While lying here in line of battle we received what, under the circumstance, was a very peculiar ration, namely, one of salt mackerel. Had we been in camp, where such food could have been properly pre-

Lieutenant William E. Axtell.

pared, it would have made a very acceptable change; but in line of battle the boys scarcely knew what to do with them, and many of them were thrown away. This came near proving a *casus belli* to two members of Company E, one contending that the other should have given them away if he did not want to use them, and the other, that he had a right to do as he pleased with his own. Nations have met in shock of battle for less cause, but fortunately in this case, though words waxed plentiful, mediation brought about a peace ere blood was spilled.

At dark on the evening of the 28th, Mott's Division re crossed the James, and after marching until near daylight, halted in the woods in rear of the Eighteenth Corps, who were to join Burnside at the mine. We remained under cover of the woods until dark, when we marched silently into the works and relieved the Eighteenth Corps. Our position was upon the bottom-lands just to the south or southeast of the Appomattox river. The suburbs of Petersburg could be plainly seen, whenever it was possible to raise the head above the breastworks, but that was a hazardous undertaking and seldom indulged in, for the enemy's main works were not over four hundred yards distant, and each showing of a blue cap above our works called forth a volley from the rebel guns.

The writer's curiosity at this point came near costing him his life; hearing something drop on the outer edge of the parapet he foolishly put his head above the works to see what it might be. It happened to be a bomb, which, at the instant of looking, exploded. It was a close shave, but close shaves were common occurrences in the trenches in front of Petersburg.

Our works at this point were very strong and well supplied with bomb-proofs and traverses for the protection of the men. The mine was to have been sprung at daylight, but a defect in the fuse delayed it until twenty minutes to five. At that time a low, rumbling sound and the simultaneous discharge of eighty heavy guns and mortars and as many field-pieces told us that the work was accomplished. The explosion was a complete success, causing an opening one hundred and fifty feet long and about twenty deep. The enemy's redoubt was rendered a complete ruin. Eight magazines, each charged with a thousand pounds of powder, had been exploded; but, unfortunately, the assault, though at first promising success, proved a failure; or, as General Grant termed it, "a miserable affair." Had the assault been entrusted to leaders who would have led instead of hiding in bomb-proofs in the rear there is no reason why Petersburg should not have fallen at that time.

After the assault at the mine orders came to McAllister to demonstrate on his front with the view of ascertaining whether the enemy's line had been weakened enough to give hope of a successful assault. To have sent men over the works would have been sending them to almost certain death. So McAllister adopted a novel yet effectual method of ascertaining the strength of the forces occupying the works in our front. The brigade was formed in two ranks and the men were instructed to place their caps upon the muzzles of their guns and at the command "March" the guns were to be raised so that they were visible. The command was then given in a loud voice, "Fourth battalion, battalion of direction, forward, guide center, march!" At the command "March" three cheers were given and the caps were raised enough to give the enemy the idea that we were preparing to move over the works. The fire that followed this demonstration showed very plainly that the rebel works were too strongly manned to make a successful assault possible. A few caps may have been wounded, but the men being under cover were not hurt. During the day, however, eight men in the brigade were wounded by shells from the enemy's batteries across the Appomattox; one lost a leg and two had arms shot off.

At dark we were relieved by the Ninth New Jersey, and, after withdrawing, marched back to the camp occupied previous to our march to the north bank of the James. We were ordered to "fix up" camp, and there was a good prospect for a long rest; but we knew that it could not last very long, for Hancock's Cavalry, as the Second Corps was facetiously called, was seldom long at rest. It was thrown here and there, wherever a point was threatened or an attack was to be made.

Thursday, August 4th, was set apart by the President as a day of fasting. Accordingly, orders were issued that all work not a military necessity should be suspended, and that religious services should be held by the chaplains throughout the army.

In the morning Colonel McAllister had service at Brigade Headquarters, conducted by Mr. Sovereign, Chaplain of the One Hundred and Twentieth New York, and in the evening services were held at the regiment by Chaplain Cline.

On the evening of the 5th we were called out hurriedly and marched in the direction of the Eighteenth Corps. The heavy firing from the direction of their position indicated that an attack was being made. But the firing soon ceased, and we were ordered to about face and return to camp.

The days passed, with nothing to break their quietness but the usual routine of camp and fatigue duty, until half-past two on August 12th, when we broke camp and marched to City Point, reaching there at eight o'clock in the evening. The day had been very warm, and the dusty roads made the march a trying one.

About noon on the 13th the corps began to embark upon transports, and by four P M. all were aboard and the transports steamed down the river. Speculation ran high—we were going to be sent on some distant expedition—Washington and the Valley perhaps; anyway, we were to leave Petersburg and vicinity. "The wish was father to the thought," for we were anxious to be sent to a new field of action. A few miles down the river, then anchors were dropped, and the boats lay to. As the time passed the men's spirits went down—leaving did not look so certain. It might be a ruse after all. But when ten o'clock came all speculation was ended, for anchors were weighed and the boats steamed up the river, past City Point and on to Deep Bottom, where we arrived about one o'clock on the morning of the 14th. It was found necessary to construct a temporary wharf before the troops could be landed. This was done as speedily as possible, and at two o'clock we began to disembark.

All were off and massed upon the river bank at eight o'clock. Two regiments were then thrown out as skirmishers, and advanced across the plain, the troops following in line of battle. A few small posts of the enemy were found in the edge of the woods, but they were soon driven away, and we occupied the works near what was called the Tavern and Pottery, on the New Market or river road. The skirmishers were again advanced, and drove the enemy across the field and through the woods to the protection of their main line. The Second and Third Brigades were massed near the gate-posts on the New Market road. General Barlow, who was in command of the First and Second Division, was to attack near Fussell's Mill with the greater part of the two divisions. But owing to the length of his line he took to the assault but one brigade, of Gibbons' Division, which after repeated attempts failed to break the enemy's line. At five P M. McAllister was ordered to report with the Third Brigade to General Barlow, but did not reach him until the fighting was over for the day.

At daylight on the 15th the brigade re-joined the division on the New Market road. During the afternoon it was advanced up the road and massed in the edge of a wood from which the enemy's camp could be plainly seen. At seven o'clock in the evening Colonel Schoonover was ordered to take the Eleventh New Jersey and post them in an oak grove near the bridge-head. It was accordingly moved to that position and a strong picket placed on the New Market road. During the night it was joined by the One Hundred and Twentieth New York. At ten A. M., 16th, it re-joined the brigade which was found occupying the position of the previous day.

It is not within the province of the work to speak of the doings of other regiments further than is necessary to illustrate the position of our own. But when injustice has unwittingly been done a brave and worthy officer, a short digression, intended to place the credit where it is due, may be pardoned. On the 16th the Eighth New Jersey, then numbering not more than a hundred men, supported by the Eleventh Massachusetts, was deployed and sent forward to develop the enemy's position. They advanced under a terrific fire to within a short distance of the enemy's main line, losing in the movement sixteen in killed and wounded. Foster, on page 147 of "New Jersey and the

Rebellion," says, "The Gallant Eighth, under command of Colonel Ramsey, advanced steadily under a deadly cross-fire from the rebels, who opened all their guns and musketry," etc. This charge was not led by Colonel Ramsey, but by Major Virgil M. Healy, of the Eighth, to whom should be given the credit.

But to return to the Eleventh. No move was made on the 17th. At seven P M. on the 18th the regiment returned to the oak grove near the bridge-head, where it was soon after joined by the rest of the brigade. About ten o'clock in the evening we were relieved, and, re-crossing the James by the lower pontoon, massed on the neck and waited for our pickets. At one o'clock in the morning of the 19th the march was resumed and kept up until after daylight, when we halted in rear of the Ninth Corps. At eleven o'clock we moved into the works between Forts Morton and Mickle, relieving a brigade of colored troops.

We found the works in a filthy condition, and spent the 20th in cleaning them up. Our division extended from the right of the Petersburg and Norfolk Railroad to Fort Alexander Hays, near the Strong house, having relieved nearly the entire Ninth Corps. The Third Brigade was upon the right of the division. At that point the lines were very close together, and safety required that we should keep entirely under cover, as the least exposure drew the fire of the rebel sharpshooters. One man was wounded on the 20th while on fatigue duty. The fire of the sharpshooters and pickets was maintained day and night, and during each of the two nights that we lay in the trenches at that point we were treated to a brilliant pyrotechnic display by the artillery.

On the 21st an experiment was made to ascertain the strength of the rebel line in our front. A few pieces of light artillery were brought into the works and began firing, and at the same time a demonstration was made similar to the one practiced on July 30th. It proved a decided failure. The rebels crept into their holes and did not fire an answering shot.

At two P M. we were relieved by a portion of the Eighteenth Corps and were ordered to the left of the Jerusalem plank-road to connect with the Ninth Corps. We reached our position about dark, and spent the night in throwing up breastworks. When daylight came we found that we were on familiar ground, being just in rear of the position held during the latter part of June and first of July.

It will be remembered that General Mott's Division left the north bank of the James river on the night of the 18th. General Hancock, with the First and Second Divisions, remained until the evening of the 20th. They reached their old camp on the morning of the 21st. After a brief rest they were ordered to the "Strong" house, then to the "Gurley" house, in rear of Warren's position.

On the 22d, General Hancock, with the First and Second Divisions and Gregg's cavalry, was charged with the destruction of the Weldon Railroad as far south as Rowanty creek. It was this movement that brought on the battle of Ream's Station. The work had been accomplished as far as Malone's bridge road, three miles south of Ream's Station, when, learning that a large force of the enemy were advancing against him, he took position behind the slight works at the station which had been thrown up by the troops sent to the relief of General Wilson in June.

About the time the attack began on Miles' Division at Ream's Station (two P M. on the 25th), Mott was ordered to send all his available force to the help of Hancock. Accordingly the Second and Third Brigades, with a battery of artillery and a squadron of cavalry under McAllister (Mott remaining with the First Brigade in the trenches), was ordered to march down the plank-road to its intersection with the Ream's Station road and there report to General Hancock. We reached the designated point, which was about four miles from Ream's Station, at five P M. Aids were dispatched to notify Hancock of our arrival; but before orders could be received from him General Meade came up in person and ordered McAllister to advance his force (which had been increased by a regiment of cavalry) along the plank-road towards the Blackwater—to take a good position and throw cavalry pickets well out. By dark we were in position and awaiting the attack of the enemy's force that was supposed to be moving towards us. After dark, Hancock withdrew and McAllister's command covered the rear. Had McAllister's command been sent direct to Hancock, no doubt the result of the battle would have been different.

We returned to our old camp and resumed the round of picket and fatigue.

The only loss sustained during the above-mentioned movements was the capture of our First Assistant Surgeon, J. Down Heritage. In a letter to Colonel Schoonover the Doctor has related the event and what followed so graphically that I will quote it as written:

"*Col. John Schoonover:*

"MY DEAR SIR—You will remember that we—that is, our division—were ordered out in the afternoon to guard a road leading to the rear of Ream's Station, where the Second Division, I think, had been engaged during the afternoon and had been defeated by the rebels. This road led over the 'Blackwater' river, or creek, and yourself and I rode out in front of where the regiment was posted (directly across the road to the bridge) I suppose, a mile to the front. We saw no enemy and returned to the command. The cannonading was still going on on our right, and as we were off the line of travel to the rear, and could get no tidings of how the fight was going, and as there was no probability of an engagement of our division, I suggested that I should go down and ascertain whether we had been licked or not. You assented, and I started. I rode back until I struck the returning ambulances, but could ascertain nothing, and kept on until I went directly to the front —Gregg's headquarters—and found that we had been most beautifully whipped, and the infantry was being relieved by the cavalry. It was now becoming dark, and to make matters worse, a thunder-shower came up, when it became as dark as Erebus. A captain, who had been to Gregg's headquarters for something, started with me to return, but, having forgotten something, returned, saying to me that I was on the right road, to go on slowly, and he would overtake me. I obeyed instructions, and heard plainly, a short distance to my left, the artillery going to the rear. The road I was on had been made that day for military purposes only; and I was going along moderately, when I was halted. It being dark, I naturally thought I had struck our picket-line, as I could distinctly see the forms of men lying on the ground like pickets in a row. I began to explain that I had no intention to desert, and had ridden up to the line by mistake, intending to go to the rear, and turned my horse's head away with the intention of going off, whereupon I heard several muskets cocked, and as that always means business, I faced around again very suddenly, and was again ordered to dismount, when about the following conversation ensued:

"*Reb.*—' Dismount.'

"*Doctor*—'I'll be d—— if I do. I have only ridden up to your line by mistake, and can explain thoroughly my intentions; I have, as I have told you, no intention of deserting, and if you will send your officer here I will explain to him.'

"*Reb.*—' Corporal of the guard, send Captain here!'

"Captain puts in an appearance, when I go over the same rigmarole to him. It being so dark as to make it impossible to see anything more than a man's form, when he reiterated the order for me to dismount, I told him, 'I'll be d—— if I would,' and that I might have some cause, as I then thought, against a fellow who seemed to me to be putting on airs, I asked, 'What troop are you?'

"*Captain*—' Hill's Corps.'

"I do not remember in my life to have had the starch taken out of me quicker by two words than was done on that occasion. I, of course, upon his solemn assurance that such was the case, dismounted and walked back to headquarters, where I was turned over by the Captain to the officer of the day or provost guard, I believe. I, however, asked the Captain to let me have my blankets and overcoat and French book which I had in my saddlebags, to the latter of which he assented, and as I was studying French, so that I could make myself understood to those French recruits we received a short time before, and as I had visions of Libby and Andersonville, and a prolonged stay before me, thought that the books would be my best friends.

"The rebels soon gathered around and began to chaff us—for there were several in the squad there that night—and after standing it awhile I reminded them we were their prisoners and it was hardly fair to blackguard us when they had our lives in their hands and our mouths were consequently sealed. Whereupon they said that I could help myself, and talk all I wanted, and shouldn't be hurt. I said, 'I will take you at your word, boys, and while waiting for the column to move on had about as spicy a debate as I ever participated in, and gave them our views of the war and our perfect confidence of whipping them. They assured me that they had beaten us to-day, and intended to storm the works to-morrow and clean up the line from one end to the other I reminded them that the commanding General hardly ever gave such long notice of intended movements, but if he had done so, and they tried it, they would pile themselves up in front of them by thousands and then wouldn't get inside and I only hoped they would try it. A great deal more was said and they got in good humor over my sallies and we had rather a good time. The boys at the front on both sides were better than those at the rear.

"Well, we were marched off after awhile and bivouacked in a field in the rain and mud, and after a long while I went to sleep.

"Was aroused in the morning and was marched off, as the guard said, toward Petersburg. On the march, which was twenty-five miles this day, we were halted ten minutes every hour for rest, as were the troops accompanying us, and they informed me that it was their custom on all marches to do so.

"Every hour I went to sleep regularly, and was aroused by the guard. I found myself in a squad of twenty-five privates, with one lieutenant of some New York regiment. I had no means of writing down names, and so have forgotten all my companions on this dreary march.

"We were taken to Mahone's headquarters, near Petersburg, which the guards said was near the fort where the mine was exploded, which would bring it nearly opposite Fort Merton on our line. There we lay on the ground the second night, I with two blisters on each heel as big as an old-fashioned cent. You see, I had a pair of high boots on for horseback-riding, and, not being used to marching, it was more than I bargained for. I missed my mare sadly. In the morning I asked the guard if they were going to give us anything to eat, for we had fasted since the day before yesterday at noon then, and began to fell somewhat hollow. He answered that he did not know anything about it, when I asked permission to call an officer—for we were near headquarters

Sergeant Eliphalet Sturdevant.

—he gave me permission, when I hailed one and asked the same question, and was very coolly informed that no provisions had been made for any issue of rations, and I asked if *he* couldn't give the lieutenant and myself some 'grub.' He said he would, and soon returned with two biscuits about the usual biscuit size. I gave one to the lieutenant and kept one myself. It tasted very well though it had been baked in the ashes. I saw their manner of issuing rations the day before from their wagons. Their flour and meal was dealt out of bags by the commissary to the troops on the march. How the 'deuce' they managed to cook it I couldn't see, but I suppose by the 'ash-cake' method.

"About nine o'clock the next morning we were ordered to 'fall in,' and marched over to Johnson's headquarters, in Petersburg, and made a circuit of the town for the purpose of display. Just as we entered, there was several of our flags, captured the day before, waving, and as we passed them the lieutenant and myself raised our caps, and the squad broke into a cheer. This made the guard as mad as March hares, and they were going to bayonet them if they didn't keep their mouths shut. The whole population were along the streets, and we were jeered and chaffed unmercifully, and asked if we didn't 'want to go home to our mammies,' 'how we liked it as far as we had got,' 'your army will be all broke up now you fellows are gone.' One fellow said, 'Ain't they the worst-looking pills you ever did see?' We were a perfect menagerie for them.

"Arrived at headquarters I asked to be sent to hospital. Upon signing parole it was done and I was put in charge of a sergeant and sent to Hill's Corps Hospital, reporting to the surgeon in charge, to whom I gave my gold pen, assuring him that I did not need it and could get another whenever I was exchanged. He treated me very kindly and introduced me to the mess of surgeons, asking them to take care of me, which they did very hospitably. The first night in hospital, after the work of the day was done and before supper, they brought out from under a bunk a very curious old-fashioned stone jug, and poured therefrom a clear liquid into a cup, and with their compliments presented it to me. I recognized the 'critter' at once as 'old apple' by the smell, and though nobody had, in my presence, imbibed any of the stuff and visions of 'pizen' floated through my brain, I was too dry for one thing, and their hearty manner inspired me with confidence for another, so with a 'here's to you' I proceeded to get outside of it and felt better. They were a lot of 'jolly good fellows.'

"I was put in charge of our wounded when they arrived, to the number of three hundred, and organized a nurse corps of the slightly wounded. The rebel surgeons paid no attention to me or our wounded after I was put in charge, and only furnished me with instruments and a little morphia. I performed several very important operations. Amputation of the thigh, arm, several of hand and fingers, removed testicles from one, and many other wounds were dressed. These men had been without attention for three days when I took them, and lots of their wounds had maggots in them. For this condition they gave me spirits of turpentine and a syringe, and when this was injected into a wound it was amusing to see those maggots boil out like a boiling spring. It was a new experience to me then, and I have never seen the like since.

"I was there three days, and the wounded were removed to Richmond as fast as their wounds were dressed or operated upon. At the expiration of this time I was ordered to report at Libby Prison, and having given my parole and having taken the precaution to have a copy for myself, I was sent alone from Petersburg. I arrived in Richmond and having the greater part of the day before me concluded to see what I could of the city before reporting, and wandered around to the cemetery and through it to the hotel (I forget its name now) since burned. Saw Jeff. Davis' house, and all the time when any suspicious characters eyed me inquired the way to Libby Prison. When I began to get tired I managed to find it, and was sent to the officers' room where I found about two hundred and fifty—for I did not count them—officers confined, and went supperless to bed on the floor. I had brought my blanket and overcoat with me and was warmly welcomed to a mess which was without these necessary articles of comfort. A 'mess' there consisted of three or four who were together possessed of a plate and cup, which was used by turns; there were no spoons, knives or forks. I had a good knife and was looked upon as a very fortunate individual, and with it I made a spoon from a piece of pine board I cut from a shelf. I have it to-day. It was not at all elegant, but I could eat bean soup with it, which was the *sine qua non*. I gave my knife to one of the boys when I came away. I carried two hundred and fifty dollars through the Confederacy with me concealed in the patch of my cavalry pantaloons. Good place, wasn't it? I put it there (except a fifty-dollar note) the first night I was captured. I was never searched and could have carried it in my pocket. Nor was anything taken from me except my horse and equipments. I am not sure Uncle Sam ought not to pay me for that horse.

"I had a fifty-dollar note changed while in Libby by a colonel, who seemed to have some underground way of getting such things done, and bought ten dollars' worth of Confederate money—receiving ten for one—and with this hundred dollars sent, through the colonel, for ten loaves of bread ($10.00), one paper of Killikinick smoking tobacco ($1.00), one-half dozen pipes ($10.00), and we had a feast and afterward a smoke, and I forgot a pack of cards ($10.00, and they were second-hand at that). We had a good time after that, but how the deuce the colonel managed it I never knew. He had a commission, I think, on what he invested, but I am not sure of details at this late day. Not knowing how long I should have to stay in limbo, I began to economize, and think I limited my expenses to ten dollars a day (Confederate). I have been sorry ever since I didn't give the boys a regular blow-out, but charity begins at home under those circumstances. But when I left I loaned the boys all I had but a hundred dollars. They were all "White Diamond" fellows and took their notes with instructions who to send them to when I got safely through the lines. And I am happy to say that I was repaid to the last cent by their friends with many thanks, and had sent to me the most expensive knife I have ever owned since by the friends of the officer I gave mine to when I left.

"The rations in Libby were cornbread, about three inches by two, a thin slice of bacon on it, twice a day, bean soup twice a week "only this and nothing more." And the bean soup was made on the plan of church fair soups nowadays—much soup to few beans. It was just sufficient to keep the soul in the body and that was about all it would do. But the boys seemed to be having a good time, and as a rule took things philosophically, though there were some notable exceptions.

"One day 'Turner,' I think it was, came to the head of the stairway and called out for sugeons and chaplains to report there, and I assure you we were not long in getting ready. Money was soon loaned, blankets given to the boys, farewells said and messages received for those at home, many of them verbal and memorized. Some addresses were given and whatever could be done in about ten minutes was done. And we were marched down into the hall, given a piece of cornbread, and away to the boat which steamed down the river to Aikin's Landing, where we were taken by a circuitous route about a mile out into country and around to our vessel, and the old flag looked better than I had ever seen it look before. I have never since lost my respects for the "Old Gridiron" as the rebs called it. The boys cheered it and we had a perfect reunion when we got on board, though half of us had never seen each other before. I then met the boy, he couldn't have been more than eighteen or nighteen years old, whose leg I had amputated at the thigh, while at Petersburg, and he was doing splendidly. I never saw him after we got to Washington, and do not know whether he pulled through or not, though I would like very much to know.

"You remember that Colonel McAllister wanted to know why I didn't stop off at City Point and join the regiment. I guess not —not if the court knew itself—with a twenty-day leave of absence ahead! Well! Well! Though as a matter of fact the steamer didn't stop.

"I had a sort of a row with a rebel colonel, going up to Petersburg on the march. He was one of your peppery, hot-headed, pompous individuals, and riding up to me, he said: 'I understand you represent yourself as a Federal Surgeon.' I answered, 'yes, sir; I *am* one,' with a little emphasis on the am. Says hot-head, 'How, sir, are we to know that?' I answered, 'By my commission.' I always carried my commission in an inside pocket of my vest, which I handed to him. It was signed by Joel Parker, Governor of New Jersey, and it would have done you good to have heard that d———n fool curse Joel. He just let himself loose on Joel and swore he was an infernal renegade, and ought to be the last man to sign such an infernal document as that, with many 'cuss' words interlarded, and then gave me a dressing down for coming down to the South, and burning their houses, and oppressing men who were better than the scum of Northern States; that we ought to be ashamed of ourselves, &c. He got as mad as a man can get over that commission; there were some sentences in it that rumpled him, I forget what now, but he did go on terribly for about half an hour. I just told him that we were prisoners and it was not best for us to discuss such matters unless we were equally situated, and walked on in silence, and took his blasted billingsgate, and have been mad at myself ever since that I didn't shoot some hot shot or words into him. But I verily believe that if I had 'sassed back' he would have got off his horse and 'licked' me, or cracked me over the head with his sword ; he was a regular termagant, and as hot as pepper.

"Do you remember the Sergeant—I forget his name—who was killed at Hatcher's Run, in a skirmish nearly in sight of our camp there, a little to the left? Poor boy, he was sick and I had excused him from duty that morning. But when the regiment went out he went along and 'got left.' He need not have gone at all. I forget his name, but you will remember him, no doubt.

"J. Down Heritage."

The Sergeant alluded to by Doctor Heritage was James Roalefs, First Sergeant of Company K. The fight was at the Armstrong house, March 25th, '65. Sergeant Samuel Kerr, of Company G, was killed the same day. An account of the fight will be found elsewhere.

On September 4th, the news of the capture of Atlanta reached us, and in honor of Sherman's victory a salute of twenty rounds was fired from every gun along our line.

Chapter XIV.

Fort Davis—Poplar Spring Church—Boynton Plank-road.

ON THE 5th of September the regiment moved into Fort Davis (called by some Fort Crawford). This was the largest earthworks along the line, giving accommodation to an entire brigade. It was situated to the left of the Jerusalem plank-road, and with Fort Sedgwick (better known as "Fort Hell"), which was to the right of the road and about four hundred yards nearer the enemy's works, commanded that approach.

Soon after taking position in Fort Davis, a body of colored troops marched up the road on their way to the front. Their officers must certainly have been ignorant of the proximity of the enemy's line and the position of their guns, but they did not long remain so, for a moving column in plain sight, on an unsheltered roadway, was too tempting a mark for the rebel gunners to resist, and soon shot and shell began to fall around them. They did not wait for orders to seek shelter, but, dropping knapsacks and other impedimenta, soon became a dissolving cloud, many of them tumbling into the ditch of Fort Davis. Their frantic efforts to get out of reach of the rebel guns caused considerable amusement to the men in the fort who were watching them, but I doubt if the negroes considered it a laughing matter.

In front of Fort Sedgwick, also held by a part of McAllister's Brigade, the enemy's entrenched picket-line ran along the crest, a short distance from our main line of works. They were a little too close for our comfort, consequently it was determined to make an effort to capture their pits and compel them to seek a position nearer their own line. Accordingly two regiments of DeTrobriand's Brigade, supported by the Eleventh New Jersey and Eleventh Massachusetts, of McAllister's Brigade, were ordered to make the assault. Entrenching tools were to be carried, so that if the pits were taken they could be turned immediately. Preparations were made on the evening of the 9th of September, but it was not until one o'clock on the morning of the 10th, after the moon had set, that the line moved forward. The enemy was taken completely by surprise, and the pits and eighty prisoners were captured. They made several attempts to recapture them, but their efforts were futile. One mistake was made, however, that marred our success, which otherwise would have been complete. Colonel Biles, in the darkness, mistook the tree—a point to which he had been ordered to advance—and pushed ahead too far, thus exposing his flank. As soon as daylight enabled the enemy to see his position they made an attack upon him, capturing about forty of his men and re-taking some of the pits on our right. This resulted in placing their pickets on a line with ours and bringing one of their pits so close to ours that only the bank of dirt separated them. The casualties in the Eleventh were the wounding of Lieutenant Morehouse and three men.

On the morning succeeding the capture of the picket-line the pickets of the contending forces agreed upon a truce. Some of the rebels, in the confusion of the attack, had left their haversacks in the captured pits. They asked if we would restore them. This we readily agreed to do if they would meet us half way between the lines, to which they assented, and their property was restored. We were having a very sociable time, bartering coffee for tobacco, exchanging papers and views of the war, when an officer passed along their line. He talked for a few minutes with some of our boys on the right, and then returned to their main line of works. Nothing was said until the officer had reached the shelter of their works. Then the pickets in our front told us we would have to get under cover as they had orders to commence firing. They acted very honorably, giving us all ample time to get into our pits. Then began the fusillade, which was kept up almost continuously until the end of the siege. There was an exception to the honorable conduct of the rebels in front of us. During the continuance of the truce some of their troops, holding the line further to the right, kept picking away at us. When we asked who they were and why they did not stop firing, we were told that they were some South Carolinians who did not know any better.

For a few days after capturing these pits and until we got covered ways built, relieving picket was an extremely hazardous undertaking. It was generally done in the evening, but the enemy would somehow ascertain when the relief was going out and sweep the field over which it had to pass with an unusually hot fire, so that the relief and relieved had to run a gauntlet of bullets.

Among the men in the pit occupied by Sergeant William Hand was a German who seemed to have had no experience in the use of entrenching-tools. The Sergeant watched for a while his awkward movements with the pick. At last, becoming impatient, he told him to sit down and he would show him how to use it. The German took the seat vacated by Hand, but scarcely had he sat down before a bullet crashed through his head, killing him instantly. His body was laid carefully outside the pit, and when the picket was relieved his death was reported. Stretcher-bearers were sent to bring it in, but as the way to the picket-line was across a bullet-swept field, they failed to find it. His German comrades lamented very much that the body was not brought in. Andrew Webster, who had been in the same pit, asked why they did not go after it, and offered to accompany them, but they did not seem willing to go. It was finally brought in by Hand and Webster, at the risk of their own lives.

During the truce along the picket-line, Sergeant Webster took four canteens and a haversack and went back to Fort Davis for rations. He had the canteens filled with coffee and the haversack with crackers, then started for the front again. He had also procured a box of matches from the sutler for Robert Leo, who was in the pit with Hand. These he put in his blouse pocket. Upon reaching Fort Hill (or Sedgwick) he found that the truce had been ended and that the enemy were again sweeping the field with bullets. He did not know what to do. To cross the open field seemed like sure death. At last he resolved to risk it, and getting outside the works, crept about half the distance, or to where the ground began to descend, then arose and ran for the pits. As he arose he dropped the matches; picking them up he continued and succeeded in reaching the pits unharmed.

On the 11th of September John W. Trout, of Company F, was shot in the head and killed while looking through a loophole. He had been repeatedly warned against doing so, as the enemy's telescopic rifles made the pastime a very dangerous one.

Even at this period of the siege the rank and file of the rebel army began to realize that they were in Grant's toils. In a letter written by one brother to another, which was found in a knapsack in one of the captured pits, the writer says: "Grant has Lee entangled. The cars are running right along the Union camp, supplying their troops with everything they need, while we are starving. The cause of the Confederacy has gone up; there is no use of fighting any longer"

Some idea of the extent of the picket-firing can be had from the fact that during the three days succeeding the capture of the picket-pits at Fort Sedgwick, the Third Brigade detail expended 60,000 rounds of ammunition.

On Sunday, the 11th, Chaplain Cline held service in Fort Davis. During the progress of the service an artillery duel was raging along the lines, and just over the heads of the worshipers the bullets were whistling merrily.

The position in the fort was not altogether a safe one. Men were in some instances struck while sleeping, and many narrow escapes occurred. Colonel Schoonover, Chaplain Cline and another officer sat down to dine, and while the Chaplain was asking a blessing, a bullet whistled over the table, passing between them—rather an unpleasant *memento mori* at a feast. And yet so accustomed had soldiers become to such interruptions that they did not in the least disturb their equanimity.

Recruits now began to come in rapidly. On the 16th thirty-eight joined the regiment, on the 17th, twenty-eight, and on the 18th, sixteen. But they were not of the best material of which to make an army or fill up a depleted one. The majority of them were substitutes, and a large proportion foreigners who had been attracted by the high prices paid by those who had neither sufficient courage or patriotism to give their personal services. Very few of these substitutes ever intended coming to the front; those that did being so strictly guarded that they could not get an opportunity to escape. A large proportion deserted to the enemy. Of those accredited to the Eleventh New Jersey during the summer and autumn of '64, 247 deserted on the way, 54 to the enemy and 40 managed to remain in the rear at hospitals, convalescent-camps, etc., making during that period a total of 341 accredited to the regiment that did not add a man to its strength.

On the 24th of September the Second Corps was extended to relieve the Tenth. This move placed us in the line about one mile to the right of Fort Davis. There we remained until the first of October, when we were withdrawn and marched to the railroad near the bridge crossing the Blackwater creek, where we took the cars for the left. After reaching the end of the military road, we marched about two miles through the rain and over very muddy roads to near Poplar Spring Church, where, about dark, we went into bivouac for the night, under shelter of the wood. We were now on the left of the Ninth Corps, having been sent to its support and to extend its left—the First and Second Divisions remaining in the entrenchments.

Early on the morning of the 2d of October the skirmishers were advanced, the division following closely in line of battle. Our skirmishers soon struck the enemy, but continued to advance, pressing them back and capturing their advance line of works. The forward movement was continued for about a mile further to the enemy's main line, which was found well manned with infantry and artillery, and which opened upon us a heavy fire. As no orders were given to press the attack, we lay down and held our position until four P. M., when we moved back to the position occupied earlier in the day. During the action a piece of shell killed one man in the Eleventh Massachusetts and then struck a sergeant in the leg, tearing it almost off—it hanging by a mere shred. With the utmost coolness the sergeant took out his knife and cut it loose. As he was being carried in a blanket to the rear, he said to Colonel McAllister: "I have done my duty, Colonel, and have lost my leg in a good cause." The colonel answered, "Yes, Sergeant, you have done your duty." Then addressing those who were carrying him, continued, "Boys, handle him tenderly; he's a brave man; take good care of him." He was in good spirits and bore the pain manfully, but he died that night in the field hospital.

The 3d and 4th of October were spent in building entrenchments. On the evening of the 3d the regiment received one hundred and thirty-eight recruits, nearly all of them entirely ignorant of soldiers' duties. One in Company E, on the morning after his arrival, was told by the First Sergeant that he was detailed for fatigue duty. He wanted to know what fatigue duty meant. When told that in that instance it meant to chop down trees and shovel dirt, he replied that he did not feel very well that morning, and guessed he would not go. He soon learned that in the army it was not a matter of feeling or desire, but of obedience.

At four P. M. on the 5th the regiment under command of Captain John Oldershaw, Acting Major, moved back to the trenches between forts Davis and Alexandre Hays, and relieved Bissel's brigade of colored troops. When Colonel McAllister reported to the commander of the colored brigade that he was ready to relieve him, he asked how many pickets they had out. The Colonel commanding replied, "Five hundred, but as your troops are a part of the Second Corps you will not need more than half that number."

As we were passing the Yellow tavern on our return from Poplar Spring Church a gentleman, hearing that we were the Third Division of the Second Corps, exclaimed, "The old Third Corps! I must see those brave troops," and hastened out in the storm to see us tramping along in the mud.

At one P. M. on the 6th of October we withdrew from the trenches and formed camp in the pine woods in the rear, where

Hancock's Cavalry rested until October 26th. The name Hancock's Cavalry was given to the Second Corps by the other troops, because of the frequency and rapidity of its movements. It was thrown here, there, and everywhere—sometimes to the extreme right, then hastily again to the left, and occasionally it

Lieutenant Alpheus Iliff.

brought up in the center. On one of its hurried marches from the left to the right, while it was enjoying a brief halt, a bystander asked what troops we were. "Why," said a comrade in the ranks, "don't you know? Hancock's Cavalry! we have just stopped to let the officers change horses." In a conversation between one of our pickets and one of the rebel pickets, the rebel asked why it was that wherever they went they met the Second Corps. It was well to have a reputation for bravery and reliability; it was a high honor to be placed at the point of danger and to be called upon at critical moments, but it certainly was not always conducive to comfort.

On October 8th Lieutenant George C. Boice was killed upon the picket-line. He had posted his pickets and stood warming himself by a fire that some of the men had built—the night being quite chilly—when a rebel sharpshooter picked him off. He had been Quartermaster Sergeant from the organization of the regiment until July 25th, '64, when he was commissioned Second Lieutenant of Company G. He had fulfilled the duties of his former position to the satisfaction of both officers and men, and no doubt would have been as efficient as an officer of the line.

Desertions from the rebel army had become very frequent. Though the Richmond papers spoke of plenty of provisions in store, yet, day by day, Lee's commissariat grew scantier; and to men living in a state of semi-starvation the knowledge that but a short distance away was plenty to be had for the asking was a temptation that many could not resist. Two Floridians who entered our picket-line at that time stated that a meal's victuals cost in Petersburg thirty-six dollars in Confederate money, and that the pay of a private soldier was eleven dollars per month of the same kind of currency. Just think of working over three months for the price of one meal—that one dollar in greenbacks would buy ten and in some places fifteen in their scrip. That fact alone showed that the people of the South had lost faith in the success of their cause and believed in the ultimate triumph of the Union.

On the 19th of October Captain John Oldershaw was ordered to report to the headquarters of the First Brigade, First Division, and assume the duties of Brigade Inspector.

The Presidential election of 1864 caused considerable excitement and discussion among the troops. Though New Jersey had virtually disfranchised her soldiers they were none the less interested, and when commissioners from other States arrived and began to take the vote of their troops in the field, New Jersey troops were subjected to taunts that made them entertain anything but kindly feelings for the Legislature that had refused them the privilege. It was generally supposed that the troops from New Jersey, especially the original members of the old regiments, were largely in favor of McClellan. I have no doubt that they were so until the adoption of the Chicago platform with the nomination of Pendleton. After the action of the convention became known and the platform had been read, together with the utterances of such men as C. C. Burr, of New Jersey; Judge Miller, of Ohio; Deane, of Iowa, and others, McClellan lost friends rapidly among the soldiers. Few soldiers in the field were in favor of a temporizing policy. They wanted a vigorous prosecution of the war, realizing that it was the quickest and surest way to peace.

As I have said, the feeling of indignation among the New Jersey troops was great, owing to the action of the State Legislature denying to its soldiers the right to vote in the field. Notwithstanding this unjust and unpatriotic action, it was decided by the officers and men of the Eleventh Regiment to poll the vote of the men present and forward the result thereof to the press of the State as an expression of its choice as to who should be President. "About this time we were receiving many recruits to fill our broken ranks, the most of whom enlisted for the large bounties then being paid, and many of whom were professional 'bounty-jumpers.' It is but just to add that a small percentage of these recruits were truly loyal and made excellent soldiers. In order that it might not be said they were controlled or influenced in their choice, the commanding officer of each company selected a non-commissioned officer, who was requested to approach each man separately and ascertain from him his choice, using no persuasion whatever." Unfortunately, but one of the company poll-lists is now available, that of Company E. That is in the possession of Bishop W Mains, who was the non-commissioned officer selected by Captain Gage to canvass the company. Though the document is stained with blood from a wound he received through the left lung at the battle of Boynton plank-road, it is still legible, and shows the result to have been :

Old members of the company for Lincoln,		14
" " " " " " McClellan,	6	
Recruits for Lincoln,		15
" " McClellan,	20	
	26	29
Total,		55
Lincoln's majority,		3

The document has a further value in that it shows the strength of the company at that time and the number of recruits then with it.

On the 17th of October occurred one of those pathetic incidents inseparable from war. At the house where our division commander had his headquarters lived an old gentleman, his daughter-in-law, and two grand-daughters. When our army first occupied the territory around Petersburg, the son had been found with rebel arms in his hands and was held as a prisoner of war. The family had been very wealthy, but the war had so impoverished them that they were dependent upon our government and the generosity of the division staff for the necessaries of life. The youngest of the daughters, a young lady of about sixteen, became sick, and though our surgeons gave her every attention, died. There they were, surrounded by the enemy, cut off from all sympathizing friends, the father a prisoner, wealthy yet in want. The officers of the division staff showed their sympathy for the bereaved family by furnishing a handsome coffin and bearing the body to the family burying-ground. The band played the funeral march, and though the idea of having a " Yankee " chaplain officiate seemed repugnant, yet they consented and Mr. Stevenson, of the American Tract Society, conducted the services at the grave.

On the evening of October 24th we were relieved by Miles' First Division, and marching back joined our Second Division and massed in rear of the lines. At five o'clock on the afternoon of the 26th we marched to the Weldon railroad, near the Globe tavern, and bivouacked for the night.

At half past three on the morning of the 27th the column was put in motion. The morning was dark and stormy and the country thickly wooded, so that progress was necessarily slow. A little after daylight we crossed Hatcher's run at the Vaugn road crossing. The enemy disputed the crossing, and Smythe's Brigade, of the Second Division, which was on the lead, forded the run waist-deep and captured the enemy's works on the opposite side. The march was continued by way of the Dabney mill road—a narrow wood-road, illy adapted for the movement of troops—to its intersection with the Boynton plank-road, about one mile south of Burgess' mill, which point was reached about noon. The brigade was about massing with the rest of the division, when General Meade sent an aid with orders that we should defend the road, as the enemy were coming in that direction. Gibbons' Division, commanded by General Egan in the absence of Gibbons, had advanced up the Boynton road toward Hatcher's run.

The enemy had a battery posted near Burgess' tavern, and another up the White-oak road, which joins the Boynton road at the tavern. These batteries began to play as soon as the head of the corps came out on the open ground, near the junction of the Dabney mill and Boynton roads. Beck's Battery, however, soon silenced the one near the tavern, and Egan's Division, advancing, took position across the Boynton road, near the White-oak road. Two brigades were to the right and one to the left of the plank-road, resting on the White-oak road. McAllister's Brigade had now been sent up to strengthen Egan, and Beck's Battery had moved up so as to command the enemy's guns north of Hatcher's run. One section, however, under Metcalf, was stationed on the ridge in the rear and on the east side of the Boynton road. This section was supported by Pierce's Brigade of Mott's Division.

Their position was about midway between Egan and the brigade of De Trobriand, which was posted near the junction of the Dabney mill and Boynton roads. It being determined that Egan, supported by McAllister, should occupy the high ground north of the run, Egan's Division was advanced in that direction. The Tenth Massachusetts Battery, which had taken the place of Beck's (whose ammunition was exhausted), was posted so as to command the White-oak road. One section, however, was placed north of the barn, to cover the advance of Egan's troops. Egan moved forward without much opposition, and had secured the bridge and captured one gun, when a volley was heard from the right and rear, which left no doubt that the enemy had entered the gap between the Second and Fifth Corps and were attacking in the rear.

A brief description of the field will give a better understanding of the condition of affairs at the time of the attack. The ground occupied by Egan's and McAllister's troops, with the Tenth Massachusetts Battery, was a high, cleared field. Through this clearing, running north by east, passed the Boynton plank-road. The clearing extended north and south about one-half mile. About one third of the distance across from the southern edge of the clearing the Boynton road was entered by the White-oak road from the west, up which the enemy had a battery posted. The cleared ground extended up the White-oak road. At the northwest junction of the roads stood an unpainted wooden building known as Burgess' tavern, and nearly opposite to the east of the Boynton road a barn. Northward the ground fell away to Hatcher's run and a mill-pond, and eastward to a dense wood. To the south the ground descended to a swampy thicket, perhaps forty or fifty yards wide, south of which was another high, cleared field; commencing nearly opposite the swamp and running south and southwest was another strip of woodland.

Metcalf's section of Beck's Battery, supported by Pierce's Brigade, occupied positions in the last-mentioned clearing, or the ridge south of the swamp. Two regiments of Pierce's Brigade, accompanied by Captain Lloyd, of the Eleventh New Jersey, who was upon Pierce's staff, had entered the wood to the right of Metcalf's guns. These were struck by Mahone's Division, which was advancing through the wood toward the Boynton road, and quickly swept out of the way. The enemy came out on Metcalf's right, who only had time to turn his guns and fire a couple of rounds when they were upon him. They captured the guns and continued advancing until they had crossed the Boynton road.

In the meantime Egan had sent word to McAllister to change front and charge the enemy in our rear. McAllister replied that he had not time to change front, but would about-face and charge left in front. The order was quickly given, and the charge gallantly made down the hill, through the morass, and up the opposite slope. The Eleventh New Jersey reached the crest and re-captured Metcalf's guns. It will be remembered that we had come to an about-face, and consequently were left in front—the troops upon our left failed to reach the crest. This threw the flank of our regiment in the air, so to speak, or rather with the flank unprotected. In fact, both flanks were unprotected, *as the Eleventh New Jersey was the only regiment that reached the crest south of the swamp when Metcalf's guns were in position.* This subjected us to a flank fire from Mahone's troops in the woods to our left, and from the guns on the White-oak road on our right and from the enemy's infantry in our front. Besides, we were under the fire of De Trobriand's brigade, which had changed front and taken position parallel with the Dabney mill road, facing toward us.

The enemy, finding themselves between two fires, moved off to the right and made an attack upon our left, or more properly our right, for we were still left in front. To meet this attack we re-crossed the swamp and formed, facing east. Darkness following, the attacks of the enemy ceased. About ten o'clock in the evening orders came to move back, and though the night was pitch-dark it was obeyed with alacrity, for we had begun to think that Richmond would be our involuntary destination. A number of our wounded had been collected in the tavern and barn, near the plank-road, but as the ambulance-train was nearly a mile away many of them had to be left behind, and fell into the hands of the enemy. Among those fortunate enough to reach the rear was Bishop W. Mains and Joseph Walton, of Company E, both wounded through the left lung. Their wounds were severe, and had they fallen into the enemy's hands no doubt both would have died. Many wounded were left lying upon the field. No opportunity having occurred to collect them, they were picked up by the enemy the next morning. Among them was George W. Lindley, of Company K, one of the color-guard, who had received two wounds in the leg.

Before leaving the field Colonel McAllister visited the wounded that had been collected in the buildings near the road, and speaking of it he says: "But one surgeon made his appearance at these hospital-houses—no nurse, no chaplain, hardly a candle to light up the room. Captain Granger, a veteran captain and brave and gallant officer, commanding the Eleventh Massachusetts, that day fell, mortally wounded. He lay upon the floor suffering intense pain. He was so anxious to be taken to the ambulance I ordered his regiment to carry him, and as many others as they could, down to the ambulances, about a mile distant. We had no stretchers, it was pitch dark, and raining. Some were carried down, some left behind, and some died while being carried. On arriving at the place the ambulances were gone, and they had to be left. Captain Granger died. I had the greatest regard for him, he was so brave and gallant. He always did his duty. He belonged to the Eleventh Massachusetts."

Men lacking courage sometimes resort to queer methods to escape the dangers of the battle. Among the recruits in Company E was a substitute named Reiley. He seemed to have a great aversion to participating in the charge across the morass, and made many excuses for stopping. But Lieutenant Hand, who was in command of the company that day, noticed the man's lack of nerve and determined to keep him in. As a last resort Reiley loosened his clothing so that they dropped about his feet, thinking, no doubt, that he would be allowed to stop and arrange them, and by that time the line would be so far advanced that he could slip away without being observed. But the Lieutenant saw through his scheme and, becoming angry at the man's cowardice, gave him a stroke with the flat of his sword, then called Corporal Mains (afterward wounded) to take charge of him and bring him to the front, which the corporal quickly did. But in spite of these precautions the fellow managed to get away and allowed himself to be captured.

Lieutenant William Hand, who was in command of Company E during the battle, says: "Company E and Company H, then under command of Lieutenant Cummings, did some desperate fighting. They tried to capture two black pieces of light artillery. We had possession of them two or three times, and fought hand-to-hand for them, long after the brigade and regiment had fallen back across the swamp. But we were overpowered and driven back before we could get them off. Men never tried harder, nor did braver fighting, than the two comcompanies did for those two pieces. They deserved success, but it was not in human nature to withstand the odds that were against them."

In reading the account of this battle by Billings, historian of the Tenth Massachusetts Battery, it would seem that the infantry upon the field—and McAllister's Brigade especially—were of no practical use; that the battle was fought almost exclusively by the Tenth Battery. But his statement is so at variance with the accounts of other participants in the battle and with the reports of the officers in immediate command of the troops engaged that it is hardly necessary to notice his account. We do so only because justice to the brave men who fought and the heroes who died upon that hotly-contested field demands it. No one who knew anything about the Tenth Battery would doubt their fighting qualities, and surely they won renown enough to make it unnecessary for their historian to try to exaggerate their merits by disparaging the work of other equally brave and meritorious troops. That he has done so there can be no question, for he says in effect that Mott's troops (McAllister's Brigade was the only troops of Mott's on that part of the field) "came running back through their guns like frightened sheep, and refused to halt though repeatedly urged to do so." Thus leaving it to be inferred that McAllister's entire brigade acted the part of poltroons. He charges General Hancock with ignorance of facts, and completely ignores the account of General Egan, who was in immediate command, and under whose eye each movement was executed. Strange, is it not, that the man in the ranks (if doing his duty) should have advantages for observation and knowledge superior to the general in command, whose duty and interest require that he be cognizant of the operations over the entire field? But let us see what General Egan says:

"October 29th, 1864.

"GENERAL—Through you I beg to thank Colonel McAllister, commanding your Third Brigade, for indispensable services rendered to myself and command during recent operations. Colonel McAllister brought up his command at a critical moment, when I was almost surrounded by a force of vast disparity of strength. The defiant bearing of the enemy showed that they regarded their combinations as undoubtedly successful and waiting only final execution. My command had done everything possible when Colonel McAllister saved them. I cannot sufficiently thank him. The recounting the particulars of his service is unnecessary, as they were too brilliant not to have been made public ere this. But I beg that you will, if consistent, commend them at large to the Major-General commanding the corps, as I shall take great pleasure in doing.

"Your most obt. servant,
"T. W. EGAN,
"*Brig.-Gen. Comdg. 2d Division.*
"To Bvt. Maj.-Gen. Mott, Comdg. 3d Div."

General Egan's words of commendation should put to rest any doubts of the courage and efficiency of the Third Brigade at the battle of Boynton plank-road. But his words are confirmed by General McAllister, whose veracity was never questioned by anyone who knew him. In a letter to his family, written just after the battle, he says: "I shall never forget that day nor that battle. Surrounded on all sides, cut off from the rest of the corps, no connection with the Fifth Corps, the victorious yells of the enemy sounding in our ears—our fate seemed to be sealed. There seemed no hope of escape. It was a time of suspense and doubt. Add to all, and what was still worse, some of Egan's men were out of ammunition and none could be had. Not a spade nor shovel to throw up breastworks. But God put it into our hearts to fight on. Trusting to Him, we charged down the hill. The enemy became panic-stricken and gave way. We rushed on, and received not only the enemy's front and flank fire, but from our line in front."

He also commends the brigade in the following general order:

"HEADQUARTERS THIRD BRIGADE, THIRD DIVISION,
"SECOND ARMY CORPS,
"*General Order*, No. 5.   "October 31st, 1864.

"The Colonel commanding brigade congratulates the officers and men of the command for the manner in which they marched to the Boynton plank-road, and the gallantry displayed by them on the 27th instant, reflecting great credit on the old brigade. Your bravery and determination, as exhibited when surrounded by the enemy, is a new wreath added to the laurels of honor won by this command in the days that are past. May this, and the gallant deeds of those battles, stimulate us to do or die for our country in the great cause in which we are engaged. Let each of us resolve to do our duty, and, by the blessing of God, victory will perch upon our banners, peace will crown our exertions, and millions will do honor to those who have so nobly borne our banners through the trying scenes of this rebellion. As we shed tears for the lost comrades who have fallen by our sides, let our prayers go up to God for protection to the widows and the orphans, and our sympathies be with them.

"ROBERT McALLISTER,
"THOS. H. DUNHAM,   "*Col. Comdg. Third Brigade.*
  "*A. A. A. G.*"

There is no need to multiply witnesses. These should be sufficient to refute the unworthy insinuations made by Mr. Billings. That some stragglers, such as are found hanging on the rear of every battle, may have gone back through the guns of the Tenth Battery we do not doubt, but that any organization acted in the manner described is entirely contrary to facts.

As has been stated, about ten o'clock we reported back to General Mott, and after marching several miles over the Dabney Mill road, went into bivouac. We rested until noon on the 28th, when we resumed the march to the breastworks, and re-occupied them at Fort Morton.

During one of the operations to the left, and after the troops had been withdrawn from the entrenchments preparatory to marching, we received what, under the circumstances, was a very peculiar ration and the only one of the kind that I remember to have seen issued during our term of service, namely, a ration of dried codfish. The brigade commissary must have had a large supply on hand and been very anxious to get rid of it, for each man received either an entire fish or a very large half. Had we been remaining in camp, where they could have been properly prepared, they would have made an acceptable addition to our menu, for soaked, boiled, and minced with potatoes and made into cakes or balls, they are not at all bad eating. But what should we do with them on a march, and perhaps in battle? A column of men, each with a codfish strapped to his knapsack, would make a ludicrous spectacle. They might have been worn on the breast as bullet-protectors, but the odor was so strong that unless we had kept well to the windward of the enemy it would have warned them of our approach, and anyway, who wanted to be found dead with a deader codfish clasped to his bosom? Had we belonged to the artillery we might have used them as missiles of war, and I have no doubt that in the half-starved condition of the enemy there would have been a regular stampede from all parts of their line as soon as they found that we were using codfish for cannon-balls (patent applied for). Take it all in all, those immigrants from Newfoundland caused us considerable perplexity, until one comrade with mischief prepense quietly swiped another over the head with one. The question was solved. The blow had been struck, war was declared. From man to man, from company to company, from regiment to regiment, the wave of battle swept. None thought of saving ammunition; the air was thick with "flying fish," and so the historic battle of the cod raged until the order came to march, and the troops moved off leaving the field covered with dead (codfish).

Chapter XV.

Fort Morton.

FORT MORTON occupied a position on the line about one thousand yards to the left of Fort Haskell, and almost directly opposite Elliot's salient, the scene of Burnside's mine explosion on July 30th. It was a part of the main line of works, which here occupied a ridge, the ground sloping rather abruptly to a small stream which ran northward and emptied into the Appomattox, to the eastward of Blandford, a suburb of Petersburg. Eastward of the stream was the roadbed of the Norfolk and Petersburg Railroad. The armament of the fort consisted of four thirty two-pound siege guns, four brass howitzers, and several large mortars. A bomb-proof magazine, and another large bomb-proof for the accommodation of troops, also occupied the interior. Bunks for the accommodation of the occupants were arranged along the southern side of the bomb-proof. A wide shelf or bench, formed of timbers and earth, ran along the north side, leaving a narrow passage. Upon the shelf were piled boxes of ammunition for small arms and a number of boxes containing chloride of lime for disinfecting purposes. The odor of the latter may have been wholesome, but it certainly was not very pleasant to those occupying the bomb-proof. Company E and, I think, a part or whole of another company, which I cannot remember, occupied the bomb-proof in the fort. The rest of the regiment held the connecting lines. The headquarters were in bomb proofs, a short distance in the rear, on the eastward slope. The picket-line which here ran nearer the enemy's works than at any other point along the line, in fact so close to their main works at one point that they could not establish a picket-line, was strongly entrenched and well protected by traverses. The part of the line directly in front of Fort Morton was on the crest beyond the stream. To the north it circled eastward until it re-crossed the stream. A like formation prevailed toward the south. So that the contour of the line directly in front of the fort was nearly that of a half circle.

I have said that the line was well protected by traverses; there was an exception, however. A part of the line to the left, which

Sergeant James McDavitt.

ran down the slope to the stream, turned sharply to the southwest, and was exposed to the fire of the enemy's sharpshooters, which rendered it untenable or at least extremely dangerous during the daytime. This the writer knows from personal experience. He was at that time acting First Sergeant of the company (the First Sergeant, Augustus Tucker, having been detailed to Trenton on recruiting service the previous winter), and had no call upon the picket-line. But one afternoon, being a little tired of the fort and bomb-proof, he thought he would like to pay a visit to the boys on the outer line. He, in company with Corporal Leonard Gillen, reached the line without drawing the enemy's fire, and passed the exposed part leading down to the stream. Some men from his own company were posted south of the stream, and among them Sharp, who had constructed a miniature mortar out of a section of rifle-barrel, and was amusing himself by shelling the enemy, using minie-balls for bombs. After a few minutes conversation with the men, we started to return, but had forgotten the danger of the exposed position, and as a consequence, were walking erect, perfectly unconcerned. Corporal Gillen had just passed through the traverse, he being ahead, when a ball from a rebel sharpshooter's rifle nipped the top of the writer's cap. It was a good line-shot, but a little too high. The approach to the picket-line was protected by a covered way, and with the exception of where it crossed the stream was exposed to the enemy's fire, and men were frequently wounded at that point.

On the night of November 5th, or rather the morning of the 6th, the enemy made a desperate effort to wrest from our possession that part of the picket-line spoken of as occupying the crest beyond the stream. They succeeded in capturing a number of posts, but before they could turn them to their use, they were driven out with great loss. For the successful accomplishment of this re-capture, credit is chiefly due to Captain Charles F Gage, of the Eleventh New Jersey, who was in charge of the picket. He made a reconnoissance in the darkness, and personally located the right of the enemy's force and led the attack upon them, fighting his way from pit to pit until the line was re-captured.

Colonel Schoonover says: "Immediately in front of the fort our pickets occupied an old line of field-works, which was within seventy-five yards of the fort held by a portion of General Hill's Corps, and in the immediate command of General Gracie, formerly of Elizabeth, N. J. The nearness of our picket-line was a great annoyance to the enemy, who kept up a constant fire upon our men who held the coveted position on the brow of the hill. Some distance in rear of the fort (Morton) a platform had been erected in the top of a tall tree, where a number of men were stationed to detect, if possible, any movement on the part of the enemy.

"On the afternoon of November 5th, it was discovered from this lookout that the enemy were busy in carrying some kind of material from the rear into the fort. From this movement the inference was correctly drawn that an attack was contemplated upon our exposed picket-line. The men were instructed to be on the alert that night, as the enemy would in all probability attempt to capture the position.

"As had been predicted, the attack was made shortly after midnight, and the picket-line, composed of men from the One Hundred and Twentieth New York and the Eleventh New Jersey, were driven from their position, leaving the enemy in possession of about forty posts. The officers on duty from the Eleventh New Jersey were Lieutenants Oliver and Schoonover. While every man engaged displayed great bravery, to the coolness and skill of Captain Charles F Gage, who was in command of the picket-line, must be largely attributed the successful recapture of the lost works. He went in person, under cover of darkness, to within a few feet of the picket-post occupied by the right of the enemy's line, and, having located their position, placed his men in an angle of the works and opened fire, which, fortunately, enfiladed the entire line occupied by the enemy. There was no escape from the deadly bullets which came from that angle. The rails which they had brought to the fort and carried with them when the charge was made, gave them but little protection. The fire of our men was effective and the loss of the enemy heavy.

"The following day General Gracie requested, under flag of truce, permission to remove his dead, which was granted. It was a remarkable and impressive sight that met my eyes as I went upon the scene of the previous night's conflict. A large number of their dead lay along the most exposed portion of the line. Many of them had attempted to dig with their hands into the hard, baked soil, and instant death had left their bodies in almost lifelike positions. The fingers were still bent, the muscles unrelaxed, and their faces, cold in death, still bore the stamp of desperation."

McAllister says: "The dash was so sudden that about forty picket-posts gave way, but our brave boys turned on the enemy and re-captured about one-half of the number and turned the enemy's flank. A desperate fight ensued—a hand-to-hand contest over the breastworks; bullets, bayonets and butts of muskets were used. The battle raged fearfully. I sent fifty more men to the assistance of our gallant boys. After a struggle of a short time we re-captured some more of our pits, but in the balance the enemy fought with stubbornness unparalleled. I sent fifty more men to their assistance, and on the battle raged. It was now near the dawn of morning, and I knew the necessity of re-capturing these works before daylight. I sent fifty more men, but before they reached the scene of action the day was ours, and resulted in nearly fifty rebel prisoners for us, among them one lieutenant. The slaughter of the enemy, this lieutenant said, was terrific. They lost terribly from our enfilade fire. They carried their wounded and dead back, but some lay on the ground where they fought. They had brought shovels and picks with them, and also a cross-cut saw to cut through the timbers in the breastworks. The lieutenant said they designed turning our works and holding them. The prisoners we took were all South Carolinians, and they fought desperately and long before they would give up. The bravery, gallantry and determination of my officers and men in this contest merit my warmest praise. My loss in killed, wounded and missing is only twenty-nine. A prisoner who came into headquarters told General Hancock that they had lost two hundred."

Following are the general orders issued relative to the fight:

"HEADQUARTERS 2D ARMY CORPS,
"November 6th, 1864.

"MY DEAR GENERAL.—I was highly gratified to hear of the brave conduct of your troops this morning and of the ability and determination displayed by Colonel McAllister, commanding brigade, in re-taking the picket-line wrested from our picket-line last night.

"I am very truly your obedient servant,

"W. S. HANCOCK,
"*Maj.-Gen. Commanding.*

'To Bvt. Maj.-Gen. Mott, Commanding 2d Div., 2d Corps."

"HEADQUARTERS 3D DIVISION, 2D ARMY CORPS,
"Nov. 7th, '64.

"*Gen. Order 671.*

"The Brevet Major-General commanding takes great pleasure in expressing to the command his gratification with the good conduct of the troops engaged in the affair of the night of the 5th instant, resulting in the re-taking of that portion of the picket-line wrested from us by an overwhelming force of the enemy, the capture of forty-two prisoners, including one commissioned officer, the forcing of the enemy to leave in our hands a number of their dead, and a quantity of small arms and entrenching tools. Special mention is due to Colonel McAllister, commanding Third Brigade, who gave his personal superintendence to the operations, and to the officers on his staff who rendered him such efficient service. The conduct of the officers and men of the One Hundred and Twentieth New York and Eleventh New Jersey Volunteers, who were directly engaged, is worthy of emulation. Such gallantry always displayed would soon bring the rebellion to a close.

"By command of

"BREVET MAJ.-GEN. MOTT,
"J. P. FINKLEMIER, *A. A. Gen.*"

"HEADQUARTERS THIRD BRIGADE, THIRD DIV. 2D A. CORPS,
"Nov. 8th, 1864.

"*Officers and Soldiers of the Third Brigade:*

"The Colonel commanding brigade returns his thanks to the soldiers of his command for their noble bearing and gallant conduct in the affair of the evening of the 5th inst. Special praise and credit is due the three companies of the One Hundred and Twentieth New York Volunteers, and one company of the Eleventh New Jersey Volunteers, and staff and line officers, who so nobly led these gallant bands of brave soldiers to a successful re-capture of the lost works against an overwhelming force of the enemy. The skill, bravery and determination of the officers and men thus engaged, representing these, and nearly all the regiments in this brigade, are worthy of note, and should be placed side by side with the heroic deeds and gallantry displayed in other and greater battles. By a firm reliance in God, and by His blessing and a determination to do our duty, this conflict for our glorious Union will soon be ended in favor of its restoration.

"ROBERT MCALLISTER,
"*Col. Commanding.*
"THOS. H. DUNHAM, *A. A. A.-Gen.*"

As soon as the loss of the pits became known, Captain Gage hastened forward with a company of the Eleventh New Jersey, and placed them in position in the angle to the enemy's right, where their fire would enfilade the captured pits. General McAllister's language would seem to indicate that a portion of the pits had been re-captured before the re-enforcement of fifty had been sent forward. If this is so—and we know from personal recollection and the testimony of participants that it is—it would seem that great credit should have been given to Captain Gage and Lieutenant Charles A. Oliver. And yet, in none of the general orders do we find any recognition of the great services rendered by them on that occasion. It is not ours to discuss the whys or wherefores, but simply to state a fact.

During our occupancy of Fort Morton and the connecting works, artillery duels were of almost nightly occurrence. There was but little danger to be apprehended from the flight of solid shot or rifled shells, as the works were amply strong to resist their penetrating power, but the shriek and scream of the missiles as they passed swiftly just above the heads of the men was enough to set weak nerves in a tremble. But the noise of their flight and explosion, with the roar and jar of the guns, was a necessary element to the grandeur of the scene presented by the flight of scores of bombs circling through the air. The course of the bombs could be followed by the light of the burning fuse, and their flight would be watched with fearless interest until the downward curve would seem to indicate a near approach, when a hurried rush would be made for the bomb-proof, where, under cover, the men would eagerly listen for the jar of the explosion that told that the danger was past. But the men would not remain long under shelter; the fireworks were too grand to be missed, and dodging the "big ones" was an exhilarating sport. Enough bombs were thrown to have caused great loss to the opposing armies had they all been effective. I do not know what damage ours may have done to the enemy, but the damage from theirs was comparatively slight.

During the month that we lay in Fort Morton I think but one bomb exploded within the fort—that was during a night duel, when an attack was anticipated and the garrison was under arms. It resulted in the wounding, and subsequent death, of Ferdinand Martin, of Company H. His left leg was so badly shattered that amputation was necessary. He died in the corps hospital, at City Point, December 4th. He was a foolishly brave man, often exposing himself unnecessarily. He was so tall that when standing up on the entrenched picket-line his head would show above the works. Yet so great was his contempt for danger that he often made himself a mark for the enemy's sharpshooters. At the time he was wounded a piece of the bursted bomb struck his gun, cutting the barrel completely in two pieces. The stock-end was not found, but the other end of the severed barrel is now in the possession of Colonel Schoonover, and is regarded as a great curiosity.

A short distance to the rear of the main line of works was a grove of pine trees. There the officers had rigged up a game of General Logan's ten-pins. A cross-piece was put from one tree to another, as high as possible from the ground. From it was suspended a rope, to the lower end of which was fastened a spherical case or shell. Pins were stood up at a given distance.

The game consisted in knocking down the pins by the returning swing of the shell. Occasionally, when the game was at its height, the enemy would take a hand in it by trying to knock down the players with shell not fastened to a rope.

There was little relaxation for the men, however, while occupying this position on the line. The picket details were so heavy that the men were on duty every alternate day. This led to the only desertion to the enemy that occurred in Company E, although there were many among the substitutes in other companies—sixteen from Company I alone.

On November 10th a substitute by the name of Thomas Jones reported for duty to Company E. On the same evening an unusually large detail was called for from the company, which could not be filled except by giving one man a double tour of duty. Jones, who seemed a modest, well-meaning young man, volunteered to go in the man's place, saying that he had had an easy time of it back at the hospital and might as well get used to his duties at once. The sergeant hesitated for awhile, for there was an order against sending substitutes on picket, but, thinking the man was trustworthy, at last accepted his services, and fitted him out with a borrowed gun and equipments and sent him out with the detail. The gun and equipments were in the pit next morning, but Jones had disappeared.

Quite a scare was gotten up one day by some of the men in the bomb-proof starting the report that the enemy could be heard mining underneath the fort. We listened. Sure enough, sounds like the stroke of a pick seemed to come from below. The magazine was opened and ears laid to the ground; the same pick-strokes were heard. There were some grave faces and anticipations of an aerial flight. But the gravity turned to laughter when it was discovered that the alarm was caused by a soldier leaning against a gun-carriage and idly tapping the wheel with a spike. To those in the bomb-proof the sound seemed subterranean.

Thanksgiving Day found us still in Fort Morton, but it brought us remembrances from the North in the shape of boxes of turkeys for a Thanksgiving dinner, a treat that was highly appreciated by the boys in the trenches.

It was not often that a case occurred where one bullet caused three separate and distinct wounds, but such a case occurred upon the picket-line in front of Fort Morton. One day one of our men (whose name I cannot now ascertain) came in with a wound through the hand. After the surgeon had dressed the wounded hand, the man complained of a soreness in the upper part of the arm. An examination showed that the bullet had also passed through the arm above the elbow. The surgeon attended to that wound, and a further examination revealed the fact that the bullet had also entered the back, where it was found lodged against the shoulder-blade.

Another illustration of the curious course sometimes taken by bullets was furnished at the battle of Chancellorsville. A bullet struck a limb of a tree almost directly over the head of Lieutenant Kennedy, and, being deflected downward, wounded him in the foot.

A party of young men in Plainfield, who were neighbors and schoolmates, had often talked of enlisting, but some of them were too young for the service. In August, '62, they resolved to make the effort. The names of the party were Aaron Fatout, Henry Hand, T. O'Doane, Aaron Lines, Joseph Frazee, William Smith, Peter Cook, Andrew Webster, William Hand and John Goodwin. Aaron Fatout, at the last moment, yielded to the entreaties of his young wife and resolved to stay at home. He was killed the next day by falling from a building upon which he was at work. The rest of the party proceeded to Elizabeth, where they met Captain Meeker, under whom they all enlisted, with the exception of John Goodwin, who was rejected on account of age. The history of the eight will be found in the history of the regiment, for they each made a record worthy of mention. Goodwin was not content, however, until he became a soldier, and joined the regiment in September, '64, under the name of John A. Zuckswort.

There was an order existing in the army in those days against the wearing of boots by infantrymen; first, because they destroyed the uniformity of the troops, and, secondly, because they were uncomfortable on long marches, causing blistered feet and ankles, and consequently being the cause of straggling. John, like many another young soldier, had a strong penchant for boots, and, being either ignorant of the order or forgetful of it, had provided himself with a fine pair of cavalry boots. While on picket one day to the left of Petersburg he felt the need of tobacco, and having a surplus of coffee, struck up a trade with the enemy's picket opposite. He got some tobacco and also a Richmond paper. While the trade was being consummated the officer in command of the picket appeared. After a few questions the matter was apparently dropped. Upon returning to camp, however, he was ordered to report to Colonel Schoonover. On entering the Colonel's tent and saluting, the Colonel asked what he had in his hand. He replied, "A rebel paper." "Let me see it." The Colonel took the paper and began reading, leaving Zuckswort standing—a badly frightened boy, dreaming of court-martial, punishment, etc. After keeping him in suspense for several minutes, the Colonel looked up from the paper and said: "Young man, you must take off those boots and wear shoes. That's all; go to your quarters." He left the Colonel's tent as happy as a young boy released from school, for he had been badly frightened. But he lost his paper and boots.

In one of the minor engagements in front of Petersburg, Zuckswort (Goodwin) was severely wounded in the left hip and right thigh by the bursting of a shell. He was taken from the field by Andrew Webster and William Hand. A piece of shell was taken from the left hip, he was sent to the field hospital and from there given a furlough home. He could walk only upon crutches, so that it was a difficult matter for him to get off the cars to procure food, and as he had started upon the journey with only six hard-tack, he was nearly starved when he reached Plainfield. Upon the expiration of his furlough he was sent to the hospital in Newark, N. J., where an operation was performed.

Continuing to grow worse, he was allowed to be taken home, where he received his discharge January 25th, 1865. He finally regained his health, but was left permanently crippled.

Among a group of men from Company B cooking around a camp fire one day was Tom Terry, the drummer, Zuckswort, and a green Irishman, who, in common with most of his countrymen from the snakeless isle, stood in deadly terror of a serpent. After the Irishman had put his pan upon the fire, he asked his comrades if they would attend to it while he went after water for coffee. In his absence Terry and Zuckswort substituted another pan, in which they had coiled a dead snake. On his return he lifted the cover to see how his cooking was progressing. One glance and he dropped it in terror and started hurriedly away with the exclamation, "Holy Moses! Oh, Lord, save my soul! the devil and the snakes are in the pan!" Nor could he be prevailed upon to go near it again.

Among the recruits who came to the regiment during the summer of '64 was a substitute by the name of Daniel Popovitz, who was assigned to Company K. He claimed to have been a major on Louis Kossuth's staff during the Hungarian revolution; an officer in the English army during the Crimean war; to have been in the service of the Sultan of Turkey—in fact, to to have held commissions under nearly every government of Europe. He was a good linguist and a showy drillmaster, an art that could have been learned entirely outside of armies. On the strength of his proficiency in drill he was warranted a Sergeant over the heads of men who had been doing their duty from the first organization of the regiment, and it was reported and generally believed that a commission was about to be given him. In the meantime, notwithstanding orders existed that no "sub" should receive a furlough, through the influence of the regimental commander he was permitted to return to New York, ostensibly to meet his wife on her arrival from Hungary. If such a being existed he probably met her in Hungary, for Popovitz returned no more—only a letter stating that he had gone to his native country.

Chapter XVI.

With Warren to Hicksford—From December 7th to 12th, '64.

THE ELEMENT of uncertainty entered so largely into the life of a soldier that he could never, even for the shortest period, claim a fixed habitation. One day a camp would be laid out, perhaps in a strip of woodland. Immediately, with bee-like industry, the soldiers would set about clearing away the underbrush and felling the giants of the forest. It would be fell and chop, split and hew, and in a few days the forest would have disappeared and in its stead would stand a city of log huts, whose intervening streets, well graded and drained, would seem to have been the labor of weeks or months. Such comforts as were accessible were gathered around, and in spite of past experience the boys would begin to congratulate themselves upon having at last gone into permanent winter quarters. The duties of the day have been performed, and night, with its promise of rest, has come; fires have been fixed for the night, taps have beaten, and the drowsy soldier is about to sink into forgetfulness of the privations around him, or a slumber filled with dreams of scenes left far behind and the faces of the loved ones far away in the Northland. But hark! Upon the winter's frosty air, ringing sharp and clear, is borne the sound of hurried hoof-beats. A belated officer, perhaps, who has been to visit friends in some distant camp, or a courier with orders to or from the outposts. But no—they turn into headquarters. Every one is quickly on the alert, and comrade says to comrade, "Marching orders." The hoof-beats begin again and are soon lost in the distance. A few minutes of suspense and then comes the voices of company commanders: "Have tents struck and be ready to march at daylight." Then speculation runs wild. "I wonder where we are to be sent now?" One says we are to make an attack on the right; another, on the left, while some have decided that we are to be sent far away. To some the balance of the night brings little rest; the thoughtful ones spend a portion of it in writing letters to those at home, while others, either careless or wise, as you may consider them, get all the rest they can. Ah! that element of uncertainty as to what the hour was to bring forth— was it not one of the fascinations of a soldier's life?

We had just become comfortably fixed in camp, when December 6th brought us one of these sudden changes. Half-past six o'clock on the morning of December 7th found our division in motion, with our faces turned southward, following Gregg's Cavalry and the Fifth Corps, the Third Brigade in the rear Just as we were about to move, Colonel McAllister received his well-earned promotion as Brevet Brigadier-General for gallant and distinguished services at Boynton plank-road, on October 27th. We soon struck the Jerusalem plank-road, and turned toward North Carolina. We had not marched many miles before it began to rain heavily, making the marching extremely tiresome. The march was a very rapid one, and the halts few and short. Heavily-loaded as the troops were with blankets, overcoats and the extra clothing necessary in winter, the rapid marching told heavily upon them, and the roadway was soon lined with stragglers. Others, in their efforts to keep up with their comrades, lightened their loads by throwing away overcoats and blankets, articles which they could illy spare. At one point in particular it seemed to me that for hundreds of yards the roadsides were covered with such impedimenta thrown away by the troops in our front. It was surely a rich harvest for the ill-clad Southern bushwhackers, who were skulking in swamps and thickets awaiting our passage and an opportunity to shoot down and rob some foot-sore straggler.

Just after dark we crossed the Nottaway river on pontoons and bivouacked on the southern bank. We had marched a distance of twenty miles through rain and mud, and the order to bivouac was a welcome one. The evening brought a cessation of the rain, the clouds broke away and the stars began to look down upon a weary and wet lot of soldiers. Camp-fires were lit and soon the fragrant aroma of coffee—that panacea for many a soldier's ills—perfumed the evening air. Then pipes for those who smoked, and rest upon the sodden ground.

After the enjoyment of so many years of comfort since the war, it seems incredible that a soldier could have rested under the circumstances that oftentimes surrounded him. Sometimes he slept in line of battle, while the shot and shell were whistling and shrieking over him and the jar of guns made the earth tremble; sometimes upon the sodden ground, while rain-drops washed his upturned face; again, upon the hardened earth, while frost was binding the streamlets or the snow-flakes weaving for him an extra covering. Under conditions that to the civilian would seem the most improbable, the soldier rested.

On the morning of December 8th the roll was called long before the break of day, and at half-past six the column was again in motion. All the troops comprising the expedition had crossed the evening previous, except the stragglers, who were picked up by the cavalry that had followed to the river, and by them taken back to camp to prevent their being captured by the enemy. The day turned out warm and pleasant, overcoats were at a discount, and, as before, many thoughtlessly threw them away—an act which they very much regretted before the expedition reached camp again.

The country through which we were then passing seemed to be fertile and well tilled, but the same condition prevailed that was found in so many parts of the South through which Union troops passed. It seemed to be populated only by women, children and negroes. If a white man was seen, it was a specimen too old and decrepit to take to the shelter of the swamp and thickets. This condition did not prevail because there were no able bodied white men in the country (as many of our poor stragglers found to their sorrow), but because with guns in their hands they were lying in hiding, waiting until the column should pass beyond hearing, that they might pick off unwary stragglers and rob the bodies even to nakedness. Many murders of this kind were perpetrated, of which we knew nothing until the return-march revealed them. In the meantime the women were clamoring for safe-guards to protect their property, which in many cases, on the outward march, were provided.

Lieutenant Edwin R. Good.

After a long, hard march we neared Jewett's Station, on the Weldon railroad, where we learned that our cavalry had already burned the station, cut the telegraph and were busy tearing up the railroad. We bivouacked for the night to be ready for a hard day's work on the morrow. The weather had changed again and the north wind was bringing with it frost and ice.

Large camp-fires were lit and the night passed as comfortably as the circumstances would permit.

The boys were astir very early on the morning of the ninth, for the weather had grown so cold during the night that it was impossible to obtain much sleep, the only comfort to be had being around the camp-fires. Daylight was awaited with impatience, but with its coming we fell in line and marched down the railroad until we reached the track not yet destroyed. The cavalry had been at the work of destruction on the afternoon of the 8th, but, owing to their method of working, their progress had not been very rapid. Their plan was to pry the rails loose from the sleepers (which, owing to a lack of proper tools, was rather difficult), then lift the sleepers from their beds and put them in piles to be burned. General McAllister introduced a quicker (and what may be called the Western) method of accomplishing the same result. Although his business had been that of building railroads, he yet seemed to be well versed in the art of destroying them. The brigade was deployed in single file on one side of the road, a man to each tie; then commands were given not known in military tactics, and not taught at West Point. First, the command was, "Take hold," when every man would bend over and grasp the end of a tie; then would follow the command, "Lift up," and in a few moments the railroad would be lying upside down. The strain incident to the turning would so loosen the spikes that the removal of the rails became much easier. After the separation of rails and sleepers the latter would be piled up and set on fire. The rails would then be placed across the burning sleepers, with the ends projecting. As the center became heated the ends would bend to the ground, thus making it impossible to use them again without being sent to the mill to be straightened. Oftentimes the heated rails would be taken and twisted around trees and telegraph poles. It was heavy work, but was thoroughly enjoyed by most of the men, and sometimes quite a rivalry would exist as to who could put the most crooks in a heated rail. When the destruction of one section was completed we would move to another, and so the work went on until nine o'clock in the evening, when we were ordered to bivouac for the night, and were told that the object of the expedition had been accomplished and that at daylight we would begin our return march.

Our advance at this time was near the North Carolina line, and for many miles the railroad was utterly destroyed. During the day our pickets brought in a booty of one prisoner, nineteen head of cattle and two mules. On the outward march the rights of private property had been respected, at least by the officers and men of our division. That there was some plundering I have no doubt, for among large bodies of men there will always be found some who recognize no law but the law of might, and who, despite orders and the strictest discipline, will find ways of appropriating anything they think will be useful to themselves. Safe-guards were granted whenever the *women* asked for them, for the men, if not honest, were at least *non est*. But so peculiar was the moral bias of these people that they could unblushingly ask protection for their property while knowing that their friends and relations were lying in wait to treacherously take the lives of the friends and comrades of their protectors.

Near where we were working at one time on the 9th stood a neat farm-house, occupied, as usual, by a Southern lady. She complained that the cavalry had plundered her place and stolen seven thousand dollars in gold. She wanted a safe-guard, which General McAllister granted her. Soon afterward one of her out-buildings was found to be on fire. As the flames progressed a fusillade of small arms was heard which caused us for the moment to think that the enemy was upon us, but it was found to proceed from the burning building, in which had been concealed a number of loaded guns. For what purpose? A peaceable farmer would not need so many arms for his own protection. After that occurrence but little attention was paid to the request for safe-guards.

The night of the 9th came cold and wet—rain, snow and sleet made sleep almost impossible, and, as on the previous night, the boys spent most of their time around the blazing camp-fires.

We were bivouacked in a woods, and morning revealed the trees decked in crystals of ice. Early morning of the 10th found us in motion, with our faces once more turned northward, Crawford's Division, of the Fifth Corps, in rear of the infantry, Gregg's cavalry following. We were quite a distance in the enemy's country, cut loose from all communication with the main army, and it was expected that the enemy would try to prevent our return and that we would have to fight our way through. Preparations were made accordingly; flankers were thrown well out and every precaution taken to prevent a surprise.

It was a fine, crisp winter morning and the rising sun revealed nature in royal robes. From every twig hung pendants of crystals, and the fields and meadows that yesterday were clothed in the brown hues of decay were now decked with diamonds which sparkled with iridescent lustre beneath each sunbeam. But, oh, what miserable marching! The same sun that irradiated the twigs and grasses turned the roads to liquid mud, except where here and there an ice-coated pool lay in wait for the unwary footstep. But we had to press on, with few and short halts.

We had not marched many miles before the booming of cannon told us that the enemy was hanging on our rear, but Gregg repulsed them with his cavalry and the column pushed on.

The night of the 10th was bitterly cold, and it was the fortune of the Eleventh to bivouac on the crest of a wind-swept hill; but the writer does not remember any cold winter's night during his term of service when he slept more snugly and comfortably than he did on that same cold night of December 10th, '64. He, with four or five comrades, was fortunate enough to secure the lee side of a log for a bed-chamber. After scraping together what leaves we could (we did not pitch any tents), we pooled our blankets, overcoats and tents and made a family bed. It was the writer's good luck to get a central position, where (with the possible exception of the tip of his nose) the cold could not reach him. Judging from the restlessness of those on the outer sides of the bed, *they* were not quite so comfortable.

Early on the morning of the 11th we were again on the move toward Sussex Court House. The roads were solid in the early morning, but the heightening sun soon brought about the same conditions that had prevailed the day before. During the previous day we had heard frequent rumors of Union soldiers being found murdered and stripped along the way, but we, as a regiment, had had no ocular proof of their truth. We had not gone far on the way on the morning of the 11th, when word was brought that six or seven dead bodies were lying close together in the woods, not far from the line of march. General McAllister and a number of others went to view them. It was a pitiful sight; from all appearances they had been stripped and made to kneel in a circle, then shot—murdered in cold blood. What else could it be called but murder? When we who participated in the great conflict shall have passed away, and the historian shall weigh with impartial scales the acts and motives of the contestants, giving due weight to such barbarous acts as these and the more barbarous acts perpetrated in the prison-pens of the South, how shallow then will appear the boast of chivalry!

After proof of such murders, committed not by the regular soldiery of the South, but by the so-called home-guards, who, hidden in swamp and thicket, like beasts of prey, lay in wait for the unsuspecting straggler, and whose wives all along the line of march had been clamoring for protection for their property, is it any wonder that the remainder of our homeward march should have been lit by the flames of burning stacks and barns!

Toward night we reached the Nottaway river, where we halted. Two regiments were thrown out as flankers, and the balance of the brigade was ordered back to meet General Crawford, relieve him and protect the crossing. After Crawford's men had reached the north side, McAllister's Brigade were assembled and followed. Thirty men, however, of the Eleventh, who, under Lieutenant Hand, had been sent back to guard the roads, came near being left. They reached the bridge only in time to walk across on the string-pieces, the planking having been removed. After marching a few miles on the north side, bivouac was made for the night.

At seven o'clock on the morning of the 12th we resumed the march along the Jerusalem plank-road, and in the afternoon reached our lines and went into camp. If there was any one among us who still entertained the idea that the Southern blacks were perfectly contented with the conditions of slavery, this Weldon railroad raid was well calculated to dispel it. From nearly every plantation passed they came in squads to join the line of march. Willingly turning their backs upon the only homes their lives had known, joyfully cutting loose from all the associations that under other conditions humanity is so loth to sever, they came with smiling faces and cheerful shouts to take refuge beneath the folds of our flag, recognizing, as if by intuition, that its broad stripes and glittering stars were the symbols of liberty and equality. Ignorant as they were of the world's ways and of all knowledge of political ethics, they seemed to have learned that the blue-clad columns trudging so sturdily along the Southern highways had not sprung to arms for sectional supremacy; had not taken their lives in their hands because of hate to persons or people, but for love of the grand principle of individual liberty and national unity

It may be well to note in detail a few of the many incidents that occurred in this connection during our five days' campaign

During the 8th, on our way out, a group came hastening from a distant farm-house. It consisted of father, mother and a number of children. As they took their places along the highway, ready to join the column that was to lead them to the land of promise, they discovered that one daughter had been left behind. The father, fearful that he would be detained if he returned for her, tearfully implored some one to go. One of General McAllister's aids rode up to the house, and, getting the child, brought it to the father. His thankfulness was unbounded, and the happy family, now united, gave voice to many expressions of gratitude. Colonel Price, of the Seventh New

Jersey, with the kindness that ever distinguished him, interested himself in their welfare and had them placed in a baggage-wagon.

Again, on the 10th, on our return march, when passing a plantation, owned, I think, by a Mr. Level (who, however, was not visible, though his wife assured us that he was a first-rate Union man—I suppose he and his sons were kindly protecting our flanks to warn us of the approach of the enemy), a group of seventeen came hastening across the fields to join the Union column. They had heard of our approach, and upon seeing the stars and stripes floating in the breeze they gathered their household goods and hastened to its protecting folds. They were of all sizes and almost every hue. One, a girl of about sixteen, was very pretty and showed but little trace of negro blood; another, a year or so older, was very dark, but each called the same woman mother. Although the weather was cold enough to make the need of heavy clothing felt, these poor people were very thinly clad, the girls having on light summer clothing and only a threadbare shawl to add its protection. There were also two small children, but in the excitement of flight one had been forgotten. The older and darker of the two girls mentioned dropped her bundle and started back, saying that she would carry the child herself rather than it should be left behind. She soon returned, bearing it with her, but in an almost nude condition, its bare legs being exposed to the biting winter air. The mother carried the youngest, the daughter mentioned the next, and, though some of the party were barefooted, with smiling faces they trudged along the half-frozen highway beside the Union soldiers. A stream was reached which had to be forded. This caused a dilemma, but members of McAllister's staff, taking the youngest upon their horses in front, carried them safely over, and the happy party went on rejoicing. It was a laughable sight to see those men of many battles carrying in their arms those woolly-headed pickaninnies, but it was an act that did credit to their humanity.

Shortly after crossing the stream we went into bivouac for the night. A tent was put up for the contrabands, supper given them, and blankets with which to make themselves comfortable for the night. But the family was not complete and they could not be content. A week or two previous to our coming, one of the daughters had been tied to a whipping-post and given one hundred lashes by her mistress, after which she had fled to the woods and yet remained in hiding. Her brother had carried her food at night. The father and brother seeing the rest of the family safe with the Union troops and comfortably fixed for the night, resolved to devote the night to finding the missing one. It was a dangerous undertaking, for the enemy hung upon our rear, and if captured, the least that would have been done would have been to remand them to captivity, followed by punishment for attempting to escape. But much to the joy of all, long before dawn they returned, bringing the missing one with them.

The winter of '64 and '65 was a very cold one in Virginia, and good winter quarters were things to be desired. It was not, therefore, very agreeable, after becoming pleasantly located, with stockades well built and all things comfortably fixed to guard against the cold, to be ordered out upon some expedition or flank movement; and still less agreeable to be compelled, on returning, to locate a new position and begin again the construction of quarters, knowing that other troops who, perhaps, had not been upon any extended service, were enjoying the fruits of our labor in the camp left behind. But such seemed to be our fate during the winter of '64 and '65. Perhaps the exigencies of the service called for it, but it was disagreeable, nevertheless.

After returning from the Weldon railroad expedition, we located near the Globe tavern, or Yellow house, as it was more generally known, and attempted once more to make ourselves comfortable.

In this connection I will relate the tale of Oliver's horse, as given me by Lieutenant Hand. Lieutenant Oliver had a brother attached to one of the cavalry regiments, who, in the course of his wanderings, had become possessed of a superfluous horse. Knowing that Charles A., who belonged to the Eleventh foot regiment, must often become weary with much tramping, he made him a present of the extra steed. The Lieutenant was highly elated with his acquisition, and indulged in many a secret smile when he thought of his brother officers tramping along through mud and slush, while he, above such discomforts, rode by. Just before we started with Warren on the Weldon railroad raid Oliver obtained leave of absence. He was anxious to see home, but reluctant to leave the horse. Upon leaving, he placed it (with many admonitions) in the care of Proctor, the cook. Proctor was generally known as "Kate," and being cook for many line officers he had a generous supply of pots, pans and other cooking paraphernalia, which, when the regiment moved, he strapped upon Oliver's horse. That would not have made an overload, but the officers soon began to grow weary and piled their blankets and other impedimenta on the horse until he looked like an animated furniture van. "Kate" frequently expostulated, saying the horse was overloaded, but they either laughed at him or met his expostulations with threats of getting another cook if he could not get the horse along. That would generally silence him, for he was very partial to good living and not very fond of fighting. Sometimes the horse would tumble into a ditch, then "Kate" would have to unload to get him out; then would come all the trouble of re-packing. With many hard words, and much tugging and hauling, "Kate" managed to get the horse back to camp. Judge of his surprise and grief when, on going out the following morning to attend to its wants, he found it dead. I doubt if Oliver ever learned the real cause of his horse's demise.

For several weeks we were allowed to remain near the Yellow house, doing picket-duty, and every third day sending out heavy working details to help in the construction of Fort Fisher and its connecting lines. It was near Fort Fisher that the famous signal tower that afterward stood as a landmark for miles around was erected. All who were with the regiment will remember it

—and the signal station perched like an enormous crow's nest in the top of a giant pine tree.

On the 23d of December the regiment, with the rest of the division, was called out to witness the execution of a deserter. I do not remember to what command he belonged, but he had deserted to the enemy, and, passing northward through the lines, had been caught, tried by court-martial, and condemned to be shot. Had he manifested the same courage upon the battle-field that he did at the place of execution he would have won the encomiums of his comrades. He met his fate undaunted, and even removed the bandage when placed over his eyes. Courage is a variable quality, present at times when death seems imminent and absent when danger is remote.

Between our picket-lines at this point was a large field of unhusked corn, but the pickets on each side were so watchful that for a time neither party could harvest it. On January 16th, however, the enemy came out with the intention of having a corn-husking frolic, and as our pickets were not invited to participate, they naturally took offense at such a lack of courtesy, and drove them away with a hot picket-fire. The firing caused a general alarm and soon the whole command was under arms and in line of battle. The next day the bone of contention was removed by our brigade going out in force with wagons and harvesting the entire crop.

Although it was always uncertain how long we would remain tenants of any one camp while on the siege of Petersburg, whenever opportunity offered some place was prepared for religious services. At the Yellow house a brigade chapel had been erected, which was dedicated on Sunday, January 15th. The services were very interesting—four chaplains participating. A melodeon had been procured, the music of which, added to that of the choir of male voices, carried us in fancy back to the peaceful Sabbath services that we had enjoyed at our far-away Northern homes.

Chaplain Cline, in a letter written on December 23d, '64, speaking of the state of the regiment at that time, says: "Convalescents had joined us, so that on leaving Brandy Station we set out with 256 enlisted men and 21 commissioned officers. I cannot give you the exact number, but I think about 60 are still absent, wounded. Many of these, everyone knows, will never be fit for duty again; 24 are reported prisoners or missing in action; as near as I can tell, 30 have been killed upon the field of battle, or died of wounds received there, 5 of whom were commissioned officers—Captains Sleeper and Layton, Lieutenants Baldwin, Egan and Boice. Four other officers were discharged on the ground of disability, and two, I am sorry to say, were dismissed. This may give you some idea of the changes in our regiment since last spring. Of our Christian brotherhood—our regimental church—numbering forty-seven in May, but sixteen are with us. Five of our little band lost their lives in their country's service, fifteen are absent in hospitals or among our suffering heroes in rebel prisons, and the remaining eleven are on detached duty at Trenton, Brigade Headquarters, or elsewhere. These are the facts. The figures as I give them are full of meaning, and as I write them down my thoughts run back to last winter, and I contrast the scene as it was then with what it is to-day. How striking and how sad the contrast is!

"To-day at twelve o'clock John E. Dixon, First Maine Heavy Artillery, was shot for desertion. According to order, our division was present to witness the execution. As Chaplain Hopkins and I, with a party of men, were very busy cutting and hauling logs to complete our chapel, we were excused."

On January 17th the division was reviewed by Generals Humphries, Mott and McAllister.

On the afternoon of the 28th a party of seven contrabands, five males and two females, came in through the picket detail of the Eleventh. Their clothing was a fitting illustration of the scarcity of such articles in the Confederacy, being composed of many pieces held to their persons with bands of tar-string, and would have excelled Joseph's in the variety of colors. They had come from Dinwiddie Court House, and having had to ford many small streams, their clothing was stiff with ice and their feet nearly frozen. Strange, what hardships and privations humanity will suffer for love of freedom, even when it confers but a doubtful boon!

Just at evening on February 4th orders came to be ready to march at daylight the next morning. That night services were held in the chapel for the last time, and then the men lay down to get what rest they could, for marching orders brought with them an uncertainty as to when another opportunity would be had; and under the conditions existing in the army at that time they were almost equivalent to orders to fight.

Chapter XVII.

Hatcher's Run—Armstrong House.

THE movement inaugurated on the morning of the 5th was another attempt to grasp with the left hand of the army some of Lee's lines of communication with the South. It was supposed that the Boynton plank-road was being used by the enemy's wagon-trains in conveying supplies to their army from the lower stations on the Weldon railroad. Gregg was therefore ordered to move with the cavalry to Dinwiddie Court House by way of Ream's Station, and from there up and down the Boynton road, capturing whatever trains he could. Warren, with the Fifth Corps, was to take position on the Vaughn road, midway between Hatcher's run and the court-house, so as to be within supporting distance of the cavalry under Gregg. Humphries, with his two reserve divisions, was to take position at the crossing of the Vaughn road over Hatcher's run and at Armstrong's mill, keep up communication with General Warren, and also with the left of the entrenchments held by General Miles' First Division of the Second Corps.

By seven o'clock on the morning of the 5th the regiment was on the move. After a march of about three miles we crossed a branch of Hatcher's run and went into position near the Thompson* house. General McAllister's official report will perhaps give the best idea of the position and work of the regiment during the day:

"Headquarters 3d Bri., 3 Div., 2d A. C., "February 14th, 1865.

"Major—In compliance with orders from Division Headquarters, I have the honor to report the part taken in the operations of the 5th and 6th insts. According to orders received, we broke camp and left on the morning of the 5th, the brigade following the

---

* McAllister called it the Tucker house.

Second, commanded by General West. On passing the Armstrong house we were halted, and I was ordered by General Mott to place my brigade in line of battle near the Tucker house, across the road leading past it, and to throw out pickets well to the front, connecting them with the Second Division pickets on my left. Also to guard well my right. This was accomplished in a very short time, giving my personal supervision to the placing of the pickets and connecting them with the Second Division pickets, on the road leading through the left center of my line, as directed. After taking a survey of the whole field, and making myself acquainted with the swamp on my front and right, I returned to my command. At twelve-thirty I received orders from General Humphries to build breastworks. My men went at it with a will and soon had the works well under way. I, at the same time, extended them toward the swamp on my right to prevent being flanked. Meanwhile an order was received from General Mott to throw a regiment across the road a considerable distance from my left. This road led down towards the Armstrong mill. I placed the Seventh New Jersey, commanded by Colonel Price, and had my brigade connect with him by taking distance to the left. The works were now nearly completed.

"At 3:30 P M. a staff officer from Brevet Brigadier-General Ramsey presented a telegram from General Humphries, directing General Ramsey to relieve me in my position. At the same time the head of General Ramsey's brigade appeared upon the ground with the General leading it. I obeyed the order, and sent my Adjutant-General, Captain Finklemaier, to division headquarters for orders, in the meantime massing my brigade in the rear.

"At four P. M. I received orders to form on the left of General Ramsey. I at once commenced the movement. My right regiments were just filing in when the attack commenced on the picket-line. I then ordered double-quick, and the men moved in rapidly. Lieutenant-Colonel Willian, of General Humphries' staff, then informed me that there was a gap in the line, between myself and Ramsey, caused by General Ramsey closing to the right. My rear regiment, the Eleventh New Jersey, Colonel Schoonover, intended for the left of the line, was taken off and hurried into this gap. They received a fire from the enemy, and returned it, causing the left of the enemy's line of battle to falter and lie down. The fire was taken up all along the line as fast as my troops were formed. The pickets on my new front having run in without firing a shot, left the enemy right on us before I had my line completed. Regiment after regiment, as fast as they wheeled into position, opened on the rebels, causing their line to

Private A. B. Searing.

halt and lie down.* The left regiment, the Eighth New Jersey, under Major Hartford, had no works, and were exposed to a terrible fire in their exposed position, but they stood nobly and fought splendidly. Not a man of this regiment, nor indeed of the whole brigade, left for the rear.

* The pickets on our front at this time belonged to the Second Division.

"Major Hartford and his regiment deserve especial credit for the gallantry they displayed in getting into position under the severe fire and holding it, without works, while two regiments of the Second Division, that had been lying for hours a little to my left, on the approach of the enemy gave way without firing a gun, leaving a still larger space between my left and the Second Division. After completing the line on my left I rode along the line with my Adjutant-General, Captain Finklemaier, encouraging the men to stand firm and the day would be ours. The One Hundred and Twentieth New York, Colonel Lockwood, was on the right of the Eighth New Jersey, and he and all his officers were on their feet doing the same. The Seventh New Jersey, Colonel Price, came next. This regiment was formed at a different angle so as to enable them to pour an enfilading fire on the enemy's lines, and prevent them from advancing into the gap. I gave the order and it was executed handsomely, and added very much to the repulse of the enemy. Had it not been for this and the aid of the artillery of the Tenth Massachusetts, commanded by Lieutenants Green and Adams, which was throwing its fire across the swamp at right angles with the enfilading fire, all would have been lost. Those artillery officers deserve great credit, and I have the pleasure of mentioning them favorably.

"The enemy advanced with the yell so well known to all, and fell back; again they advanced with a determination to break my line, but my line stood firm and rolled back the tide of battle in a highly creditable manner. Prisoners said they advanced in three lines of battle. From all I could see and learn, I think that was the case, though the woods prevented our seeing their movements.

"In riding along the line I found Chaplain Hopkins, of the Eleventh Massachusetts, using a gun and firing constantly, and encouraging the men to stand firm. He is deserving of mention.

"Before the battle ended General Humphries and a part of his staff came upon the line and was an eye-witness to the scene. It was pleasing to see how the appearance of the corps commander inspired our men to new effort.

"The third attack of the enemy then attempted ended in a complete route, and, night closing in, they fell back to the woods, leaving their dead behind them. During the latter part of the engagement two regiments of the Second Division came up to the support of the left of my line, and at the close the whole of the Second Brigade formed on my left. A number of prisoners came in during the evening and were forwarded. During the night our pickets were thrown out, and, tired and exhausted as the men were, most part of the night was spent in building breastworks on the left of the gap; the rest laid on their arms during the night.

"On the 6th the strengthening of the line was continued : our picket-line was advanced, and details were sent out to slash the timber and bury the enemy's dead. During the afternoon part of my command was sent out on a reconnoissance toward the enemy's line, which they discovered to be about one and a half miles from our own.

"February 7th, packed up and remained under arms until dark; one-fourth of the men remained under arms all night.

"In conclusion, permit me to say my officers and men did all that could be desired of them ; the former, regardless of their own personal safety, encouraging the men to stand firm, the latter firing low, as directed. To mention some would be doing injustice to others. I must, however, not omit to mention Captain J. P. Finklemaier, who fully sustained his previous reputation for bravery and gallantry in action, advancing and encouraging officers and men everywhere under the most terrific fire. Also my aids, Captains Charles F Bowers, A. A. D. C., and Lewis M. Morris, Brigade Inspector, and Lieutenant W Plimley, who went with a will into the thickest of the fight whenever ordered. Subjoined I have the honor to submit a list of casualties :

"Seventh New Jersey, 1 man wounded. Eighth New Jersey, 11 enlisted men killed, 2 officers and 35 enlisted men wounded. Eleventh New Jersey, 1 enlisted man killed and 1 wounded. One Hundred and Twentieth New York, 2 enlisted men wounded. Total killed, 12 enlisted men. Wounded, 2 officers and 39 enlisted men ; total, 53.

"R. McAllister.

" To Major R. Driver, A. A. G. 2d Div. 2d A. C."

As will be seen from General McAllister's official report, it was one of the fortunate chances of war that saved the Eleventh from taking position in the open ground on the left of the line.

Had not Ramsey's closing to the right left a vacancy that the Eleventh was hurried in to fill, its roll of casualties no doubt would have grown to greater proportions. The difference between the loss sustained by the Eighth New Jersey (which was on open ground without breastworks) and the other regiments of the brigade shows the great benefit to be derived from even a slight line of works when troops are acting on the defensive.

Although General McAllister's report gives only general commendation to the officers and men of the brigade, except in the case of Major Hartford and the immediate members of his staff, I think as much could be said for all the officers of the brigade. I am certain that no officer or man belonging to the Eleventh shirked a duty. Conspicuous among them for coolness of bearing and seeming disregard of danger was Colonel John Schoonover and Captain Charles F Gage. We know that it was impossible to have mentioned by name all enlisted men who bore themselves gallantly through battle, but we of the ranks sometimes felt that unnecessary praise was lavished upon those in office, who, after all, did only their duty and what their superior position gave them opportunity to do. A good leader no doubt is a prime essential to a good army, but no matter how brave and capable a leader might be, he would be helpless without brave and trusty men to follow. We know that the *morale* of a regiment or brigade was often lowered by hearing (in general orders) extravagant praise given to some favorite officer, who at best did nothing but his duty, while the soldier in the ranks was spoken of in vague and general terms. The American soldier in the war of the rebellion was not a machine, as are the majority of the soldiers in European armies, but a man who had volunteered for a specific purpose, and who, though obeying orders, would not subordinate his thinking and reasoning faculties to authority, and he was apt at times to listen with disgust to the extravagant praise lavished upon those who had been fortunate enough (through political or other influences) to secure a pair of shoulder straps. He recognized the fact that without a union of parts there could be no perfect whole, and that the

T

humblest man in the ranks who did his whole duty deserved as much as he who commanded and directed—for each did only as much as circumstances or ability enabled him to do.

In the attempt to break through our lines at this point, three of the enemy's divisions, parts of Hill's and Gordon's Corps, under General Gordon, were engaged. They were confident of success, and General Gordon, in conversation after the war, expressed surprise that his repeated attempts had been foiled by only one brigade and a battery of artillery.

During the battle, while the enemy's lines were pressing hard upon us, Chaplain Hopkins, of the One Hundred and Twentieth New York, began to sing the "Battle-cry of Freedom." The song was taken up by the brigade, and there is no doubt that as the strains of music rose above the battle's din many hearts resolved anew to "rally 'round the flag" whenever danger menaced it.

Just before the opening of the battle, and while General McAllister was directing the formation of the Seventh New Jersey, a horseman in the uniform of a Union major approached him with the remark: "General, I almost took a rebel officer." The General replied, "Why did not you altogether do it?" "He was well armed," said the major. "So are you," said McAllister, "and who are you?" "I have charge of the picket-line in front," he replied. "Then you belong to the Second Division," answered the General, and gave no further thought to the major at the time. On looking around for him some time afterwards, for the purpose of making some inquiries in regard to the pickets, he found that he had disappeared. Then it occurred to the General that he might have been a rebel spy. Events that occurred after the war had ended proved the surmise a correct one. In a conversation between the Generals, after the war, speaking of this battle, McAllister asked Gordon if he had sent an officer in the uniform of a Union major to ascertain our position. Gordon replied, "Most likely I did."

Another interesting incident in connection with the battle of February 5th was disclosed after the war had ended. Lieutenant

U. B. Titus, ordnance officer of the Third Division, Second Corps, learned from Lieutenant Jones, who had held a position on General Gordon's staff, that when McAllister and staff rode out to inspect the picket-line they passed near a number of Gordon's men, under Lieutenant Jones, who were lying in ambush. They had their guns leveled, when Lieutenant Jones ordered them not to fire, remarking, "That man looks too honest to be shot down like a dog." Had they fired, probably not one of the party would have escaped. General Gordon, in conversation with McAllister afterward, corroborated Lieutenant Jones' story.

Lieutenant U. B. Titus, the ordnance officer of the Third Division, Second Corps, says: "During the fight I received an order from General McAllister for ammunition, with the accompanying request to hasten it with all speed, as his regiments had nearly exhausted their supply. I at once advanced with a load of powder-coated Yankee pills to a spot as close as practicable in the rear. In the course of issuing the ammunition and upon the line I met with the General. Taking me by the hand, he exclaimed, 'Lieutenant, you have brought us just what we want; we are giving it to them to day.'"

I will here say, by way of explanation, that wagons containing ammunition were seldom hauled to the extreme front. They were taken as close as was consistent with safety, and from that point the ammunition was distributed by hand. On this occasion Lieutenant Titus, realizing the urgency of the case, did not wait for ordinary details to do the work, but personally assisted in carrying the ammunition to the line of battle.

Discouraged with the failure of their third attempt to pierce our lines, the enemy retired behind their works. It was then night, but it brought little rest to the tired soldiers, for most of the night was spent in strengthening the works, not knowing but the morrow might bring a renewal of the conflict.

On the 6th, our pickets were pushed farther to the front, but no material change was made in the position of the regiment, the work upon the lines being continued. Details were sent out to bury the dead, and others to slash the timber on our front.

During the afternoon a part of the brigade went on a reconnoissance toward the enemy's line. Their main works were found to be over a mile from us.

On the 7th of February we packed up and stood under arms until night, and a part of the regiment was kept under arms *all* night. This order of thus spending the nights became more and more frequent as the time approached for the final movement. Some part of the command would be on duty constantly during the hours of darkness, and an hour or two before daybreak the entire regiment would be called out. It was a wise precaution, no doubt, but it was not very pleasant to be awakened at a time when slumber was soundest and sweetest.

During the succeeding days we built a second line of works, and made ourselves as comfortable as circumstances would permit.

On February 21st a salute of a hundred guns was fired in honor of the fall of Charleston and Columbia, South Carolina.

Desertions from the enemy's ranks had been very frequent, an average of about ten a day coming in on our brigade picket-line alone.

On the 24th another salute was fired in honor of the capture of Wilmington, North Carolina.

Among the deserters who came in our line on March 1st was an old man who said he had served three years and was tired of it, and as his home was near Wilmington, and as that place was now in possession of the Union troops, he would try to make his way home again. Another, a young man, had been enrolled since '61 but had escaped the army until that winter, when they had hunted him with bloodhounds from the mountains, where he had fled for safety, and to keep from taking up arms against the Union. Many of the deserters who came in on this part of the line were from Cook's Brigade of North Carolinians. On the second of March, between the hours of one A. M. and ten P. M. seventy-three came in through our brigade picket-line. Even to the dullest mind the fact was plain that the Confederacy was falling to pieces.

An unusually bright and intelligent-looking man was brought to headquarters one morning by the picket-guard. Colonel Schoonover inquired of him if General Picket was not becoming alarmed at the frequent desertions from his division and whether any steps had been taken to prevent desertions from his line. He replied that "the usual number of men on a picket-post was three, but it had recently been increased to four by adding a man who was known to be reliable." "How, then," it was asked "did you get away?" "Oh," he answered, "I was the reliable man on my post last night."

On the evening of March 4th the Rev. Dr. Hale, of Pennington, N. J., arrived at brigade headquarters, as the guest of General McAllister. Some extracts from the Reverend Doctor's account of this visit may be of interest to the reader as showing the impression our mode of living made upon the mind of a civilian. He says:

"I left Pennington on Friday, March 3d, for the seat of war in Virginia, Dr. Welling acting as escort; passed through Trenton and Philadelphia to Baltimore, going thence by steamer via Fortress Monroe, and arrived early on March 4th at City Point, the headquarters of the Army of the Potomac. In a freight-car, on rough boards supported by boxes, we were conveyed slowly to our destination, the Tucker house, near Hatcher's run, on the railway built by the government for the transportation of troops, provisions and ammunition. This was a distance of about thirty miles in a southerly direction. Arriving about sunset, we were cordially welcomed by General McAllister and assigned quarters in the spacious parlor of the Tucker house, with the General and his surgeon. A large open fireplace, well filled with logs and sticks of pine, furnished a bright fire to cheer us and keep off the cold. Window-sash and window glass had long since disappeared, and the places of doors and windows were supplied with canvas. The next day, being the Sabbath, I preached morning and evening in the chapel of the brigade. This was a structure unique and attractive, tastefully put together throughout with unhewn pine logs, poles and branches, with fixed seats and pulpit of the same, and carpeted with small green branches, all so well arranged as to make a comfortable house of worship. This was the handiwork of the soldiers of the brigade, by order of their sympathetic, upright Christian commander.

"If there were any church-members who entered the army leaving their religion behind them, General McAllister was not one of them. He was nowhere and at no time ashamed of Christ. He was equally firm in the practice of abstinence from all intoxicating liquors, and he neither used alcohol himself nor offered it to others. Although his rigid temperance principles were not agreeable to some, yet they could not withhold their respect from one who, in so manly a way, acted according to the dictates of his conscience. No efforts were spared by him during his four years' service as an officer in the army to persuade his men to be habitually and thoroughly sober. Had all the officers and men of the Union army indulged less in stimulating beverages we would have had fewer defeats and a shorter war, with a smaller expenditure of money and an immensely less sacrifice of precious lives.

"One of the most painful scenes witnessed was the military execution of a private, who had been tried by court-martial for desertion, convicted and sentenced to be shot. A hollow square was occupied on three sides by the regiments of the division in command of General Miles. To the middle of the fourth side was led the prisoner, an Irishman, attended by a priest. After a short religious ceremony the condemned man was seated on his coffin, then, at a signal by an officer, the fatal shot was fired and instantly he fell dead. As soon as the surgeon pronounced him dead he was placed in his coffin and buried in a grave already opened near by. The penalty for desertion is just and essential to the safety of the army, but some of these poor ignorant men are too stupid to know when they are breaking the law.

"Among the heroic ladies to whom the nation owes a debt of lasting gratitude is Miss Helen Louise Gilson, who came into the army under the protection of her uncle, Mr. Fay, of Boston,

Mass. She was a fine representative of those Christian women of high intellectual culture, energy of character and patriotic devotion, who helped to carry our nation through the war and at the same time infused a more elevated moral tone through the army. Upon the close of the war Miss Gilson returned home and was married to Mr. Hamilton Osgood.

"The severe labors, exposure, cares and anxieties of her army life had broken down a naturally strong constitution, so that she lived only about one year. A handsome monument has been erected over her grave in Mount Auburn cemetery by the Third Corps Union, under the direction of Dr. E. L. Welling, chairman of the committee appointed for that purpose."

On March 11th there was a review of the corps by Generals Meade and Humphries. The 25th of March brought the prelude to the campaign of '65, which ended with the surrender of Lee at Appomattox. A little after four A. M., while Company E, of the Eleventh, was taking their turn at standing under arms in the breastworks, heavy firing began upon the right. Soon the entire brigade was under arms and orders were issued to pack up and be ready to move at once. The enemy had made an attack upon the Ninth Corps at Fort Steadman, broken through our lines and captured the works. The capture of the picket-line at that point was made easy because of the existing order to permit deserters from the enemy's lines to bring their arms with them. Groups of men, representing themselves as deserters, entered the Ninth Corps' picket-line in front of Fort Steadman and captured the pits, thus opening the way for the assaulting column.

Our camp was soon stripped of canvas, knapsacks packed and the men ready for further orders. No movement, however, was made until about ten o'clock, when the Eleventh Regiment was ordered to demonstrate against the enemy's picket-line to the left of the Armstrong house. We marched out in front of the works and entered the woods to the left of the open space. Skirmishers were thrown out and advanced to within two hundred and fifty yards of the enemy's pits.

Colonel Schoonover, thinking the enemy's position too strong to be assaulted with only one regiment, so reported to General McAllister, who then sent the One Hundred and Twentieth New York to his assistance, which was placed in position to the right of the Eleventh. Three companies, however, of the One Hundred and Twentieth were ordered to the left to protect the flank.

General McAllister, who had up to this time remained with the front line, received orders from General Mott to place the two regiments under command of Colonel Schoonover and return to his headquarters, where he (General Mott) was waiting to see him. The line was soon pushed forward to the edge of the wood, from where the enemy's picket could be plainly seen across an open field. Schoonover gave the order to charge, and the line, led by its commander, sprang forward at a double-quick, and although the advancing line was subject to an artillery fire from the left and a severe musketry fire from the front, the pits were quickly reached and captured, with about one hundred prisoners.

As some of our men reached one of the pits still held by the enemy, one of them placed his gun nearly against the breast of one of our men and pulled the trigger, but fortunately the cap failed to explode. Our Union soldier attempted to retaliate, but his gun, too, played him false. Captain Thompson (who was never far from the front) then appeared upon the scene, and with a blow from his sword laid the rebel stunned and bleeding at his feet.

The enemy kept up a rapid artillery fire for some time, and a continuous musketry fire from their main line of works, less than six hundred yards distant. The fire from one of the enemy's redoubts to our left so enfiladed the line of picket-pits as to render them untenable while the fire continued, while everyone who showed himself was subject to a fire from their main line of works. In front of their main line at this point was a strong palisade, and in front of that nearly four hundred yards of slashing.

General Smythe's Division should have connected with our left, but at three in the afternoon had not yet done so, consequently our left flank was unprotected. About that hour the enemy advanced under cover of the woods and by a sudden dash succeeded in capturing a portion of the line on our left.

It will be remembered that three companies of the One Hundred and Twentieth New York had been sent to the left flank. Upon these companies fell the weight of the flank attack, with the inevitable result that some were captured and others driven from the field. This is written intending no disparagement to the gallant men of the One Hundred and Twentieth, for no other troops could have acted better when taken on flank and rear. The result of this attack, however, left the left flank of the Eleventh exposed and the presence of the enemy there in temporary confusion. But the men were quickly rallied, and, advancing again, recaptured the part of the line lost. Lieutenant-Colonel Lockwood, of the One Hundred and Twentieth New York, who was division officer of the day, displayed great gallantry in rallying and advancing his regiment during this movement. Soon after the re-establishment of the line the Eleventh Massachusetts reported to the front, and was placed by Colonel Schoonover in the wood upon the left. We also made connection with General Smythe by taking distance to the left. As the distance to be covered was about six hundred yards, it left our line very weak.

About six o'clock in the evening the enemy again advanced with a strong force, through the wood, upon our left. They moved with great rapidity, and with a rush and a yell were upon us and, capturing pit after pit, succeeded in re-taking the entire line, with about eighty prisoners. General McAllister coming up with the Seventh and Eighth New Jersey the lines were re-formed, but General Smythe having withdrawn his front no further advance was made. The firing continued brisk all along the line until long after dark. The shells shrieked through the woods, cutting away branches of trees and scattering the fragments around us, but at last the noise of the battle ceased.

We remained in position until one o'clock on the morning of the 26th, when we were ordered to return to camp, leaving a strong picket-line to hold the position.

The Eleventh New Jersey and the One Hundred and Twentieth New York captured during the day one hundred and fifty prisoners, and lost in killed, wounded and missing one hundred and forty-five enlisted men and two officers. The loss to the Eleventh was sixty-four. The killed were Sergeant James Roalefs, of Company K, and Sergeant Samuel Kerr, of Company G. The body of Sergeant Roalefs was left between the lines. The next day Chaplain Cline went, under a flag of truce, to recover it, but the enemy had buried it. Sergeant Kerr had but recently rejoined the regiment as an exchanged prisoner. He had one of the main arteries severed by a bullet and bled to death before surgical assistance could be reached.

During the advance through the wood Company E was upon the skirmish-line. Among its men there was one who, though he had been with the regiment from the date of its muster into the service, I think had never passed through a battle. By some hook or crook he would always manage to escape the eyes of the officers and get out, but would invariably turn up smiling when the danger was over. I believe he had a genuine desire to pass through an engagement, but timidity was so ingrained in his constitution that whenever the opportunity offered he could not pluck up courage to do so.

On the day in question Captain Gage, of Company E, was acting Major, and the command of the company devolved upon Sergeant Marbaker. He resolved that, if possible, he would keep an especial watch upon the man mentioned. During a halt that occurred in the wood, the Sergeant passed to the right of the company. While there the line advanced again. Making his way back towards the left, he found his man absent; no one seemed to know what had become of him. The Sergeant, determined to find him, went back to where the line had been halted. He was found in company with another, huddled behind a big pine tree. When asked what they were doing there, they expressed the utmost surprise that the line should have advanced without their knowledge. They were escorted to their places again, and though one managed to slip away afterward, the one who was under especial charge was kept in place until the fighting was over and the company returned to camp. After finding himself safely in camp he came to the Sergeant and thanked him for having kept him in line, saying, "I can now honestly say that I have been through one battle." I have related this incident to show that some who shirked did so not because they chose to be cowards, but because nature had endowed them with an excess of timidity they could not overcome. I believe the man mentioned had a desire to become a good soldier, but he simply could not.

As opposed to this, I noticed among the recruits in the same company who were passing through their first battle experience a man (Richard Porter by name) whose face was blanched and whose limbs were trembling with fear. He evidently realized to its full extent the danger that surrounded him, and yet, paradoxical as it may seem, though terribly afraid, he had the courage to face the danger.

The New York papers in their reports of this engagement—for probably the first time—gave the Eleventh the credit it deserved, the "Herald" being especially commendatory. Just previous to the action of the 25th, for some breach of discipline, Lieutenant Alonzo Merritt had been placed under arrest. When the fighting began he was in camp with Lieutenant William Hand, then acting quartermaster. Hand asked him how he would like to go out and help the boys. Merritt was ready in a moment, and he and Hand both came to the front and took part in the battle. Merritt conducted himself so gallantly that he was released from arrest, and no charge made against him.

On returning to camp, after the fighting of the 25th, we again put up tents and took up the routine of camp duty. But we knew that our quiet could not long remain unbroken. Every one felt that the operations of the 25th were really the initial movements of the campaign—that the subsequent days of rest were but the inhalation of breath before the final struggle—for "final" we felt that it would be. The frequent desertions from Lee's army during the winter told us that many of his veterans had lost all hope for the success of the cause for which they had fought so long and gallantly. We knew that he still had a

Corporal A. S. Talmage.

formidable army of tried veterans, behind works that were unusually strong, and that the sacrifice of many lives would yet be called for before the end should come. Yet we were anxious for the commencement of the campaign, that it might be sooner ended. Consequently there was but little grumbling when the order to pack up and move came on the morning of the 29th.

"HEADQUARTERS 11th REGIMENT, NEW JERSEY VOLS.
"CAMP NEAR HATCHER'S RUN, VA., MARCH 27, 1865.

"CAPTAIN—In accordance with circular from Brigade Headquarters of this date, I have the honor to report the operations of my command on the 25th inst. as follows :

"About 10 A. M. I was directed by the Brevet Brigadier-General commanding to take my regiment and make such demonstrations against the enemy's picket-line on the left of the 'Armstrong House' as would develop the strength in his main works.

"I entered the woods on the left of the open space and advanced a skirmish-line to within about 250 yards of the enemy's picket-line, when I determined, after viewing the ground, that one regiment was insufficient to make a successful attack. The One Hundred and Twentieth New York was accordingly sent forward and placed on the right of the Eleventh New Jersey. Three companies of the latter regiment I deployed to the left in the woods to protect my flank. The line was then advanced quickly to the edge of the woods, when a charge was ordered and the men went handsomely forward under a raking fire of artillery from the woods, capturing the enemy's picket-pits with nearly 100 prisoners. The enemy kept up a rapid fire of artillery for some time and a continued fire of musketry from the main works, which were less than 600 yards distant. I do not think there was more than a thin single rank behind the works at the time. The redoubt on the extreme right of the enemy's line so completely enfiladed the line of picket-pits that it would have been untenable had the fire been continued, while every man who showed himself received a volley from their line of works. At this point the enemy have about 400 yards of slashing and a palisade 30 yards in advance of the works.

"About three P. M. a force of the enemy advanced under cover of the woods on the left of the line and succeeded in capturing a portion of the line. The men were rallied a short distance in the rear, the line advanced and the pits re-taken with a few prisoners. Much credit is due to Lieutenant-Colonel Lockwood, of the One Hundred and Twentieth New York Volunteers, then Division Officer of the Day, for the gallant manner in which he assisted to advance his regiment at this time. A short time after the line was re-established, the Eleventh Massachusetts reported to me and was placed upon the left, in the woods. About this time I saw General Smythe, who desired me to connect with his right and protect his flank, as he was about to make a charge upon the enemy.

"As I had previously received orders from General McAllister to make this connection, I attended to it in person. I was obliged to extend my lines at least 600 yards to accomplish this, leaving it weak through the woods.

"About six o'clock in the afternoon the enemy again advanced through the woods on the left with a strong force and rushed upon the line with a yell, capturing pit after pit toward the right, and finally succeeded in re-taking the entire line and about eighty prisoners. The men were re-formed along the pits occupied at present by the picket-line, where they remained until withdrawn, about one A. M. on the morning of the 26th. The Eleventh Massachusetts was withdrawn, as directed, with the same division. I deem the conduct of the regiments engaged in the capture and re-capture of the enemy's line during the day was all that could be expected. Too much praise cannot be given them for the manner in which they first charged and captured the line. The officers, without exception, behaved nobly. I desire to mention particularly Major Scott, Captains Holmes and Newkirk, and Adjutant Russell, of the One Hundred and Twentieth New York; Captains Gage, Morehouse and Thompson, and First Lieutenant Oliver, of the Eleventh New Jersey. These officers deserve much credit for their personal bravery and efficiency. A more cordial and earnest-working officer than Major Scott I have never met. The reports of Lieutenant-Colonel Rivers, Major Scott and Captain Gage are enclosed.

"Very respectfully,
"Your obdt. servant,
"(Sd.) JOHN SCHOONONER,
"*Lieut-Col. Comdg.*

"To Capt. J. P. Finklemaier, A. A. G., 3d Brigade, 3d Division, Ind. Corps."

Following is the official report of the part taken by the Third Brigade, Third Division, Second Army Corps, from March 29th to April 14th, 1865:

"HEADQUARTERS 3D B., 3D D., 2D A. C.,
"April 15th, 1865.

"*Captain A. W. Keene, A. A. G. 3d Div., 2d A. C.:*

"In compliance with orders from Div. H. Q., I have the honor to submit the report of operations of this command from Mar. the 28th to date. Pursuant to orders, the brigade broke camp on the morning of the 29th, and with the rest of the division moved to the left. Our movements on the 29th and 30th consisted in advancing our lines cautiously, the enemy's skirmishers falling back before us. On the 31st we moved further toward the left to relieve the division near Boynton plank-road, where the enemy was found strongly entrenched, three of their forts commanding the road. An assault on one of these having been ordered at 12 M., the 11th Mass., Lt.-Col. C. C. Rivers, and the 120th N. Y., Lt.-Col. Lockwood, supported by the left wing of the 8th N. J., Maj. Hartford, and the 11th N. J., Lt.-Col. Schoonover, advanced. The regiments charged through heavy slashing to crest of the hill overlooking the enemy's works, and succeeded in driving the enemy from and occupying a part of their rifle-pits, capturing some fifteen of their pickets. The attack was made under a severe fire from the enemy's batteries and sharp musketry from their pits. After remaining there under the enfilading fire, the enemy's artillery sweeping the entire front, for one hour, orders were received to withdraw, which was a more difficult task than the advance. The men were drawn off almost one by one under a severe fire from the enemy's sharpshooters, not, however, without the loss of many men killed, wounded and captured. At dark the brigade was ordered to the left of the Boynton plank-road, and took a position near a run in the woods.

"April 1st, at 5 A. M., the brigade was ordered to occupy the line held on the afternoon of March 31st. After dark we again returned to the line in the woods held the previous night. Heavy skirmishing was sustained all night, and when on the 2d of April, at 3 A. M., orders were received to withdraw to the position occupied the day previous, the enemy opened a most galling fire of artillery and musketry on our line. A general attack on the enemy's line having been ordered on the 2d of April, Gen. Mott directed me to send out and attack the enemy's picket-line in our immediate front. The 8th N. J. was selected accordingly, accompanied by myself and staff. On reaching our picket-line, the enemy opened a terrific fire of musketry, shell and canister upon us. The regiment steadily advanced and succeeded in capturing the enemy's whole picket-line in our front, 165 prisoners and 200 muskets. The enemy's artillery fire still continued, which, however, was soon silenced by our men pouring a well-directed musketry fire into their main line. The 11th Mass. and 11th N. J., whom I had ordered for support, advanced. The enemy was observed to withdraw their guns and leave. In the subsequent charge on the enemy's main works, another lot of prisoners were captured. Major Hartford succeeded in first planting our flag on the enemy's redoubt at 9:30 A. M. The whole command behaved most gallantly in this charge and our men were seen grappling with the enemy, who in some places offered the most stubborn resistance.

"This over the command moved, with the rest of the division, toward Petersburg, in front of which the enemy bivouacked for the night, and where news was received of the evacuation of Petersburg and Richmond. April the 3d, orders having been received to pursue the enemy, we left, in connection with the division, the front of Petersburg, taking the river road toward the Danville railroad, which we crossed on the morning of the 5th, marching on the left of said road. We passed Jettersville on the morning of the 6th, where the enemy's line was discovered in our front. The 11th Massachusetts, on the left of the Division skirmish line, rendered valuable service. The balance of the brigade was formed at once in line of battle and marched forward for several miles, the 2d Brigade, Gen. Pierce, on the right, the 6th Corps on the left.

"At 3 P. M. a charge was ordered, which was executed in very handsome style. We succeeded in driving the enemy from our front, and the 120th New York and 11th Massachusetts, with the balance of the brigade, materially assisted in capturing the enemy's wagon train and quite a number of prisoners.

"On the morning of the 7th we crossed the Appomattox at High Bridge about two miles from Farmville. The enemy again made a stand, and skirmishing was sustained all day. During the night of the 7th the enemy left our front. We rapidly pushed him toward Piedmont coal mine, New Store and Lynchburg road, toward Appomattox Court House, where, at 3 P. M. of the 9th, official intelligence was received of the surrender of General Lee. The troops were then consigned to three camps, and remained so until the 10th. The 8th New Jersey was then ordered to escort the ammunition train back to Burksville. The rest of the brigade, having followed the division toward Farmville, on the 11th, was ordered to act as rear guard to the artillery train, with which it arrived near Burksville on 14th, about 4 P. M.

"During this short and eventful campaign all the officers and men of this command have exhibited such commendable bravery and endurance that it is almost impossible to make a distinction. I cannot, however, omit to mention particularly the brave and gallant conduct of the following officers, and to recommend them for brevet promotion : Lt. Col. John Schoonover, 11th N. J., and Capt. John P. Finklemaier, A. A. G., to date from the 21st of Jan., on which date both officers have been recommended for brevet promotion, in just appreciation of their valuable services during last summer's campaign. They have since, on the 5th of February, near Hatcher's Run, as well as throughout this campaign, fully sustained their previous reputation, and are so well known throughout the corps for their gallant and efficient conduct in the field, that I deem it my duty to renew the application for their well-earned promotion. Maj. Hartford, 8th N. J., for gallantry exhibited on the 2d of April ; Col. Francis Price, 7th N. J.; Lt. Col. Lockwood, 120th N. Y.; Maj. Scott, 1st Lt. and Adjt. ; E. McRussell, 120th N. York; Capt. Chas. F Gage, 11th N. J., have exhibited commendable bravery on all occasions during the campaign. Lt. Wm. Plunley, A. A. D. C., on my staff, for his brave conduct on the 2d of April with Maj. Hartford.

"Robert McAllister,
"J. P. Finklemaier,   "Brig. Gen. Comdg.
"A. A. G."

"Headquarters 3d Brig., 3d Div., 2d A. C.
"Gen. Order No. 7.   "April 12th, 1865.
"To the Officers and Men of this Brigade:

"It is a pleasure for me to again congratulate you on the brilliant success of this campaign, and the noble manner in which you have acquitted yourselves in the different affairs in which you have participated. I must favorably mention the One Hundred and Twentieth New York, temporarily commanded by Major Scott, and the Eleventh New Jersey, commanded by Captain Charles F. Gage, all under command of Lieutenant-Colonel Schoonover, for their gallantry in taking and re-taking the enemy's picket-line, with a large number of prisoners, on the 25th of March, under a severe fire of artillery and musketry. The Seventh New Jersey, Colonel Price, for timely assistance rendered late in the evening, in establishing the broken line and making connection, under fire of the enemy.

"The Eighth New Jersey, Major Hartford; Eleventh Massachusetts, Major Dunham, and One Hundred and Twentieth New York, Lieutenant-Colonel Lockwood, all under command of Colonel C. C. Rivers, for gallantry in developing the enemy's forces on the Boynton plank-road on March 31st.

"The Eighth New Jersey, Major Hartford, for the capture of the picket-line, on the 2d of April, with a large number of prisoners and arms, under a galling fire of shell and musketry, and planting our flag on the enemy's redoubt. The Eleventh Massachusetts, for their gallant advance with the division skirmishers on the 6th. The Eleventh Massachusetts and One Hundred and Twentieth New York for their early connection with the Second Brigade in the advance on the evening of the 6th, and the balance of the regiments for their promptness in throwing out skirmishers and their handsome advance which drove back the enemy and assisted in capturing the wagon-train. While all were not engaged at once, each did its share in helping to secure the great result, of which you may all feel proud, and can now rejoice over the greatest victory of the war. But in our rejoicing let us not forget the gallant dead, that our prayers may go out daily for the widows and orphans, and our hearts open to their wants in sympathy and benevolence.

"ROBERT McALLISTER,
Brig.-Gen. Comm'd'g.

"J. P. FINKLEMAIER,
"*A. A. G.*"

Chapter XVIII.

Capture of Petersburg—Amelia Springs—Farmville— Lee's Surrender.

AFTER waiting until the Army of the James had taken our places in the entrenchments, we moved by the left flank down the Vaughn road, across Hatcher's run. Marching two or three miles, we halted, faced to right and threw up a line of works. Soon the order came to advance, and with skirmishers thrown well out we moved slowly and cautiously toward the enemy's lines, passing in the meantime an old line of rebel works. This movement continued until dark, when we were again ordered to move by the left flank. A heavy rain-storm had set in, which, with the darkness and heavy undergrowth in the forest, rendered marching very difficult. After passing a deserted rebel camp we were halted, and lay in line of battle the remainder of the night. A night's rest, obtained under such conditions, is not a very pleasant one, nor conducive to sleep; at least, it would not be to a civilian. But neither mud nor rain was sufficient to keep a tired soldier from sleeping. They would catch a few winks under the most unfavorable of circumstances and on the most unpromising of beds. I remember having obtained a passable night's rest upon a wagon-tongue, with head and shoulders crowded upon the hounds and legs twisted around the pole.

The rain was still falling heavily on the morning of March 30th. A hasty breakfast over, we again moved forward in line of battle. Our advance led through woods and swamps and across the Dabney mill road, about midway between Dabney's mill and the junction of the road with the Boynton plank-road. Soon after crossing the Dabney mill road our skirmishers struck the enemy's pickets, but pressed them back, and we continued advancing until we reached the vicinity of the Crow house, where we halted and hastily threw up a line of works. We remained in that position until near two o'clock on the morning of March 31st, when we were ordered to fall in, and the movement by the left flank was again taken up. The rain had ceased, but the mud made marching wearisome work. Daylight found us at the Boynton plank-road and near the enemy's works, which had been built on our old battle ground of October 27th. Just to the left of our brigade stood the white-oak tree under which Hancock had his headquarters at the commencement of that battle and from which the enemy had driven him.

The old battle-ground was hardly recognizable. From each side of the Boynton road frowned a formidable battery—one occupying the field upon which we had been so nearly captured and from which we made the charge on October 27th—while stretching westward along the White-oak road, now a heavy line of earthworks, to the right and left the timber had been slashed so that the features of the entire field had been changed. I think but few at first recognized it as the place which a former visit had cost us so dearly.

About 12 M., an assault having been ordered upon the enemy's works at this point, the Eleventh Massachusetts and One Hundred and Twentieth New York, supported by the Eleventh and Eighth New Jersey, were formed under cover of the wood and ordered forward. They charged through the slashing and reached the crest overlooking the enemy's main line, capturing a portion of their picket-line and a few prisoners. During the advance a terrific artillery fire had been poured upon them, one spherical case wounding fifteen men in Companies B and I of the Eleventh New Jersey. Among the wounded was Sergeant Owens. Owing to an enfilading fire from the enemy's batteries, the position attained was found to be untenable, and after holding it for about an hour the line was ordered to fall back to their former position. This was found to be a more dangerous undertaking than the forward movement had been. From some parts of the line the men had to return one at a time, running the gauntlet of the enemy's fire until they had regained the shelter of the woods.

Some time after this assault the Eleventh Regiment was moved by the left flank to the open ground near the Boynton plank-road, and in direct range of the enemy's batteries. There it lay for some time with no other protection than that afforded by a few rails. The enemy opened upon it a severe artillery fire, but fortunately no one was injured, though there were some very narrow escapes. The writer, while standing in rear of his company issuing ammunition, was splattered with dirt by a bursting shell.*

About dark we were moved still farther to the left and took position in the woods, to the left of the Boynton plank road. Some parts of the line occupied that night by the Eleventh was very swampy, so much so that the men had to cut brush with which to build a staging to keep themselves out of the water.

About five o'clock on the morning of April 1st the regiment was moved back to the position occupied on the previous afternoon. At dark, we again returned to the position in the woods held the night before. Heavy skirmishing continued through the night, and when, at three o'clock on the morning of the 2d, we were again ordered to re-occupy our line on the right of the road, the enemy opened on us a severe musketry and artillery fire.

At 7:30 an assault upon the enemy's lines was ordered. The Eighth New Jersey leading, captured the enemy's picket-line and a number of prisoners. It was followed closely by the Eleventh New Jersey and Eleventh Massachusetts. As the line advanced the enemy was observed to withdraw their guns; the

---

*While the regiment was lying in this exposed position under the heavy shell-fire from the enemy's batteries, General Grant and staff rode along the lines within easy range of the enemy's guns. Evidently inferring from the large escort that it was an officer of high rank, at least thirty guns were trained upon the cavalcade as long as it was in sight. This may seem like a needless exposure on the part of the commanding general of an army, but it is a notorious fact, and the history of the war will bear me out in the assertion, that no officer, no matter what his rank, who never came near enough to the enemy to hear the whistling of a bullet or feel the jar of a bursting shell, made a record for himself which is looked upon by posterity as especially brilliant.

line then pushed rapidly forward and soon their main works and a number of prisoners were in our hands.

Near where we entered the enemy's works stood a small, unpainted house. It was tightly closed and showed no signs of occupancy. James P Myers, of Company E, then serving as a stretcher-bearer, knocked at the door and, receiving no answer and supposing the house to be empty, delivered a blow with the end of his stretcher which burst the door open. The room seemed to be unfurnished and untenanted, but from the semi-darkness a voice cried, "Young man, don't come in here." Peering through the gloom he discovered a figure clothed in bed-ticking—the figure of a woman, so old and bent and wrinkled that she seemed more like a wraith than a human being. Startled by the ghost-like appearance, Myers beat a hasty retreat, saying, "Don't be afraid, old woman; I won't hurt you."

Others may have investigated the premises, but Myers was satisfied with one glimpse of its uncanny occupant.

Leaving the works in our rear, and the old battle field of the "Bull-ring" to our right, we crossed Hatcher's run and passed up to the Boynton plank-road, which we followed towards Petersburg, the enemy flying before us.

The Sixth Corps, having entered the enemy's works opposite Fort Fisher, swept to the left as far as Hatcher's run, then facing about marched in the direction of Petersburg. The Second and Third Divisions of the Second Corps (Miles with the First Division having followed the enemy out the Claiborne road toward Sunderland Station) were ordered to continue in the same direction, and connect with the left of the Sixth Corps. The Third Division consequently continued up the Boynton road for several miles until connection was made. It was then late in the day and it was ordered to bivouac for the night.

On the morning of the 3d of April, it having been ascertained that Lee had retreated during the night, we were ordered to take up the pursuit. By eight o'clock A. M. we were on the march by way of the river road. The march was kept up as rapidly as the state of the roads would permit until half past eleven in the evening, when a halt was ordered for the night. At six o'clock on the morning of the 4th we were again in motion, following the Fifth Corps towards Jettersville. Merritt's cavalry, coming in from our right, interrupted our march. After the passage of the cavalry the column was again pushed rapidly forward until near night, when it went into bivouac.

The men were then entirely out of rations and the trains were eagerly looked for, but at two o'clock on the morning of the 5th, when the march was resumed, they had not yet reached us. Shortly after crossing Deep creek, Merritt's cavalry, which had been near Bevel's bridge, on the Appomattox, again interrupted the march. The infantry filed out of the road to allow the cavalry to pass, and remained at that point to await the coming of rations. About 8:15 the trains came up and rations were issued. The men were given time to get breakfast, but at ten o'clock orders came to move forward. Toward evening we reached the vicinity of Jettersville, where we found the Fifth Corps entrenched. It was supposed that Lee was concentrating his army near Amelia Court House; dispositions were therefore made to attack him at that point.

On the morning of the 6th the Second Corps, in conjunction with the Fifth and Sixth, was ordered to advance toward Amelia Court House. Our division was to the left of the Richmond and Danville railroad. After proceeding a few miles it was found that Lee was in full retreat toward Lynchburg, having passed our left during the night. The line of march was therefore changed, the Second Corps taking the direction of Deatonsville. The enemy's rear guard was found posted on high ground beyond Flat creek, near Amelia Springs. After a sharp brush, during which General Mott was wounded, they were dislodged, and the advance continued. A running fire was kept up until near dark, when they again made a stand on the high ground eastward of Sailor's creek. The First Brigade, which had been leading, was then placed upon the reserve, and the Second, under General Price, and Third, under General McAllister, formed in line of battle and pushed forward. The enemy made a spirited resistance, but were soon driven from their position.

On reaching the high ground overlooking Sailor's creek the cause of the enemy's stand at that point was discovered. Parked on low ground, east of the creek, was a train of one hundred and fifty wagons. The drivers had just begun to pull out, but, our line pressing swiftly down the slope, they escaped only with their teams, leaving wagons and contents in our hands. The wagons were loaded with miscellaneous stores, some even containing female clothing. Many of the boys secured trophies of this capture, such as books, surgical instruments, and other pieces of portable property. The writer obtained a military map of Virginia (since lost), and a Signal Corps glass which he gave to Lieutenant Berry, from whom it was stolen. By the time these movements were completed darkness had fallen, and the troops bivouacked for the night. Beside the train mentioned the corps gained, during its day's operations, three pieces of artillery, thirteen flags, and about seventeen hundred prisoners.

On the morning of the 7th we pushed forward to the Appomattox, which we crossed at High bridge. The enemy had set fire to the railroad bridge at that point, and were making an effort to destroy the wagon bridge, when Barlow's Second Division reached the ground. Barlow's men advanced at a double-quick and drove the enemy away, saving the wagon bridge. Four spans at the north end of the railroad bridge were burned, but the balance was saved, General Humphries says, "chiefly by the efforts of Colonel Livermore and his party, who put out the fire while the enemy were skirmishing under their feet."

After crossing the Appomattox we took a road leading to the northwest, and which runs into the old Lynchburg stage-road about four miles north of Farmville, thus leaving Farmville to our left. Barlow's Division, however, continued up the railroad toward that place.

About one o'clock we struck a large force of the enemy entrenched near the old stage-road. It was afterward ascertained that nearly all that remained of Lee's army was concentrated there. Our lines were kept pressed up close to the enemy, and heavy skirmishing continued through the afternoon and into the night.

One Southern writer, speaking of how closely they were pressed on this occasion, says: "The enemy seemed to be ubiquitous; the firing increased in rapidity and extent, until three sides were at once set upon by the enemy. I never was so bewildered as on this occasion."

Preparations were made for an attack in the morning, but when the morning of the 8th dawned it was found that Lee had again retreated.

About 6:30 we again took up the pursuit by way of the Lynchburg stage-road. We passed New Store about sundown. About two miles beyond we halted for a rest. After a rest of a couple of hours the column was again put in motion and continued the march until after midnight, when we bivouacked. Having marched in all about twenty-six miles, being without food, the men were nearly exhausted.

Negotiations for the surrender of Lee's army had been pending since the evening of the 7th, when Grant's first letter was sent by General Humphries through the lines near Farmville.

When we halted at midnight on the 8th, Longstreet's troops were less than three miles in advance of us.

The supply-trains reached us on the morning of the 9th, and after rations were issued the column was again put in motion. The head of the corps soon came within sight of the enemy, and preparations for an attack were being made when a truce was called. It was then about eleven o'clock.

The hours dragged slowly along; anxiety was intense. Every man knew that the truce indicated a continuance of the negotiations for surrender and that the end could not be long delayed. Every man was on the *qui vive* for news. If an officer came galloping from the direction of the enemy, the men would say excitedly, "Here comes news; now we'll know!" and when he passed by with no announcement of surrender, every countenance would drop.

Torn with hopes and fears, the hours passed slowly away until four o'clock came. Then from the direction of Lee's army came, at a rapid gallop, a group of officers. As they drew near, Meade, bare-headed, with his hair streaming in the wind and wildly waving his cap, was seen in advance. Every man was quickly on his feet. As the commander of the Army of the Potomac dashed past, he cried out: "Lee has surrendered! Lee has surrendered!"

Instantly the wildest excitement prevailed. The feelings that had been so long suppressed burst forth in the wildest cheers. Guns were fired and caps darkened the air. Officers were called upon and compelled to speak, but could scarcely be heard, for every patriotic sentiment elicited the wildest applause. The artillery began to boom as if a battle were raging; but soon *its* voice was silenced for fear its tones, sounding of joy instead of carnage, would lacerate the sensitive feelings of the conquered.

It was late in the night when the camp settled down to quietness, and calmer thought brought a full realization of what the surrender of Lee's army meant to us. It meant an end to the bitter struggle that had sown our land with the graves of our noblest and best; that had brought sorrow to thousands of home-circles and clothed tens of thousands in the habiliments of mourning; that had bent the proud head of the father and silvered the dark tresses of the mother; that had ravished the roses from the cheek of the maiden and stifled the joyous laughter of children; that had filled the country and towns with men maimed and crippled by the stroke of the weapon or broken and shattered by disease; that had left desolate ruins where once stood happy homes. It meant peace—peace in its full, broad significance; peaceful nights, with no shot of picket or shriek of shell to break our slumber; no bray of bugle or rattle of drum to call us hurriedly to arms; days undisturbed by the roll of musketry or the thunder of cannon, with no dread of assault or enemy in ambush; no more long marches through dust or mud—through stifling heat or pinching cold, with blistered feet and aching limbs. It meant rest, and finally—home!

Two days previous to breaking camp for the final campaign men were detailed from the regiment to accompany the supply-train. The men detailed from Company E were A. B. Searing and Lambert Sharp, better known as " Bully." " Bully " was one of the most incorrigible foragers in the regiment, and he did not always confine his operations to property belonging to the enemy. After his first night's duty at brigade headquarters he returned to camp bringing three canteens of whiskey. It was not until the boys had drank freely of it that they asked how he obtained it, well knowing that it was not by any usual method. The answer, if true, was not very assuring to sensitive stomachs. He told them that he had bored a hole in the barrel, sucked it out with a straw, and then transferred it to the canteen.

Molasses, when it could be procured, was thought to add a desirable flavor to hard-tack. When passing New Store a barrel with its head knocked out stood on the roadside. " Molasses, molasses," ran along the line, and tin-cups were quickly loosened from haversacks. As the barrel was reached cups made a hurried dip, but you can imagine the strength of the language used when, instead of Porto Rico, it was found to be tar!

Any lover of tobacco who passed through Farmville had no need to want, for it was found there in abundance, and in almost every form then known to the manufacturers of the weed. Our trains passed through the town, and some of the wagons being empty, Sharp, with his usual enterprise, loaded on a goodly supply of tobacco, which he generously distributed among his comrades in the company as soon as he met with them.

Before resuming the account of our return from Appomattox to Burksville Junction, and from Burksville Junction to Washington and on to Trenton, we will take up Lieutenant William Hand's narrative of his service with the supply-trains during this last and memorable campaign of the Army of the Potomac.

On February 1st, '65, Lieutenant William Hand, then of Company I, was detailed as Acting-quartermaster of the

Eleventh New Jersey, which position he retained until the regiment was mustered out of service. After receiving this appointment, however, Lieutenant Hand participated in two of the battles in which the regiment was engaged—at Hatcher's run February 5th, and the Armstrong house, already noted, March 25th, '65.

Lieutenant W. H. Egan.

Lieutenant Hand says: "From April 3d to the 9th we were constantly on the move. We started with six good fat mules to each wagon, but before the surrender of Lee they were nearly all worn-out. We used all kinds of devices to keep them going. Every day we would make the loads of two or three wagons as light as possible and send them on ahead to issue rations to the men. Then they would have a chance to rest until the train came up, when those teams would be put to heavy loads and the tired mules to the lighter wagons and sent forward again. We did the best we could to keep the men in rations, but it was very difficult, as the men were marching day and night and our mules were fast giving out with constant work and no rest. We threw out everything that we could do without, and pressed into service everything in the shape of a horse or mule that we could find. It was a common thing to see quartermasters and sergeants and wagon-masters tugging at wheels or unloading and loading wagons to get them out of the mud. Sometimes we would put two or three teams to one wagon, pull it out of a mud-hole or over a hill, and then go for another.

"I was sent to the front one day with rations. We loaded wagons as light as we could, and, putting six of our best mules to each, started on the jump to overtake the men. We reached them about sundown and issued the rations. They were then ordered to make themselves comfortable for the night, but before they had time to make their coffee, another order was received directing every one to press forward at once, and engage the enemy wherever and whenever he was found, without waiting for additional orders. 'For,' the order stated, 'General Lee will surely surrender to-morrow if he is pressed.' He was pressed, and surrendered.

"Our train was at Farmville when the surrender took place. We were ordered immediately back to Burksville Junction.

"Our train started on the morning of the 10th of April, but I was detailed to remain in Farmville in charge of a large quantity of ammunition that was taken from the wagons to make them lighter. I was to wait for some empty wagons that were at the front issuing rations; on their return I was to bring the ammunition in them. We expected them about ten o'clock in the morning, so I kept no rations for myself, nor horse. I waited all day until dark, then I saw army headquarters come into Farmville, and I reported to the Quartermaster-General. He referred me to Major Johns, who told me that all the wagons were loaded heavily with captured guns and equipments, and that there was no possibility of taking our ammunition. So I left it there and started for Burksville. It was very dark, the road was as bad as a road can get, and I had never been that way before, but I thought my horse would naturally follow the road the wagons had gone.

"It was a dreary, dismal ride, and I was entirely alone. Several times I had to get down and feel for the tracks of the wagons to make sure that I was on the right road. At last I reached Burksville and found our wagons. Under one of them, asleep on the ground, were my two Sergeants, Crisp and Titsworth. It was about daylight, and knowing that 'Ed' would soon be up to take care of my horse I left him standing and crawled in between the two sergeants, and, although I was very hungry, was soon fast asleep. It was the first time in eleven days that I had had an opportunity to take off my shoes and go to sleep right. Even then I was not allowed to sleep long—I was called up at eight o'clock for breakfast, my sergeants having invited me to breakfast with them. And how I did eat! They had some good steak and coffee; I thought it was the best that I had ever tasted. After breakfast I went to sleep and slept the remainder of the day.

"That evening the regiment came and the line officers with whom I usually messed set 'Kate' to work cooking a big kettle of beans. As they were cooking, each officer began to season them to suit his own taste, until at last, with so many bosses, the beans were about spoiled. Then Captain Smith capped the climax, as he usually did, by stirring them with a big bar of soap. So we had no beans that night. Then, to change the program, we sat down and played euchre for sutler's goods. We soon had Lieutenant Rockhill elected for twenty-seven dollars' worth, and we voted that he should purchase that amount for supper, which he did, and we had a royal supper—without beans.

"Among other things that had been thrown out to lighten the wagons was a Dutch oven belonging to Colonel Schoonover.

He felt very badly over the loss of it, and scolded me for throwing it out. I promised to get him another, and rode out in the country to look for one. I found some colored people using one in a large farm-house—there were no white people on the plantation. I offered to buy the oven, but the boss darkey said they 'couldn't spar it no how.' I offered a dollar, then two, and so on up to five, but he would not sell. I thought Colonel Schoonover's comfort was of more importance to me than theirs, especially as I was only acting quartermaster and we had a long march before us to Washington. If the Colonel appointed another Quartermaster I would have to march. If I retained my position I would have a horse to ride, so I must have that oven; and, as I could not buy it, I confiscated it. I just dumped the contents on the table and took it to camp and presented it to the Colonel.

"About this time we met an intelligent contraband who wanted to come North. We engaged him to assist our cook, black our shoes, keep our tents in order and make himself generally useful. He wanted to know what we were willing to pay for his services. Captain Smith suggested that if we fed and clothed him $100 per week would be about the right figure, and as no one objected, he thought that he was properly installed into a good job at a pretty fair income. After a while he began to look around for some money, but he never could seem to meet the particular officer whose duty it was to pay the assistant cook for that particular week. There was a good many of us, and somehow he always tackled the wrong one. The one he wanted to see always happened to be absent when he wanted to see him; or, if he found him, it was not his week for paying the assistant cook. We brought him along to Trenton and left him there, but he never could learn the proper method of collecting an assistant cook's salary.

"While we were in camp at Burksville a new horse was drawn for the use of the adjutant. He was a beautiful dappled-gray, but he was a bad one, and the adjutant could not ride him.

"One day Adjutant Berry was sick and Lieutenant Alonzo Merritt was acting. He had about enough commissary aboard to make him feel very brave, so he brought out the gray horse 'to show him,' as he said, 'who was adjutant.' Then we had a circus. Merritt was very sorry that he happened to be adjutant before he got through. It was great amusement for the men, but hard on Merritt and his clothing. He received many a fall before he gave it up, but he failed to convince the horse that *he* really was adjutant.

"Captain Gage afterward trained him and made him quite gentle. Then I exchanged with Adjutant Berry, he taking my black horse and I the gray. I was very proud of him, but on the road from Richmond to Fredericksburg he suddenly became very lame and I was obliged to leave him. I took my saddle and bridle on my back and for about half a day trudged along on foot, being a subject for laughter from every quartermaster and sergeant on the road. At last I met a sergeant who had captured a bony-looking specimen, apparently about twenty or thirty years old and weighing about five hundred pounds. I thought he might carry me until I could get something better, so I bought him for thirty dollars. I found out afterward that he was only four years old, and after he had been fed awhile and got strong he could outrun any horse in the regiment. I brought him home and sold him for ninety dollars, and he was afterward sold for two hundred and fifty.

"In passing through Richmond on our way back to Washington, I, in company with other quartermasters, rode about the city, visited Belle Isle, Libby Prison and other places of interest, and talked with many people along the streets. Most of the people with whom we talked told us that at the time General McClellan first appeared before Richmond there was nothing in the world to prevent his taking the city; that everything was prepared for evacuating it and that the Confederate army and the people were greatly surprised when it was learned that he was falling back.

"On our way we crossed the old battle-field of Fredericksburg, and we then saw how very difficult it would have been for General Burnside to have taken the heights. In looking down from the position occupied by the Confederates, the wonder seemed to be how the Union army got so far as they did without losing more men—though God knows it lost enough.

"When we left Washington for Trenton an opportunity presented itself—and I could not resist the temptation—to get even with a wagonmaster who had refused me a ride nearly three years before, when I was very sick. I was in charge of the transportation and I had provided a car for the officers, one for the non-commissioned officers, and the remainder of the train for the private soldiers.

"Our wagonmaster was making himself comfortable with the non-com's, when I ordered him out and told him to go with the soldiers. I would have liked to have made him walk had I had the authority.

"When we reached Trenton we did not meet with as enthusiastic a reception as some other regiments had received, and the men felt somewhat disappointed. One day, as I was passing from camp to my boarding-house, I saw Jimmie Butler, of Company B, throwing water from the canal to the bank as fast as he could with his cap. I asked him what he was doing. He said he was going to flood the city and drown them all because they had not entertained us as they should. But, fortunately, before we left the city the ladies gave us a handsome collation and saved the city from destruction by flood."

Chapter XIX.

Our Return March—Burksville—Washington—The Grand Review—Trenton—Mustered Out.

ON April 10th we began our return March, acting as rearguard to the artillery. We reached Burksville Junction at four P. M. on the 14th. Many members of the late Army of Northern Virginia accompanied us on the march, and while many expressed delight at the termination of the war, others were extremely bitter and made many foolish boasts of what they would yet do.

At Burksville camps were laid out and preparations made for a few weeks' rest or a march southward to meet Sherman's army, as circumstances might dictate.

The spirit of content and satisfaction that follows a consciousness of duty well done, a task faithfully performed, pervaded the entire army. The glow of joy and hope beamed from every face, when suddenly the news came that President Lincoln had been assassinated, and the army was plunged into mourning. Each felt as if he had lost a personal friend, one in whom he had reposed the supremest confidence—and, indeed, such was Lincoln to every true soldier of the Union. The humblest private in the ranks, had he a grievance, had he met with injustice, felt that if the matter could be brought to "Uncle Abe's" attention he would meet with justice; but justice tempered with mercy. The news at first engendered bitter feelings toward our conquered foe. But calmer thought and the evidently sincere regrets expressed by many of our late antagonists, convinced us that the death of our noble chief was looked upon by the better class of Southern people as a new calamity.

On the 19th the entire brigade assembled to hear an obituary sermon upon the late President. The brigade flags at half-mast, the regimental standards draped, the muffled drums and low booming of minute-guns told of an army in mourning.

While in camp at Burksville, a number of our old members, who had been absent sick or as prisoners, re-joined the regiment. Among them was Sergeant Alpheus Iliff, of Company E, who had been captured on the 10th of May, '64, at Spottsylvania. He had been reported missing, and his family mourned him as one dead. It was therefore a surprise to his comrades to learn that for seven months he had been suffering the tortures of Andersonville and Florence. He was the only prisoner from Company E who was taken as far south as Andersonville who returned to tell of his sufferings.

On Tuesday, May 2d, we broke camp at Burksville and turned our faces northward. After a march of about eleven miles we encamped for the night between Jettersville and Amelia Court House.

After an early breakfast on the morning of the 3d, we resumed our journey. Passing Amelia Court House, we marched to the Appomattox river, which we crossed on pontoons, and halted for the night a short distance beyond.

The extreme heat on the 4th made the march a very fatiguing one, and quite a number were overcome by the heat. The line of march led through a fine agricultural country, which showed comparatively few marks of war's devastation. White inhabitants were not so scarce as they had been along the lines of some of our previous marches, but could often be seen curiously watching the passage of the columns of blue. One old gentleman gave expression to his amazement by exclaiming, "You Yanks must have a right smart heap of men." At sundown we halted for the night.

The rain was falling heavily on the morning of the 5th, but notwithstanding we were early on the way, and at noon reached Manchester, opposite Richmond. Here Major Halsey re-joined us, having been absent sick, and took command of the regiment, Colonel Schoonover being absent on leave.

We lay near Manchester until Saturday, the 6th, when we marched through the town and down to the James river, which we crossed on pontoons, the bridges having been burned by the enemy when they evacuated the city. The line of march led by Libby Prison, the scene of so much suffering and cruelty, also by "Castle Thunder," almost as notorious, and through some of the principal streets and past the capitol, on the steps of which stood Generals Meade and Halleck. The colored population gave us a joyous welcome, but the whites looked sullen and disappointed. We soon left the city behind and encamped for the night near Mechanicsville.

We were off again at an early hour next day, crossed the Chickahominy, passed Hanover Court House and did not stop for the night until the Pamunkey had been left two miles behind us.

The night of the 8th we bivouacked on a plantation owned by James Lucknow, and the evening of the 9th found us on the border of Spottsylvania county.

Early dawn of May 10th found us again on the march. Crossing the Ta river we marched through the village of Thornburg and continued the route by way of the Massaponax church to near Fredericksburg. Our march led us across the rivers Ta, Po and Ny, which with the southern branch, the Mat, united form the Mattapony river.

At eight A. M. on the 11th we again fell into line. Marching through Fredericksburg we crossed the Rappahannock on pontoons to Falmouth, and took the road to Hartwood church, near which well-remembered locality we halted for the night.

Our route on May 12th was over a very rough road to Cedar run, over which we were ferried in a pontoon boat, thence to Broad run, which we forded. The march was kept up until near midnight, when we halted near the Orange and Alexandria railroad.

On the 13th we marched to three miles beyond Fairfax Court House, by way of Manassas Junction and Centerville, fording, on the way, Silver run, Kettle run and Bull Run river.

The 14th, being the Sabbath, we were given a day's rest. Chaplain Cline held service under the shade of a large apple tree. Colonel Schoonover returned and resumed command of the regiment.

At two o'clock on the afternoon of the 15th we moved on again, and after a march of about eight miles went into camp near Four-mile run, where we remained until orders came to start for home.

Though the war was over, and no enemy menaced us, yet for some inexplicable reason the march from Burksville Junction to near Washington had been pushed with as much vigor as if the fate of the nation depended upon our reaching a certain point at a given hour. Through rain and mud, dust and heat, early and late, the march was kept up, to the extreme limit of endurance and beyond, for, in fact, men who had escaped the deadly missiles of the enemy on hard-fought fields, met death from sun-stroke on this homeward march, over roads where no enemy lurked in ambush or disputed our way from well-manned earthworks.

Who was to blame I cannot say. Certainly the government was not so penurious as to hasten, in this manner, the discharge of the men who had served it so long and faithfully.

A rumor was current at the time that a wager existed between the staff officers of the Second and Fifth Corps as to which should first reach its place of destination. If the rumor was true those responsible should have been severely punished.

Both corps left Richmond on May 6th, and from there to Fredericksburg their routes were nearly identical. But from there on the Fifth had much the shortest route, it going direct to the Occoquan at Wolf Run Shoals, and thence to their place of encampment, while the Second Corps, as has been shown, diverged northward by way of the Hartwood Church to the Orange and Alexandria Railroad, and then by way of Centerville and Fairfax Court House.

On Sunday, May 21st, Chaplain Cline delivered a very touching sermon. He recalled with much feeling our long association, the difficulties under which we had often met to worship God—sometimes in the trenches, where the deep voice of the cannon and the sharp crack of the rifle mingled with the voice of prayer and praise. He exhorted all to "become as faithful soldiers for Christ as they had been for country."

The 22d was spent in polishing-up for the grand review.

On the 23d occurred the grand review of the Army of the Potomac. At seven A. M. we left camp and marched across the long bridge and up through the city to the east of the capitol, where we remained until nine o'clock, when the signal for the column to move was given. The line of march led up Pennsylvania avenue. The sidewalks were thronged with citizens, whose enthusiasm knew no bounds. All along the line of march the heartiest cheers greeted us, while from nearly every window flags and handkerchiefs were waving; flowers were scattered in profusion, so that nearly every soldier carried a bouquet in the muzzle of his musket. On the steps of public buildings were grouped the children of the public schools, who sang patriotic songs as we marched by. Theirs were the first childish voices that many of us had heard for nearly three years, and the sweet tones of their voices echoing above the strains of martial music seemed to us a guarantee of peace and home. As we passed the reviewing stand occupied by President Johnson, Generals Grant, Meade and others, someone proposed three cheers for the officers and men of the Eleventh New Jersey, and they were given with a will. In many places banners were displayed bearing the motto, "The public schools of Washington welcome the heroes of the Republic. The only National debt we can never pay is the debt we owe to the victorious Union soldiers."

After passing the reviewing stand the march was continued to Georgetown, where we re-crossed the Potomac on a pontoon bridge laid just below the aqueduct; then through Arlington to camp, which we reached thoroughly tired-out with the day's march and excitement.

On May 25th the camp was visited by Mrs. General McAllister and daughter, Mrs. Dr. Welling, Dr. Kirk and wife, Hon. Marcus L. Ward, Hon. John Hill and others. In the evening the camp of the Fifth and Second Corps, occupying opposite positions, were brilliantly illuminated.

On the 30th we marched to Bailey's cross-roads, where the corps was reviewed by many distinguished officers, both civil and military, among whom were President Johnson, Secretary Stanton, Generals Meade, Hancock and Humphries, Admiral Farragut and others.

We had not been many days in camp near Washington before the knowledge of our presence reached the camp of the convalescents, situated near by, and the various hospitals in and contiguous to Washington, and men who had been absent for months, some because of wounds and sickness and others for unexplained reasons, began to report back to their commands, all anxious to accompany the regiment and be with it when it should report back to the State.

Every regiment had a class of men who, while apparently healthy, would manage in some way to get back to hospitals or convalescent camps and remain there for months, or eventually get transferred to the veteran reserve corps. Only those skilled in that system of soldiering knew of the methods employed to win the favor of the surgeons in charge so as to be reported month after month as unfit for duty. Doubtless they made themselves useful in some capacity, but a capacity that could have been filled by those less fitted to stand the rigors of campaigning. The aggregate of this class of men would have made a respectable army as to size, but hardly as to courage, and perhaps it was a wise provision to keep them in the rear, as they would have been only a detriment to the brave boys in front. Some of this class, who had been absent so long that they had been dropped from the rolls, came walking into camp as smilingly and as self-conscious as if their individual exertions had brought about the final end of the war, and only that the war was ended, and no good purpose could be served by their punishment, were they allowed to escape.

One afternoon during our march northward from Fredericksburg we encountered one of the most terrific thunder-storms that we had met during all our experience as soldiers. The thunder rolled like volleys of artillery, and the vivid electric sparks leaped from gun to gun till the regiment at times seemed to be marching through sheets of flame. To add to the consternation, a team attached to one of our baggage-wagons was struck, and, I think, the entire team killed. While the storm was still raging we were ordered to go into bivouac. We managed to put up tents, but they were almost useless, for the beating rain came through them as though they were sieves, and streams poured underneath. To lie down was impossible, so we huddled beneath our rubber blankets as best we could and waited for the storm to pass.

As we approached Washington, and long before we came in sight of the dome of the capitol, venders of pies, cakes, bread and the various luxuries to which we had long been strangers, began to meet us. They scented the prey from afar, and knowing how lavish soldiers were with money, calculated to return with empty wagons but well-filled pocket-books. If so, one who pulled out along the road as the Eleventh was passing, returned to Washington a sadly disappointed man. Peering into the wagon one of our men discovered that it was loaded with what the boys denominated soft bread, in contradistinction to hard-tack. As usual, it was in sheets of eight or twelve loaves. To fix bayonet was but the work of a moment—a rapid charge and a sheet was captured. The movement was quickly followed up, and soon the entire load was marching with the column, and the vender turned his face homeward with a lighter wagon, but not much heavier purse.

Again, while lying in camp, we were visited by another with a load of radishes and onions. He drove into camp, halted, and turned his back to his horse and made ready to deal out green groceries to purchasers. Some one slyly gave the horse a prod with a bayonet which started it off at a double-quick. The huckster, who was leaning against the tail of the wagon, turned one somersault and the wagon, colliding with a stump, another, while radishes and onions flew about promiscuously, to the profit of the boys, who quickly gathered them up.

On the 2d of June General McAllister issued the following farewell order to the officers and men of the old Third Brigade:

"HEADQUARTERS THIRD BRIGADE, THIRD DIVISION,
"SECOND ARMY CORPS,
"*General Order, No.* 10.   June 2d, 1865.
"*To the Officers and Soldiers of the Third Brigade:*

"As we are about to separate, allow me once more to congratulate you upon your past and brilliant career, which now becomes a matter of history. The war is over, the contest ended. The glorious old flag of our country, consecrated by the blood of our fallen heroes—under the folds of which you have so often, so long and so gallantly fought and bled—now floats in triumph all over our land. The war brought us to the field—peace returns us to our homes. Our work is done, and we go to enjoy with our friends in the several States represented in this command the fruits of our victory. New York, New Jersey and Massachusetts have an interest in you as their representatives, and will do full justice to the old Third Brigade. In parting with you I feel more than I can express or language convey. We shared each other's dangers, toils and fatigues on the march, in the battle, in the charge, with victory or defeat. Ties of more than an ordinary kind bind us together. Good-bye, comrades in arms; God bless you and the widows and orphans of those who have fallen by our sides, and if we never meet again on earth may we meet in a brighter and better world.

"ROBERT MCALLISTER,
"J. P. FINKLEMAIER,   *Brig. Genl.*
"*A. A. G.*"

On Sunday, June 4th, Chaplain Cline preached his last sermon to the Eleventh Regiment south of the Potomac. It was, in fact, his farewell talk to the men with whom he had been identified for nearly two years and for whose welfare he had worked so earnestly. It was a touching effort, eloquent with reminiscences of the camp and the march, the battle and hospital.

Between twelve and one o'clock on the morning of the 7th of June we were notified that transportation had been procured and that we would start for home at four A. M. There was no more sleep that night, and tents were struck and knapsacks packed long before morning. The recruits who had served but a short time were notified that they had been transferred to and consolidated with the new men of the Twelfth, and would have to report to that regiment. The most of them received the news calmly, for they knew that the war was over and at the farthest their stay would be for only a few weeks. But one Joseph Lee,

The above cut shows the effects of a bullet from the rebel lines upon a Testament in the pocket of Sergeant Thomas Blackwood, of Company C. Sergeant Blackwood now resides in Trenton, New Jersey, and still has in his possession this highly-prized book.

a drafted man belonging to Company E, was very anxious to get home, and could not believe that he was to be left behind. He was assured by his comrades that he would have to remain, but he would not believe them. Going to Sergeant Marbaker he asked if it was true that he could not go home with the regiment. The Sergeant told him that it was, but assured him that he would not have to remain long; that, as the war was ended, the remainder of his stay would be only a picnic. But he could not become reconciled to the idea, and exclaimed: "I'll never get home! I know I'll never get home! I'll die, I'll be d——d if I don't! I'll die, I'll be d——d if I don't!" Though the man's distress was evidently real aud his determination to die pathetic, the men could not help but laugh at his manner of expressing it. He did get home, however, in spite of his expressed determination not to do so, being mustered out with the rest of those transferred to the Twelfth on July 15th. Besides the enlisted men transferred to the Twelfth were several commissioned officers of the Eleventh: Captain T. J. Thompson and Lieutenant U. B. Titus to Company A of that regiment; Lieutenaut E. White to Company C; Lieutenant George H. Johnson to Company D, promoted to first lieutenant of Company B June 24th, and Second Lieutenant Watson P Tuttle to Company I of the Twelfth.

At four o'clock on the morning of the 7th of June, '65, we turned our backs upon our last encampment south of the Potomac, crossed the long bridge for the last time as soldiers, marched past the capitol and to the Soldiers' Rest, where we breakfasted. A train of box-cars stood ready to receive us. We climbed on board and waited. Slowly the hours dragged away, and no movement. "Are we never going to start?" is the cry. At last, about two o'clock in the afternoon, we pulled out for the North. The box-cars were stifling, and all who could climbed on top. At Baltimore there was a long delay, but at last we were again under way. We passed through Wilmington and reached Philadelphia about two o'clock on the morning of the 8th, stacked arms on Otsego street and breakfasted at the Volunteer refreshment saloon. Stretched across the street near the saloon was a large flag bearing the motto, "The City of Brotherly Love Welcomes with Hearty Cheer the Returning Braves." And here let me say that during the long years of war no city in the Union did more—if as much—for the soldier than did the City of Brotherly Love. No worthy Union soldier had need to go hungry upon her streets or want for a place to lay his head. The hands of her inhabitants seemed never to grow weary of ministering to his comfort, and their purses were ever open to supply his wants.

After daylight we marched to the ferry and crossed to Camden, where our feet pressed again the soil of our native State. After some delay we again boarded the cars for Trenton, which was reached about nine A. M. We left the cars on East Canal street, below State, and forming into line were marched up State street to the capitol, where we very impatiently listened to speeches by Governor Parker and General McAllister, after which we were marched down to Camp Bayard.

Camp Bayard was situated on Coleman street, Chambersburg, (now a part of the city of Trenton). It contained a large brick building, then used as a barracks (now as a cracker bakery). The building and parade-ground were inclosed with a high board-fence, with the gates or "sally-port" on Coleman street. Guards were placed all around the camp and orders issued to permit no one to go out without a pass. The men paid but little attention to the order. For nearly three years they had been amenable to discipline, had submitted to orders that they had sometimes thought unjust, and all without grumbling or a sign of insubordination, but now that they were practically at home, the war over, and no real necessity existing for such strict orders, they looked upon them as an unwarranted stretch of authority. Many of them lived in the city, but a few minutes' walk from camp; others had homes but an hour or two's ride away, and they did not feel like submitting quietly to being penned-up day after day. As a consequence, though no demonstration was made, the camp was deserted by all who lived within easy reach of home. Some of the guards had even placed their guns in their quarters and wandered off. The writer had charge of the guard on the sally-port. Home was only sixteen miles away—he had not seen it for three years—should he stay in camp over night? No; the temptation was too strong. Turning the guard over to a friend (Sergeant George W. Lindley) he reported to Captain Gage that he was going home. The captain suggested that he had better have a pass and gave him one; but, pass or no pass, home would have been reached that night. That was the feeling of the majority, and guards were practically useless. On returning to camp, Lindley informed the writer that his guards had nearly all left him before morning. Those who remained in camp on the 9th were treated to a fine collation by the ladies of the city. The next day the following card appeared in the "State Gazette":

"CAMP BAYARD, June 10th, 1865.

"*Editor State Gazette:*

"DEAR SIR—I desire, through the columns of your paper, to return the thanks of the members of the Eleventh and Twelfth Regiments to Mrs. M. Whittaker, Mrs. Waufold, Mrs. Willet Dunn, Mrs. Robert S. Johnson, Mrs. Captain Corey, Miss Martha Young, the Misses Buckman, and Mr. George James, for the splendid repast given us at camp on Friday evening. This act of kindness is duly appreciated and will be long remembered.

"JOHN SCHOONOVER,
"*Bvt. Col. Commanding.*"

On the 13th a dinner was given to the Eleventh and Twelfth Regiments in Bechtel's Hall on Front street. Speeches were made by Governor Parker, Hon. Marcus L. Ward, General McAllister, Colonel Schoonover, Mayor Mills and others.

We lay in Camp Bayard a week, awaiting our pay. Though our discharges had not been given us, they had been made out and dated the 6th, on which date we were mustered out of the service of the United States. We were no longer under pay and the men were anxious to reach their homes and again take up the duties of citizenship. The delay may have been necessary, but the men could not understand it and grew very impatient. Several times a date had been set for payment, but the time would pass by without any sign of receiving it. On the afternoon of the 14th, without consulting with officers, nearly two hundred men of the Eleventh and Twelfth formed in line and marched up to the State House to ascertain *just when* they were to be paid Being assured that it would not be later than the next afternoon, they quietly marched back to camp. On the afternoon of the 15th, at 2 o'clock, we marched up Broad street, signed the rolls, received pay and discharges and once more became citizens of the State of New Jersey.

Chapter XX.

Account of the Imprisonment of Corporal Aaron Lines, of Company B.

Aaron Lines, of Company B, was captured by Ewell's men on October 14th, 1863, during the retreat from Culpepper—the movement familiarly known as "the race." A short time previous to this movement he had made application to be transferred to the cavalry—as a weakness of the chest made him fear that he would not be able to bear the strain of long marches. But his application was refused, the Adjutant saying that such men as he could not be spared from the regiment. His fears proved true, for during the hurried movement back to Centerville heights he was compelled to fall out, and, as stated, was picked up by Ewell. He was taken to the rear, as Ewell was forming for the attack upon Warren at Bristow. As he was passing through the rebel lines Ewell, who was sitting on his horse near by, asked him how many corps we had in there. Lines answered, "I do not know." He was turned over to a lieutenant in command of the rebel provost-guard and put with a squad of other prisoners who had been picked up on the march. As the rebel lines advanced the prisoners were also moved forward and kept but a short distance in rear of their line of battle, so close that during the engagement they were under fire from the Union guns. During the temporary absence of the lieutenant in command, a major, with an Irish orderly, rode up and dismounted. They were followed by about fifty dilapidated "Johnnies" on foot. The major, with foul oaths, commanded the prisoners to take off their shoes. The order was very reluctantly obeyed. Lines, who had on a very good pair, hesitated until the major in person approached him and ordered him to take them off. He asked if that was the way they treated prisoners of war. "Yes," replied the major, "this is the way we treat you d— Yankees, who come down here to rob us and burn our homes." Lines answered,

"Perhaps I may some time see you a prisoner." That made the representative of chivalry so angry that he reached for his revolver. Lines, without further hesitation, took off the shoes and handed them over. About that time the lieutenant returned, and was seemingly very indignant at the major's treatment of the prisoners, and threatened to have him placed under arrest. But the major expressed his willingness to assume all responsibility, and the dialogue ended. The shoes were quickly appropriated by the waiting crowd, who in turn threw their old ones to the prisoners; but many of them were left on the ground, as they were not worth picking up.

When Lee's army turned to retrace their steps the prisoners, now barefooted, were marched ahead, through woods and ravines, over stones, briars and bushes. Their feet soon became so lacerated and swollen that it was almost impossible to rest their weight upon them. But still they had to press on, keeping pace with the mounted guard. Some gave out and died by the wayside. They were nearly starved, but no rations were given them until they reached the Rappahannock. They forded the river and were hurried on through our old camp to Culpepper and the Rapidan.

Lines says: "I cannot find words to describe my feelings, either mental or physical. I am no longer craving something to eat. I reel as I go; the bottoms of my feet are scoured with the mud and gravel until they are perfectly raw; my legs seem paralyzed! When I get warmed up I experience the most excruciating pains from the ends of my toes to the hip-joints! How can I endure it? I seize a stick from the roadside to help hold myself up, and, by grasping it with both hands, I relieve somewhat the weight from my feet!"

They reached the Rapidan after dark and were placed on board of cars and taken to Richmond, where they arrived in the day-time. As they were marched up to Libby, men called from the upper stories, "You have come to h—l; if you have any money hide it!" They were packed in so closely that when they lay down they had to lie partly across each other. After three or four days had passed, and after clothing and persons were thoroughly searched for money, Lines, with a number of others, was sent to Belle Isle. The lower part of the island, toward Richmond, was nearly covered with dilapidated Sibley tents. These were crowded full of prisoners, but were not sufficient to accommodate near the numbers that were collected there. Those unfortunate enough to be crowded out had to stand the inclemencies of the weather as best they could. Autumn passed and the icy-blasts of winter began to sweep over the island, chilling to the bone the half-clad, unprotected men. No wood was given to those in tents, and not until some had died from exposure to the cold was any given to those who were without shelter, and then it was issued in such small quantities that it was practically useless. Had it been equally divided among the whole number it would have amounted to a stick about the size of a man's fore-arm per capita each day. The rations were ferried over from Richmond, and consisted of about four or five ounces of bread, a microscopic piece of pork, a pint of water colored with about a tablespoonful of boiled peas (called soup), and occasionally a little molasses or sorghum. So hungry would the prisoners become that they would stand for hours upon the river-bank straining their eyes to catch a glimpse of the boat that was to bring them temporary relief. Many were without blankets—Lines was fortunate enough to have kept his—but there was none to spare to put under them, and they were compelled to lie upon the frozen earth. After a few minutes of such repose the side next the ground would be nearly paralyzed with cold. All night long men could be heard double-quicking up and down through the camp to keep from freezing. Upon one occasion it was so cold that a cup of water that Lines had placed near him froze solid and cracked open on the top during the night. Many had their hands and feet frozen. Clothing was sent through the lines by the United States Government, but those that received it almost immediately traded it to the guards for food, being better able to stand the piercing stings of frost than the gnawing pangs of hunger.

Lines, when captured, had a pair of home-made stockings which had been sent him by his mother but a short time before. These, with leather sewed upon the bottoms, constituted the only foot-covering he had for nearly a year. It was rumored that thousands of rations had been sent through the lines for the prisoners by the United States Government, but if so the only portion of it received by Lines was a piece of pork about half an inch thick and two and a half inches square and a few crackers, about one-half a ration as issued to the Union soldier.

Around the upper part of the camp at Belle Isle was built a breastwork about four feet high; the guards were placed outside of that, and, as at Andersonville and other places of confinement for Union prisoners, they appeared to take delight in shooting anyone who went anywhere near the so-called dead-line; they seemed to shoot through mere wantonness or love of bloodshed.

No people of modern times, and no civilized people of any time, have exhibited more brutality in their treatment of helpless prisoners of war than did those of the South in charge of the various prison-pens during the late war of the rebellion. That prisoners should sometimes have gone without a sufficient supply of food in a land that was taxed to its utmost to furnish food enough for its armies and inhabitants could be excused, but that they should have gone shelterless and fireless in a land rich in timber cannot be overlooked. There was no excuse for their being deprived of proper facilities for cleanliness and being compelled to use water poisoned by the fetid drainage of cesspools, in a land ribboned with pure streamlets and deep-flowing rivers.

It is the right of all prisoners of war to escape if possible, and for their captors to re-take them if they can, but it is not the right of any civilized people to hunt men with bloodhounds, like beasts of prey, and stand by rejoicing while the savage brutes tear and lacerate unarmed and emaciated captives. It was not their right to punish men—who were only flying from almost certain death by starvation—with the stocks, beneath a burning sun, until over-burdened nature gave way and death came to their relief, nor to place iron collars around the necks of honorable soldiers and cords upon their thumbs and tie them up so that only their toes touched the earth, and leave them for twelve hours to suffer the most excruciating tortures, so that when cut down they fell a mass of helpless quivering flesh upon the ground. Words cannot describe the various tortures, the untold and untellable miseries that Union soldiers were subjected to in the prison hells of the South, commanded as they were by monsters and guarded by brutes. Time will not erase the blot from Southern honor, nor eternity be any too long to bleach out the stains made by the flow of the blood of the helpless.

On the 22d of February, '64, a number of prisoners, among whom was Lines, were given three days' rations, which consisted of a cake about nine inches in diameter and two and a half inches thick, made of corn meal. They were then taken from Belle Isle and marched to the railroad, where they were loaded in box-cars, about sixty to a car. They were told that they were to be taken to a point of exchange. But day after day passed and they knew, by the rising temperature, that they were journeying southward. Through the day the doors of the cars were kept slightly open so that the air inside was comparatively pure; but at night they were tightly closed and locked, and the air, breathed over and over, soon became foul and suffocating. The prisoners begged that the doors might be opened only a few inches, but the guards were deaf to entreaties, and though a number died of suffocation before the journey was ended, no change was made in the condition of things.

The journey seemed interminable, suffering as they were from hunger, thirst and want of air. But at last, after being a week upon the way, they reached that inferno of Southern contriving, Andersonville prison-pen.

Andersonville is situated in Sumter county, Georgia, on the Georgia Central railroad, and about sixty miles southwest of Macon. The prison-pen, which, at its largest, contained about twenty-five acres, was surrounded by a stockade of pine logs sixteen feet high, the lower ends firmly imbedded in the ground. The inner fence or dead-line consisted of narrow pine boards nailed to posts. Along the stockade at intervals platforms were built for the guards. Another stockade about six feet high extended around outside, to be used as breastworks in case of an attempted rescue. At the corners earthworks containing cannons were so constructed as to enfilade the sides. Through the center ran a stream, bordered by swamps, toward which the ground pitched from either end. Upstream, outside the stockade, was situated the cook-house, the refuse from which and washings of utensils were thrown into the stream from which the prisoners were compelled to get their water-supply. The water was often coated with a greasy scum so nauseating that only the greatest thirst could induce men to drink it. But this was not the worst. For a long time no conveniences for the men's necessities were provided, and the swamp on either side of the stream became the depositories for human excrement through which the prisoners had to wade to reach the water.

One writer says: "No provision was made until very near the close of our incarceration towards carrying off the refuse or sewage. The filth that accummulated through the long summer months can neither be described nor imagined. Most of it collected in and about the three acres of swamp, and I have seen that three acres one animated mass of maggots, from one to two feet deep, the whole swamp moving and rolling like waves of the sea." (A causeway was afterwards built to the stream.)

At one time near thirty-five thousand men were confined within the inclosure. Some few had tents. Some fortunate enough to have kept their blankets, made shelters of them; some ripped up whatever clothing they could spare and sewed the pieces together to make shelters from the intense heat of the sun. A number of prisoners were sent out to work during the day. On returning they would sometimes bring in slabs of pine from four to five feet long and about eight inches wide. Some of the men would buy or trade for these slabs and with them would construct huts by digging a hole in the ground. A crotched stick would be set up at each end, a ridge-pole laid on and one end of the slabs rested upon the pole and the other on the ground; the slabs would then be covered with earth and one end walled up with mud. This style of building, in the dialect of the prison, would be called a shebang. Others built huts of mud, into which they would crawl like burrowing beasts. But the pen became so crowded that there ceased to be room in the higher part of the ground for even these primitive shelters, and the island in the swamp was also occupied. But there were thousands who were absolutely without shelter from the burning heat of the sun and the beating of the rain (and during the month of June, '64, it rained nearly every day,) and the heavy dews at night. These unfortunates lay around in the little shade cast by the rude structures of their more fortunate comrades. The ground became so impregnated with filth that, after every heavy rain, maggots would issue from it and crawl over the surface. It was impossible to keep clean, as soap was seldom issued; during the ten months only about one-quarter of a pound per man was given, and there was only the greasy water of the run in which to cleanse clothing and persons, consequently the most lothesome of vermin preyed upon their bodies.

The rations consisted of meat and mush, alternated with meat and meal, occasionally stock peas. Sometimes sorghum molasses, one tablespoonful for a ration. It took a week of saving to accumulate enough for a taste. The meat was what was called corned beef, or rancid bacon, a day's ration weighing from two to four ounces. It was often issued so spoiled as to be unfit for food, yet it was greedily devoured by the famishing prisoners. The mush was thrown loosely into wagons and carted to the prisoners, who received it on their blankets, they being about the only receptacles of sufficient size that they possessed. The meal was in sacks, and one pint of meal, or its equivalent in mush, was given for a day's ration. It was a nice point to issue the rations equally and impartially. To facilitate the work there was a commissary appointed for every three hundred men, who drew the rations for that number. They in turn issued them to commissaries representing squads of twenty-five, who issued them to the men. Even then dissensions would arise, for the starving men would quarrel over a crumb and fight for a bone. And, indeed, a bone, even when meatless, was an acquisition.

Lines says he used to start out early every morning hunting bones. After he had found enough to fill the small fruit-can that was his only cooking-utensil, he would break them up and, by boiling, extract what little substance they might contain, thus making a dish of bone-soup; but he was not always successful in getting enough, for many others were engaged in the hunt.

Up to July 1st, '64, the rations were issued raw, and though the surrounding country was heavily timbered, little wood was supplied for cooking purposes. To be sure, squads were sent out, but they returned with little more than enough to supply their personal wants, and any surplus could only be procured by purchase or barter. The stumps that had been left standing when the inclosure was built were hacked entirely away by the knives of the prisoners, and even the roots were dug up and utilized.

Words cannot describe the appearance of the thousands who were compelled to inhabit that place of torment. Men, hollow-eyed and cadaverous with starvation, bearing but little semblance to human beings, dragged their tottering limbs around day after day. Others, too feeble for self-help, with limbs swollen and distorted, and covered with scurvy sores, or rotten with gangrene, worms eating them long ere the breath had left their bodies, lay apathetic, waiting for the end. Did they pray, it was only for speedy death.

But let me turn again to the account given by Lines. "Look any direction and our eyes would meet distressing sights. Men dead and dying, and we could render them no assistance, for it was all that we could do to care for ourselves. Words cannot describe it, as it was during the summer months. From one to three hundred died daily, diarrhœa and scurvy being the prevalent diseases. Scurvy would first appear in the gums, then would follow pains in the legs and arms, the calves of the legs would swell, turn yellow, then black and blue spots would appear, which finally became running sores. The cords of the legs would become so contracted that it was impossible to stand without the aid of a crutch, and then only upon the tips of the toes. I have seen fly-blows in the corners of the eyes and mouths of men before the breath had left their bodies, and the sores upon their persons were filled with maggots. I have helped to take off their clothing and try to wash them when the smell was too horrible to be endured. Under these terrible sufferings the minds of many gave way and they became as groveling idiots.

"One day a man passed me entirely nude; he turned to pass between two brush arbors; a stick passed from one arbor to the other about a foot from the ground; he could easily have stepped over it, but instead he lay down and with great difficulty crept under it. Another, who had lost a leg at Chickamauga, deliberately walked across the dead-line and sat down; his comrades tried to call him back, but he did not heed them, and they dared not go after him; as soon as the guard saw him he took deliberate aim and blew out his brains.

"I did not receive any soap during the thirteen months that I was at Andersonville. Our mothers would not have known us, so dirty were we. It was impossible to keep clean. We were nearly eaten up by vermin—they were in the sand, in the blankets, in fact everywhere; two or three times a day I would strip myself and search every inch of clothing, but it was in vain.

"During the month of August a sudden and terrible thunderstorm arose. It was like a cloud-burst. So heavy a body of water fell that it swelled the small stream until it covered the swamp and swept away a part of the stockade. As the storm began to cease the guards opened with their batteries and sent the shot screaming over our heads. They no doubt thought that we would endeavor to escape through the breach and fired to frighten us. The stockade was quickly repaired. During the height of the storm the lightning, which was incessant, struck in several places, at one place killing a number of men. At one place where it struck—on the east side, between the dead-line and the stockade—a stream of clear water issued from the ground, and continued to run, affording thereafter a plentiful supply of pure water.

"I will leave the scenes of horror within the stockade and turn to those in the so-called hospital. The hospital was an inclosure of about three or four acres, surrounded by a high board-fence. One side rested upon a swamp. Within the inclosure was erected a few tents. The death-rate there was something terrible. I, with twenty-three others, was placed under a strip of canvas stretched over a ridge-pole. In two weeks I was the only one left out of the original twenty-four. But as fast as one would die the vacant place would be filled. The patients all lay upon the ground, except those in the gangrene ward. The stench from that ward was horrible, and could be smelled fifty yards away. The suffering of the patients was beyond my powers of description, and the sights so pitiful that they have remained indelibly impressed upon my memory. Would to God that I had never witnessed them, or that forgetfulness would come and blot out the memory of the many horrible scenes of suffering that I had to look upon while powerless to relieve. I saw one man with gangrene on the side of the neck, the bone and muscles exposed; at last the arteries were eaten off, and death ensued from bleeding. I saw another, with his thigh swollen to the size of a nail-keg, with a hole eaten in it in which I could lay my head. Another, naked while the nurse was treating his sores with nitrate of silver, who seemed to be but a mass of putrid flesh from the crown of his head to the soles of his feet. These are but three cases, and perhaps not the worst that could have been found among the many hundreds of Union soldiers who suffered and died of that terrible malady at Andersonville.

"Out under the stately pines stood the operating tables where day after day the knife and saw were kept busy cutting off decaying members. This method was generally successful, for death followed and brought a permanent cure. I was suffering with scurvy; no sores broke out upon me, but I was racked with excruciating pains and could scarcely move. When but two of

Gettysburg Monument.

us were left of the twenty-four, my comrade and I would crawl down to the edge of the swamp and rub each other with sand, which afforded temporary relief. I found that he was fast sinking, and one morning I found him dead by my side, under the blanket that we had occupied together. I helped to lay him out in the street ready for the dead-wagon. I took from his pocket a knife and tuning-fork, which I still possess, but would gladly return to his friends did I know where to find them. His name has passed from my memory, but I know that he was a member of a Connecticut regiment, and had been captured at Plymouth, North Carolina.

"With the exception that we in the hospital were a little better sheltered we had but few advantages over those in the stockade or pen, for medicines were either not to be had or were given in such small quantities as to be useless. The doctors would pass around mornings to ascertain the nature of the disease. If it was diarrhœa, he would advise the drinking of oak-bark tea, a remedy hard to get in a pine forest. If scurvy, he would prescribe Irish potatoes, if we could get them. Fortunately, I had one dollar and fifty cents which I had obtained by the sale of a bucket. With that I bought one dozen potatoes and ate one a day, raw, and soon got better. As soon as I was able I did what I could to help those who were helpless. Among them was a boy of sixteen who lay dying upon the cold, damp ground. He was entirely helpless, and at his request I would frequently turn him over that, by a change of position, he might get a little ease; but so sore was his body that he would cry like a little child when touched.

"Oh, what pitiful sights! And though years have passed and my eyes fill with tears when I recall them, I still seem to see the death-dews gathering upon the brows of the dying and hear the vain but pitiful cries for mother, sister, wife and loved ones.

"There were times when every tent and substitute for a tent in the hospital inclosure was full, and the new patients would have to lie out in the streets until death made a vacancy for them—entirely helpless. The flies would gather upon festering sores and the maggots held revel in their yet living bodies. The grim reaper daily gathered in his scores, and the dead-wagon on its rounds never wanted for a load. They were piled into the wagon, one upon another, like sticks of wood, and hurried to the graves, which were long trenches about seven feet wide and two feet deep, in which they were laid side by side.

"I will relate one or two more acts of uncalled for cruelty that I witnessed before I close. The prisoners were in the habit of trading to the guards for food whatever they could spare from their scant stores. One day I saw a comrade with a pair of shoes bartering with a guard, who, at that point, was stationed within the enclosure near the swamp. While in the act a rebel officer and detective came along. The detective seized the shoes and threw them on the ground, at the same time applying the most abusive epithets to the prisoner. The prisoner remonstrated, whereupon the detective seized the officer's sword and dealt him a severe blow across the temple and again upon the thigh and then drew back as if to thrust him through the heart, but after cursing for a while he returned the saber to the officer and passed on. How my blood boiled at the indignity and how earnestly I wished that I could be upon equal footing, if only for a minute, with the cowardly dastard; but I was helpless.

"Again, one day, I heard the sharp crack of a rifle, and hastened in the direction from which the sound came. I saw lying about ten or twelve yards from the board-fence (this was within the hospital enclosure) the dead body of a comrade; his crutches lay on each side where they had fallen from his hands. No one was near him; they did not dare to go. I asked of a comrade standing near the cause of the shot, and was told that the dead comrade had asked the guard outside something relative to trading for food. The answer was a minie-ball. There were large spaces between the boards of the fence at this point, but I noticed that the ball had passed through the board and entered the left breast of the crippled soldier, causing almost instant death. You can imagine my feelings as I gazed upon the fast-stiffening body of my comrade, and then upon the murderer of a helpless invalid as he walked unconcernedly up and down outside the palisade."

There were several hundred prisoners outside of the prison-pen on parole of honor, some engaged in the cook-house, others chopping wood, digging graves or burying the dead. For three months previous to leaving Andersonville, Lines was engaged in this outside work.

Chapter XXI.

Letter from Rev. E. Clark Cline, Chaplain Eleventh New Jersey Volunteers—Lieutenant Baldwin's Head-board.

MY STORY, if I should tell it, I should have to say, does not begin as early as I have often wished it had. I seemed to be so hindered in getting to the front by a series of providences that it was not till August, 1863, that my commission came and I hurried to join you. I can never forget the warm welcome given me by both officers and men and the respect always shown me and, I think, the work I came among them to do, from the beginning of my regimental life till I, with all my comrades, was mustered out. I am fully conscious how far I failed in doing for the noble fellows all they needed and deserved, but with the knowledge I then and since gained I feel I could serve them better if we were to go out to service again. Let them try me and see. I don't know whether there were more Christian men in the Eleventh than in other regiments— my personal acquaintance with other regiments was not sufficient to enable me to say—but I do know we had many noble, godly men among us. Some of these came to the army thinking it was nigh impossible to lead a religious life there—and we who were there well know that it was not an easy thing—but they found that God's grace was as present in the army, and as mighty to help, as at home. And not a few who had been hiding their colors came out bold and bright, standing up for Christ and doing Him faithful service.

I wish you could get a picture of a prayer-meeting around a camp-fire, smoked on one side, frozen on the other, yet as enjoyable a meeting and as fruitful of good as any ever held in the finest churches at home, if we dare be the judge. And if you could put the General and other officers of various ranks among the attendants and participants in the service of the meeting, the picture would be truer. I would like to recall the revivals in the army in the winter of '63 and '64, and much of a like work in the subsequent year also, but it is a difficult task to describe such an experience, especially after the lapse of more than a quarter of a century and amid surroundings so different from those that are now our lot.

My little tent, when in camp, would be crowded with the boys through the day when not on duty—and at night as well, wanting to know the way to be saved. Our meetings, either around an out door fire or in our log chapels, were largely attended, and many of the boys at that time enlisted again—now as soldiers of the Lord—and were better soldiers of their country for it. Officers, too, took up the cross and professed Christ, and became happy Christians and valuable helpers to me. I can't give you their names—I had better not try to do so. I couldn't mention them all, and I ought not to omit one worthy a place in this distinguished roll. Some are still living; I thank them for their help. Some are dead; their memory is sweet to this day. And some who did not take an active part in this religious work, yet aided me much in their hearty recognition of its value and in doing what they could to make it as easy for me as possible. Perhaps I ought to name as such helper the Colonel who was so much of the time in command of the regiment.

A regimental temperance society was organized on December 15th, '63, with Dr. Welling as its first president. He delivered an address before the society and a large audience assembled with it. The address was published. This temperance society was quite a feature in army life. I guess I had better not tell you who were members of the society, for in publishing them you might draw special attention to those who did not join, and then the readers into whose hands the history might fall would draw their inferences; that would not be fair. This society was the means of good. I find that twenty-six signed the pledge on one day, sixteen on another, fourteen on another, and it kept growing.

Only a few days after I joined the regiment I found that there were some deserters of the Union army in our division guard-house. Daily visits to them, and oftener sometimes, under such circumstances—knowing their guilt and seeing the possible penalty of their crime staring them in the face—you can imagine my experience, just on the field, was sad and trying. Personal interviews, and occasionally a public religious service, were not without their profit, I trust, to these men. Efforts made in their behalf with the authorities resulted, at first, in a stay of execution, and, finally, in their pardon. But the experience of those days, with the terrible strain on my feelings, I shall never forget.

I have referred to my work that lay directly in the line of the religious and spiritual welfare of the regiment. Any one familiar with army life, looking back on work of this kind, must recall the hindrances in its way. With no place of worship except an occasional log-chapel when in winter quarters, and this often vacated by a move of the army almost as soon as built, and so almost always obliged to hold our meetings in the open air, and this when we were lying quiet for any length of time; when it was cold and uncomfortable, the men often engaged so as not to be at leisure to attend; the restraints of home and home influences taken away; the temptations many and strong—some would think the fruit of Christian work would be small. But I dare say that the attendance at our religious services, with all the discomfort often connected with it, and other difficulties in other respects in the way, compared favorably with the attendance of Sabbath services and prayer-meetings at home, with all the attractions and comforts and social helps that at home are in its favor—and the results of religious services were very much, and circumstances considered, in the measure, what we find them at home. They encouraged the men, gave them stimulus and strength for the hard service in camp, and the stern ordeal of facing the enemy and bravely fighting him on the battle-field, and of resisting the trying temptations of army life, and led them, in more cases than we shall ever know till we shall meet them in heaven, from sin to the Saviour, and from a wild, reckless, wayward life, to that of a humble, happy, useful Christian. Of course in such things we cannot use figures—that is God's province alone—but we can speak of the great interest shown in their own personal salvation, and in the salvation of others, by both officers and men, especially in the winter of '63 and '64, and even up to the abandonment of our camp near Brandy Station in May, '64, and on the march, and in the battles of the campaign that followed.

I have referred to the visits of the men to my little tent to ask the way into the new life, their avowal there and in the public meetings of their enlistment in the Christian army, and of the new Captain under whom they intended to fight. And that they held out in the new life, was in most cases true of our soldiers as of the citizen Christian at home, with the experience of over a quarter of a century now in the quiet and helpful success of church life at home. I think as many maintained their Christian characters, with all the disadvantages of their army surroundings, as I have found men doing here. Some of them deserve a story to be written of their Christian soldier-life, as has been written of Havelock and Headly, Vicars and Adjutant Stearns, and many others, whose memory thus rehearsed will not soon be forgotten.

I seem yet to hear the dear boys singing and praying, and testifying their love for Christ, and of the help they felt He gave them in the hardships and dangers of the army. Even on the march, when possible, we used to gather for a prayer-meeting, and we separated to take up the march again or go into battle.

I find in diary of May 10th, '64: "Resting on march after dark; went to right of the regiment, sat down with Captain Sleeper and Sergeant-Major Lanterman on a blanket and began to sing; the boys gathered around and we had a good prayer-meeting; closed with singing 'Oh, that will be joyful, joyful to meet to part no more,'" etc. Little did I think it would be a parting meeting with Captain Sleeper, Lieutenant Egan, Sergeant-Major Lanterman and many others.

Another means of good to the soldiers during the war was the religious reading-matter so generously furnished by the Christian

Commission—for which our gratitude is ever due—and distributed by the Chaplains. Thousands of religious papers and tracts and Testaments and hymn-books—they did more than help while away leisure hours; they made the little tent more like home, gave food for the mind, stimulus to their hearts and fresh courage for their wearing work, and led many to Christ and built up for these a strong Christian life.

How shall I tell you of my experience in the hospital with the sick and wounded—the times we shall never forget, when we sat down by the little hard bunks on which the dear men were breathing out their lives, with no wife or mother or sister to care for them when they felt their need so much—doing what we could for them, but not able to take the place of their loved ones, whom they longed so to see, but dying without it. Then, too, gathering the wounded after the battles, the rows lying on some hillside till the hospital could be reared; or, they cared for and often from necessity hurriedly to be sent for further treatment; some, no help for them; some crying for water; others groaning from pain; others, in their delirium, and though nearing death, thinking they were on the battle-field and fighting as bravely as ever. Oh, those were dreadful days! I can't tell you of them as they were.

Then the burying of the dead; that, too, hastily, if they were to be buried at all—still, always taking time for a prayer and the burial service. In the hurried movements of the army and many to bury after battle, no material from which to make a coffin, we had to be content to wrap them in their blanket or overcoat and lay them thus in the grave, and always, even then, if possible, marking the spot with their name, regiment and company. When in camp and dying from disease more care could be taken, and if nothing better could be found, empty hard-tack boxes taken apart and put together would make a coffin. I think it was only one, perhaps two, that was not buried of our regiment from September, '63, to our mustering-out at the close of the war, and this one or two could not be found after the battle. All credit to the noble fellows who helped in this work.

The dead were removed in the winter of '65 from along the lines of battle to more permanent spots, which were fenced, in the rear. I wish they all could have been sent home and buried with their kindred—how many more thousand graves would there have been to decorate then—but of course this could not be; still, the dear boys and their friends who gave them to their country deserved it. But they will be found at the resurrection.

I received from Titsworth, who brought it from brigade or division headquarters, the mail and distributed it in the regiment. This daily pleasurable event—and still more pleasurable if we weren't so situated as to get it daily—you can recall as vividly as I. Yes, we can hear again the joyous cry, "Here comes the mail!" as the Chaplain was seen with loaded arms wending his way from company to company. We can see *his* look of pleasure as some comrade with smile-lit face received from his hands the looked-for and welcome letter, and hear his words of condolence when forced to reply to eager questioning, "No, nothing for you to day." We can see the eager opening of envelopes and the smile broaden to a laugh as the record of some simple doing at the home far away was read. We can see the envious look, or the shadow of grief and disappointment that seemed to say, "Well, they have forgotten me, they don't care for me any more," creep over the faces of those who were so unfortunate as to receive no token from home. We can see those selfish in their pleasure, or too proud to publicly give way to emotion, steal quickly away to the privacy of their tents or some secluded place to read and re-read the loving messages.

Oh! those loving messages received in the days when we were soldiering, written, as they often were, in irregular characters, for the mother's hand would tremble and her tears blot out the lines as she tried to pen words of love and encouragement to her boy so far away. But youth sometimes forgets that mother's love is best, and even her loving words are for the time forgotten, and the heart throbs to the ever new but "old, old

x

Fac-simile of the last communication sent by the Regimental Commander to the skirmish-line. Captain C. A. Oliver was in command.

story." Father's, mother's or sister's letters may be passed to comrades, boyhood's friends, but hers, never. They were read in secret, conned over upon the picket-post, and just before the clash of battle the hand would instinctively go to the blouse pocket to learn if the precious missive was yet safe. And after the red tide had swept to its full, and ebbed away, leaving its human wreckage cast upon the battle-shore, how often those loving missives were found clasped by stiffened fingers and stared at by glassy eyes. The writers could not tell, they could not know, the joy that came with those messages from home But there was some that brought no message of joy; that told of loved ones lying on beds of pain, or with eyes closed and hands stilled forever. How strong then the temptation to brave all authority and court dishonorable death for one sight of the loved one's face. But all honor to the soldier that so few in selfish grief forgot honor and duty.

I will relate an incident illustrating the grand patriotism of the boys, and, occuring among the first experiences of my army life, it impressed me very much. Corporal Joseph Frazer, of Company B, was mortally wounded at Locust Grove. He was taken to the division hospital, and seeing he was not to live he sent this dying message to his mother, "Tell my mother I die for my country."

I have spoken of a chaplain's work, and it often came to him with the wounded on the battle-field, binding up their wounds as well as we could do it with the appliances at hand, giving them drink, loading them in ambulances, or getting them on stretchers, or anything else that was handy, to be carried to the rear, to the temporary field-hospital. A good sample of this work was on the day of the battle of Spottsylvania Court House. Let me tell it just as I jotted it down at the time:

"What wounded I saw—the dead and dying all around—Captain Goodfellow, Judge-Advocate, wounded; got an ambulance for him, and helped carry him down the hill; Captain Warren, First Massachusetts, mortally wounded; had a few words with him; Captain Ayres, killed; Colonel Schoonover and Captain Sleeper, both reported killed; hunted for the bodies at the front; carried back wounded soldiers; at one time left all alone with the dead and dying; a wounded man from the Twelfth New Jersey praying for the blessing of Christ, and rejoicing in His presence with Him. Went to the field-hospital to look after our wounded; found that the report of Colonel Schoonover's death had reached there and that preparations had been made to send his body home! went back to the front again, determined to have his body, if possible; went to the extreme front; bullets whistling among the trees; not finding the Colonel's body, came back. I met Captain Starboard, who said the Colonel was alive—he had seen him five minutes before. Oh, how glad I felt! Hastened again to the hospital with the joyful news. Early next morning (Friday)—too late that night to do anything more—went to the front again; found the bodies of Captain Sleeper and Lieutenant Egan, and brought them to the hospital; buried Cole and Castner. I was detailed to go to Belle Plain with the bodies of Captain Sleeper, Lieutenant Egan and Captain Evans, Seventh New Jersey; the wagons were all in use taking off the wounded. Near midnight I went to the division hospital to see if I could get a wagon there, but all were in use. I was sorry—I so much wanted to get the bodies home. Early Saturday morning had to bury them, as we were about to move."

Such was the fate of war. How trying it was!

We all remember Lieutenant Baldwin. What a bright fellow he was, a genial, warm-hearted man and good, brave soldier. The winter we lay at Brandy Station his wife died. I saw him quite frequently after his return from her funeral. But the best and most satisfactory talk was on the afternoon of May 3d. He called to see me at my tent and we had a good time together; talked about his brother—then a missionary to China—of a possibility of his going there sometime to assist his brother in the printing work of the missionary station; of our Regimental Temperance Society, which he joined, signing the pledge that afternoon. Then we turned to the subject of personal religion, in which I thought he seemed unusually interested. But we were soon interrupted by a call of an orderly from Brigade Headquarters, where he was serving as Acting-Adjutant, and soon after we broke camp and were on the march. As he was at the head of the brigade and engaged in his pressing duties I did not get to see him again till the 10th, when, as the brigade was forming to make a charge on the enemy, he rode up to my side and said, "I want a good long talk with you the first chance that we have." I never saw him again to have the talk; the hard, continuous fighting kept us apart, and on Sabbath, the 15th, he was instantly killed.

We had an experience at the field-hospital after the battle of the Wilderness. After that awful fight we had many wounded on our hands. Was attending to some men when orders came to send all wounded men away. Carried them down to the road and began to load them in ambulances when an orderly came riding up and saying: "Captain —— said that the wounded should be unloaded and the teams sent off, the enemy was in possession of Ely's ford." Some said "the man is a spy," and began to question him; others were in favor of listening to him; and others still said, "go on with the loading." There was great excitement there for a while, with all those poor fellows to care for and not knowing what we were to do. But we did what our hearts prompted us to do—load them in the ambulances and do the best we could to get them to the rear where they could be kindly cared for—and it proved to be the right thing.

I often think of that charge the army was put in line to make at Mine Run. I recall it here, not to go into particulars, but to remind you of the sober faces on us all that November morning. How fearfully cold it was! I find that I have a record that it was reported that men had frozen on the picket-line Sunday night or Monday morning. Well, when the order came, and we got in line and knew what we were to do, a gloom fell on us all. Hardly one, I dare say, as he thought where and into what he was going, expected to come back alive. Money, pocket-books, watches and messages were brought by the men until I did not know what to do with them all. Ah! it was a time of terrible suspense and serious thought. I understood that on another part of the line the men wrote their names and addresses on strips of paper and put them in their pockets, that they who found them dead might identify them. And the fearful strain and trial lasted all day, even to our brave men—and they were brave—ready at any time to die for the country and the cause of the Union. What a relief it was when the order was countermanded and we moved back. If that charge had been made, what a chapter in history somebody would have had to write! I believe to-day, as I believed then, from what everyone said, that men thanked God for deliverance that day who had never prayed before.

That whole campaign—less than a week in length—was a hard one. We left our camp on Thanksgiving day. It was a beautiful day. We marched all day, crossing the Rapidan, and skirmished nearly all the time. Our Thanksgiving dinner was eaten at eight o'clock that night—nothing since five o'clock that morning. After a sort of sleep and rest, advanced and soon found the enemy, and the battle of Locust Grove was the result.

I was with the regiment awhile, then, as the wounded needed care, assisted in carrying them to the hospital—I remember we had to remove this once during the fight—on stretchers, on boards, on doors they were borne back. The fighting did not last so long, but the wounded seemed a good many for the time. I tried to get some one to help me back with a poor fellow, but as all were engaged, I helped him on my horse, and while I led the old black, saw to the carrying of another. That night with the wounded was a sample of our battle-field experience. The field was covered with wounded men. We built a fire and made them as comfortable as we could; but what comfort! The air cold and damp, and many of the poor fellows without blankets and lying on the cold ground. As I passed from place to place I met the continued cry, "Can't you dress my wound?" "Can't you give me some water?" while all around was heard groanings and cries of pain. A good part of the time I was with one of our boys. How he suffered all that long night—not a wink of sleep. Though the doctors gave him repeated doses of morphine, he could not lie down, but sat up and cried and cried with pain. But this was not the only one; the field was covered with them.

Next morning we found another of our men wounded in the head and nearly dead; we could scarcely see him breathe, yet thought he might recover if something was done for him. So we got a stretcher, laid him on it and covered him with blankets, expecting to take him to the hospital, but on the way saw some ambulances and had him put in one; but the poor fellow died. So it went.

These few incidents are but samples of many of like nature that occurred. They serve to show the scope of a chaplain's work, and prove that the position was far from being a sinecure when filled by such a man as E. Clark Cline. I do not know whether other chaplains were as conscientious as he. I do know that none could have been more so. His heart was in his work. He did not wait for duty to drag him from personal comfort and prod him onward. He sought for duties—often made them— and then performed with heartiness and earnest patriotism; and all in a manner so unostentatious that the veriest scoffer could not help but say, "Truly he is a Christian."

Quoting further from his letter, he says: "I find in one of my monthly reports the following: 'We have been much cheered by an order from these headquarters confiscating all moneys found in the hands of gambling parties, and appropriating the same for the use of the sick; and the energetic efforts of the commanding officer of the regiment have been used to the carrying-out of the same.'"

In another report reference is made to the work of grace in the regiment in the winter of '63 and '64, as follows: "With a rest of some months, with nothing to disturb the attention save a light picket duty on the picket-line, and an occasional reconnoissance, our chapel, after it was built, was crowded every night with eager worshipers and earnest seekers after truth. We believe many found the 'pearl of great price,' and learned of that wisdom which is more precious than rubies. Their courageous fight against sin proved in whose service they had enlisted, and their valiant testimony for Christ showed that they were contending for the crown of eternal life. A singing-class, and frequent gatherings of staff and line officers for this interesting service, I find noted in my diary. Lieutenant-Colonel Schoonover, Adjutant Beach, Captain Sleeper, Captain Kennedy, Dr. Heritage and Sergeant-Major Mount were among the singers. This not only helped to while away the time of camp-life, but proved in many ways helpful to all who shared in it.

"In speaking of our religious work I hesitate to mention the names of those who were earnest helpers in it for fear that some deserving ones will be omitted. Still, some of the dead I can name; chief among them was Captain Sleeper, of Company I. In a slip cut from a Red Bank paper, after his death, I find I was reported saying this about him: 'I have learned to love him as a brother. How he did help me in winning souls to Christ; how brave he was for his Saviour, as well as for his country. Everybody loved him—all mourn his loss.'

"I remember Lieutenant Egan was just beginning to take hold of Christian work when he was removed from us by death. Lieutenant Boice, on duty as Commissary Sergeant so long, was not privileged to be with us in our religious meeting in the regiment, but I remember one night he stood up among his comrades and confessed Christ, and began then a faithful service for Him, and kept it up till his sad, sudden death on the picket-line.

"Then there was Jeremiah Dunham, of Company D, killed at Locust Grove. The Sabbath before, he was at our prayer-meeting and gave us some very interesting statements in relation to Bible history, which he had heard made by a missionary from Palestine. We talked of our plans for conducting our Bible-class in the future, and expected he would be spared to tell us more.

"Occasionally a visitor in camp gave us help. Prominently among these was the Rev. George Hale, D. D., then pastor of the Presbyterian church of Pennington, N. J. How the men listened to his stirring sermons and his temperance addresses and talks at our prayer-meetings, and profited by them! Hon. John Hill, of Boonton—what a friend to the soldier, and how we enjoyed his visits to the camp! Mr. Titsworth, the father of *our* Titsworth boys, came down and helped us; Rev. Dr. Duryea preached in our chapel; Rev. Mr. Smith, brother of Captain Smith of the Eleventh Massachusetts, did the same; Rev. Mr. Renker, of New Jersey, did also. And who does not remember Uncle John Vassar and his grand work in the army! Human panegyric is too feeble to pay the tribute which is his due. I never knew another like him.

"My brother chaplains with whom it was my privilege to work I remember clearly: Rev. Mr. Sovereign, Fifth New Jersey; Rev. Mr. Moore, Sixth New Jersey; Rev. Mr. Hamilton, Seventh New Jersey; Rev. Mr. Hopkins, One Hundred and Twentieth New York; Rev. Mr. Twichell, Second Excelsior; Rev. Mr. Eastman, Third Excelsior; Rev. Mr. Beck, Twenty-sixth Pennsylvania; Rev. Mr. Watson, Eleventh Massachusetts.

"It is not easy to tell of the work done in saving souls, lightening burdened hearts, making men happy, comforting the sorrowing, helping the weary to rest, making their life in the army, so humble and hard, often as much like home as possible. These are things which the Lord does, and in which we feeble men are but little instruments. To tell how many meetings were held, and sermons preached, and talks made in prayer-meetings, and visits made to the boys and visits received from them, and papers and tracts and Testaments and other books given to the men, all this were easy; but to tell the fruit of all this in souls brought to Christ, and joy filling human hearts, and better lives and nobler service for the country, and triumphant deaths, is not my portion to do. This is the history of the Eleventh New Jersey that is to be read in the better world. I would like to tell you of my correspondence with the mothers, or wives, or sisters, as the case would be, of deceased soldiers. What letters these broken-hearted ones did write! Ah! there were patriots at home as well as in the field."

The above cut brings to mind an interesting incident in the life of a soldier when surrounded by the dangers and vicissitudes of actual warfare.

The successful charge by the Second Army Corps upon the enemy's works at the Bloody Angle, near Spottsylvania Court House, took place May 12th, 1864. On the Sunday following, May 15th, the brigade to which the Eleventh Regiment was attached occupied a line of works in the extreme front, as an advance guard, the army being massed some distance to the rear preparatory to another advance in the direction of Richmond. Some time during the day, General Rosser, commanding a brigade of rebel cavalry in our immediate front, brought up a battery and commenced an enfilade fire upon our line.

The works which we occupied were constructed of small pine logs and earth, with an occasional traverse. Lieutenant-Colonel Schoonover and his Adjutant, Lieutenant J. C. Baldwin, were sitting side by side and leaning against one of these traverses.

Several shells had dropped into the Twenty-sixth Pennsylvania, on the right of the Brigade, killing a number of men, when suddenly one forced its way through between two of the logs composing the traverse, crushing Baldwin's head and causing instant death. The shell rolled ten or twelve feet away, but fortunately the fuse went out and no explosion took place.

Colonel Schoonover, fearing that the enemy might gain possession of the works, had Baldwin's body hastily rolled into an army blanket and directed that it be buried in a grove of pines a short distance to the rear of the line. A board from a cracker-box was secured upon which he cut the name, rank and date of death. This was placed at the head of Baldwin's grave, and when his body was brought to New Jersey the board was brought with it. It is still in the possession of Lieutenant Baldwin's sister, Mrs. Martin, widow of the late Senator Martin, of this State. She has kindly furnished the plate for this work.

Chapter XXII.

Sketches.

BREVET MAJOR-GENERAL ROBERT MCALLISTER, the subject of this sketch, was born on a farm situated in Lost Creek Valley, Juniata county, Pa. Previous to the War of the Rebellion he took great interest in military matters, and rose through the various grades to the rank of Brigadier-General, and had command of the Brady Brigade of the uniformed militia of Pennsylvania. When the rebellion broke out he was in New Jersey, building a tunnel through the Oxford hills, at Oxford, Warren county, for the Delaware, Lackawanna and Western Railroad Company. When Sumter was fired on, his partner was left in charge of the heavy contract, and McAllister raised a company at Oxford, went to Trenton, was commissioned by Governor Olden as Lieutenant-Colonel in the First New Jersey Regiment, serving in that capacity until July 28th, 1862, when he was appointed Colonel of the Eleventh Regiment. He was temporarily in command of the First Brigade, Second Division, Third Corps, also of the Second Brigade, Second Division of the same Corps. On the 24th of June, 1864, he took command of the Third Brigade, Third Division, Second Corps (Second New Jersey Brigade), filling that position during the remainder of the war. On the 27th of October, 1864, he was appointed Brigadier-General, by brevet, for gallant and distinguished services at the Boynton Plank-road, and on the 13th of March, 1865, was brevetted Major-General for meritorious services during the war. He was mustered out of the service on the 6th of June, 1865.

He was present at the first Bull Run, rendering efficient service in arresting the retreat of our forces. He participated in the battles of West Point, Gaines' Mill, Charles City Crossroads, White Oak Swamp and Malvern Hill. At Gaines' Mill he was in command, the regiment suffering severely in that engagement. His bravery was conspicuous at Fredericksburg, and he was specially mentioned for his gallantry at Chancellorsville and Gettysburg, being severely wounded in the latter engagement. After an absence of ninety days he returned to the field and participated in all the engagements of his brigade from that time until the close at Appomattox.

In the engagements of Hatcher's Run and Boynton Plankroad General McAllister, by his coolness and intrepidity, won the special commendations of his superiors. Foster, in his History of New Jersey and the Rebellion, truthfully says: "General McAllister was not merely conspicuous for courage on the field in the hour of battle, he was hardly less distinguished for the blamelessness of his life in camp and his conscientious devotion to his duties as a Christian. He was one of those who carried their religion with them to the field, and illustrated in the midst of all its jostling vices, all its clamorous temptations, the virtues which religion nourishes and enriches."

The following extract is copied from the report of the fourth annual reunion of the Second New Jersey Brigade Society, held at Camden, New Jersey, April 9th, 1891:

"And hardly had the badge of mourning been removed from our flag before the angel of death came in our midst and took from us that splendid soldier, our old Commander, our late President, Major-General Robert McAllister. No braver soldier went a-field. He was the bravest among the brave. No one performed the duties to the letter as he. No duty unperformed."

We pause to shed a soldier's tear upon his grave. He died as he had lived, the Christian General and the gentleman, beloved and respected by all who knew him.

Chaplain Cline says of General McAllister: "He was a self-denying, laborious officer, often performing duties which men in the same position generally placed upon subordinate officers, doing this for fear all might not be done right. And he knew no danger—always in the extreme front, never asking anybody to go where he had not been first himself. I could give many instances of great bravery and devotion to his work,

348 THE ELEVENTH REGIMENT,

but will mention only one. During those fearful battles of the wilderness, he worked so hard and was so careful and anxious, both day and night (as he always was in time of special danger),

General McAllister's Monument at Belvidere, N. J.

that he was entirely exhausted, but would not give up. Two horses had been shot under him, he had received a blow on an old wound sustained at Gettysburg, and was suffering from this, but he would not listen to his friends and take the rest he absolutely needed.

"After the enemy had retired from our immediate front, he did go back to the hospital to get a quiet night's sleep, but next morning, early, he was at his post again. His conduct was regulated by a pure love of country and strict conscientiousness. There was no affectation in his fervid patriotism; no absorbing ambition for military renown in his desire to meet the foe, but a quiet determination and an inflexible firmness which were not always seen. He brought to the service a character mellowed by religious culture, and was throughout a Christian officer; loving the approval of conscience more than the plaudits of men."

He died February 23d, 1891, and was buried at Belvidere, New Jersey, where, through the generosity of his fellow-citizens, a handsome monument has been erected to his memory. It was dedicated May 30th, 1894.

JOHN SCHOONOVER, Brevet-Colonel Eleventh New Jersey Volunteers, was born at Bushkill, Pa., August 12th, 1839. He received his education from the common schools of his native place and the instructions of the Rev. J. K. Davis, of Smithfield, Pa. At the age of sixteen he began the work of teaching and preparation for college. The outbreak of the rebellion found him thus employed at Oxford, Warren county, N. J. Soon after the proclamation of President Lincoln calling for seventy-five thousand men to serve for three months, Schoonover joined a company raised by Captain Campbell at Belvidere. The company reported at Trenton, but so quickly had the State's quota been filled—the four regiments being completed in seven days—that they reached the capital too late for acceptance. As the company was about to return to Belvidere, Captain Campbell stepped to the front and asked all who were willing to go with him for three years to do likewise. But seven responded, Schoonover being one of the seven. The number of three-year patriots being so small, all returned to their homes. But Schoonover's patriotism was not of the kind that could rest content with the acquisition of such laurels as these, and we soon find him again at Trenton as a private in Company D (Captain Valentine Mutchler), First New Jersey Regiment, for three years. This regiment left the State June 28th, 1861. The following September Schoonover was made corporal. The ensuing winter, Colonel Torbert, then commanding the First Regiment, issued an order directing each captain to select a sergeant to prepare for examination, the one standing the highest to receive a commission as Second Lieutenant. No Sergeant of Company D being willing to stand the trial, the subject of this sketch was selected to represent that company. Four only appeared for examination, the successful one being Commissary Sergeant S. G. Blythe. Schoonover, standing second, was promoted Commissary Sergeant, dating from March 24th, 1862. He served in that position until August 2d, 1862, when he received a commission as Adjutant of the Eleventh New Jersey Volunteers, then organizing at Trenton. The Eleventh left the State on August 25th, 1862, and was first engaged in Burnside's attack upon Fredericksburg. The first engagement proved to the men of the Eleventh that their Adjutant was one on whom they could depend. During the desperate fighting of the regiment in the woods at Chancellorsville, on May 3d and 4th, 1862, Adjutant Schoonover was conspicuous for his bravery and coolness, and received honorable mention therefor. On the 2d of July, at Gettysburg, he received two wounds and six bullet-holes through his clothing, and on the 3d his horse was shot under him. He again received slight wounds at Spottsylvania and at Barker's Mills, but he never thought his wounds sufficiently severe to necessitate going to the rear. He was commissioned Lieutenant-Colonel in 1863, and brevetted Colonel March 13th, 1865, for conspicuous gallantry.

Chaplain Cline says of Colonel Schoonover: "He ever showed himself to be a man of rare excellence, of great firmness and energy, of a dauntless courage which never calculated danger when a duty was to be performed, a high sense of right and unflinching adherence to its obligations, with intellectual endowments of a superior order and social qualities which won the affection and admiration of all his associates. Kind-hearted to his command, never exacting from them any unnecessary work and always ready to do everything in his power for their comfort and happiness, he was universally beloved and honored, and there was scarcely one who would not have given his life, if needs be, to save his. Brave himself and ever in the front of the battle, he took *them* there; and in camp his regiment was in the highest state of discipline and order."

MAJOR THOMAS J. HALSEY entered the service as Captain of Company E, Eleventh New Jersey Volunteers, a company that was largely made up of citizens of Morris county. He was severely wounded in the battle of Chancellorsville, and for a time was absent from his command. Soon after re-joining the regiment he was commissioned Major, to date September 14th, 1863. June 23d, 1864, in Mahone's successful attack upon our lines, Major Halsey and twenty-six men were made prisoners. With the exception of Gettysburg and Wapping Heights, when he was absent on account of wounds received at Chancellorsville, Major Halsey had been present with the regiment in all its engagements, and received special mention for his gallant behavior at the battle of Locust Grove.

After being confined for eight months in the Andersonville prison, enduring all its hardships and privations, he again reported for duty.

Major Halsey was a man of sterling worth and irreproachable character. He was patriotic in the fullest sense of the word, and by his manly bearing and genial disposition won many friends.

At the close of the rebellion he resumed business in his native State, but later on he removed to Missouri, where he died January 20th, 1893.

DR. E. L. WELLING, of Pennington, New Jersey, entered the service as Assistant Surgeon of the Third Regiment, New

Jersey Volunteers, June 25th, 1861. He was made Surgeon of the Eleventh New Jersey Volunteers July 19th, 1862. After the battle of Fredericksburg, he took charge of the Corps Hospital, and rendered distinguished services while in the performance of this duty. He developed exceptional ability as an organizer and manager of hospitals on a large scale, and was more or less on this duty until the close of the war. He was Secretary of the Third Army Corps Union from its organization to the day of his death; served for some time as Surgeon-in-Chief in the National Guard, on the staff of General W. J. Sewell, and, on the death of Dr. W. W. L. Phillips, he was appointed to succeed him as Medical Director of the National Soldiers' Home, at Hampton, Virginia. Owing to failing health, he was compelled to resign and retire to his home at Pennington. His army comrades held him in high esteem, and he gave his country over four years of valuable and patriotic service. He died November 29th, 1897.

PHILIP J. KEARNY possessed many of the characteristics of his distinguished cousin, General Philip Kearny. He was brave, ambitious, and a thorough soldier. Entering the service as Captain of Company A, he was commissioned Major of the regiment May 3d, 1863.

Major Kearny received special mention for his bravery at the battle of Chancellorsville.

He was seriously wounded, July 2d, at the battle of Gettysburg, a ball crushing through his knee joint, from the effects of which he died at St. Luke's U. S. Army General Hospital, New York city, August 9th, 1863. In the death of Major Kearny the regiment lost one of its best officers.

CHAPLAIN E. C. CLINE was born in Warren county, New Jersey. He graduated at Lafayette College in 1857 and at Princeton Theological Seminary in 1862, and was ordained for the army July 6th, 1863, entering at once the service of the Christian Commission. From this duty he was called to the

Chaplaincy of the Eleventh New Jersey. He was mustered into the regiment September 11th, 1863, and was constantly on duty from that time until the close of the war, when he was mustered out with the regiment, June 6th, 1865.

The position of Chaplain was one of great responsibility. Not only was it his office to preach and to pray—he was the soldier's counselor. When sickness came his duties found him at the bedside in camp and hospital; on the long and weary march he gave them cheer and sometimes bore their burdens; with tireless hand and sleepless eye he assisted in the care of the wounded and was their support in the hour of death; he wrote letters for the living and looked after the burial of the dead, and communicated the sad news to their friends.

In all the varied and self-denying duties which the earnest and devoted Chaplain performed, no one in all the service was better fitted, or served more faithfully, than Chaplain Cline. The whiz of a bullet or the shriek of a shell was not an unfamiliar sound to his ears. He went wherever duty called him, and his services in camp and hospital, on the march and battle-field, are gratefully remembered by the regiment.

At the close of the war he became pastor of the church at Oxford, New Jersey, and in 1887 he was called to his present charge at Phillipsburg, New Jersey. In the church at the latter place, a handsome memorial window, in commemoration of the regiment's dead, has been erected by its members and friends. It was dedicated June 6th, 1891.

IRA W CORY entered the service as a Sergeant in Company K, Seventh New Jersey Volunteers, September 15th, 1861. When the Eleventh was organized, he was commissioned First Lieutenant of Company H. He was promoted to the Captaincy of this company in July, 1863, taking the place of Captain D. B. Logan, who was killed in the battle of Gettysburg. After Logan's death, Cory took command of his company, which, at that time, was on the extreme left of the regiment. When General Barksdale, commanding a Mississippi brigade, was charging down through the open fields in our front, word was received from General Carr by the commanding officer of the regiment to have some one bring down the mounted officer who was leading the charge in our front. Captain Cory was instructed to have his entire company execute this order, and the gallant Barksdale fell that afternoon. When asked that night where he was wounded, he replied, "All over." He was absent for a time on detached service at Draft Rendezvous, at Trenton, N. J., but was present with the regiment, with this exception, during its entire term of service. Captain Cory was a brave, thoroughly reliable and conscientious officer.

JOSEPH C. BALDWIN entered the service as Sergeant of Company K, Eleventh New Jersey Volunteers, August 11th, 1862; Second Lieutenant, Company K, February 18th, 1863; First Lieutenant, Company C, August 26th, 1863. Baldwin was a man of rare intelligence, and his genial and happy disposition made him a host of friends. He was killed at Spottsylvania Court House, Va., May 15th, 1864. A short time previous to his death he was made acting Adjutant of the regiment, and while leaning against one of the traverses in the line of works occupied by our troops, a shell forced its way through between the logs composing the traverse, crushing his head and causing instant death. A career which undoubtedly would have proved brilliant was suddenly cut off, and his death was a great loss to the regiment and deeply felt by his comrades.

CAPTAIN W H. MEEKER was born in Rochester, N. Y., May 9th, 1842, but has lived in Elizabeth, N. J., since 1848. He enlisted as Corporal May 21st, 1861, in Company A, First Regiment, New Jersey Volunteers; promoted to Sergeant, and was discharged at Mechanicsville, Va., June 12th, 1862, to enable him to accept a commission as Captain of Company B, Eleventh New Jersey Volunteers. He had command of his company in the battles of Fredericksburg and Chancellorsville, but was prostrated with sunstroke soon after the latter engagement.

He re-joined the regiment at Warrenton, Va., July 31st, 1863; was honorably discharged for disability September 3d, 1863, Special Order No. 396, War Department, the regiment losing the services of a brave and valuable officer. The following testimonial, signed by the members of his company, was handed him upon his departure from the regiment:

"*Captain Meeker:*

"SIR—In view of your contemplated departure from the field, we, the few remaining members of your company, would take this occasion to testify to your bravery and worth, regretting our inability to offer at this time a more substantial token of our regard and esteem.

"Your bearing on the field of Chancellorsville we are proud to emulate, and in your retirement to the circle of civil life we hope for you a speedy restoration to health, and at home you will bear with you our heart's best wishes for your happiness and future welfare."

THOMAS D. MARBAKER, the Regimental Historian, was born August 23d, 1846, on the Musconetcong Mountains, Hunterdon county, New Jersey. He left school at eleven years of age, commencing at that date to earn his own living. He entered the service July 19th, 1862, as a private in Company E, before he was sixteen years of age. Marbaker was a type of hundreds of young men whose exceedingly youthful appearance frequently stood in the way of that advancement to which their bravery, efficiency and endurance entitled them. He was made Corporal August 20th, 1863, and Sergeant November 1st, 1863. Sergeant Marbaker was severely wounded at Chancellorsville, but left the hospital and rejoined the regiment on its march to Gettysburg. The Adjutant, discovering that he was in the ranks marching with a running wound, advised him to at once get in an ambulance, but Marbaker, with a pluck and endurance that was surprising, remained with his company and stood shoulder to shoulder with his comrades in the great conflict at Gettysburg. He was mustered out with the regiment June 6th, 1865.

WILLIAM E. AXTELL commenced his military service as Second Lieutenant in Company H. He was present with the regiment in all its marches and engagements up to and including the battle of Gettysburg, where he was severely wounded, on account of which he resigned September 29th, 1863. He was commissioned First Lieutenant July 2d, 1863, but not mustered. In the resignation of Lieutenant Axtell, the regiment was deprived of the services of a brave and efficient officer.

SERGEANT ELIPHALET STURDEVANT entered the service August 18th, 1862, in Company E, Eleventh New Jersey Volunteers. From the start he was a soldier in whom reliance could be placed in whatever duty he was called upon to perform. He was not only a good soldier in the camp and on the march, but he filled well his part upon the field of battle. He fell severely wounded at the battle of Gettysburg; was taken to the field-hospital, where his left leg and right arm were amputated, from the effects of which he died July 13th. There was no one whose loss was more deeply felt by his comrades than Sergeant Sturdevant. A man of irreproachable character, modest and retiring in his disposition, and an earnest and devoted Christian. In his death the regiment lost one of its bravest and most efficient men. His body was taken to his native village—Rockaway, New Jersey—where he was buried with military honors.

MAJOR W H. LOYD was born in Philadelphia, Pa., January 27th, 1839, and at outbreak of the war was engaged in the stock brokerage business. He joined the First Pennsylvania Reserve Militia April, 1861, as private; Second Lieutenant Eleventh New Jersey Volunteers, August 12th, 1862; First Lieutenant, November 17th, 1862; Captain, March 16th, 1863; commissioned Major Seventh New Jersey Volunteers, October 13th, 1864, and while awaiting muster was severely wounded, October 27th, 1864, at the battle of Boynton Plank road, while serving as Brigade Inspector, Second Brigade, Third Division, Second Army Corps. During winter of 1863-4 was detached from regiment and assigned to staff duty, first as A. A. I. General, First Division, Third Corps. Upon consolidation of Third and Second Corps was appointed Brigade Inspector and assigned to Second Brigade, Third Division, Second Corps; was honorably discharged for disability from wounds, January 13th, 1865.

That Major Loyd enjoyed the confidence of his superior officers is evidenced by his frequent promotions. Upon leaving the service he re-entered the banking business, in Philadelphia, in which he is still engaged.

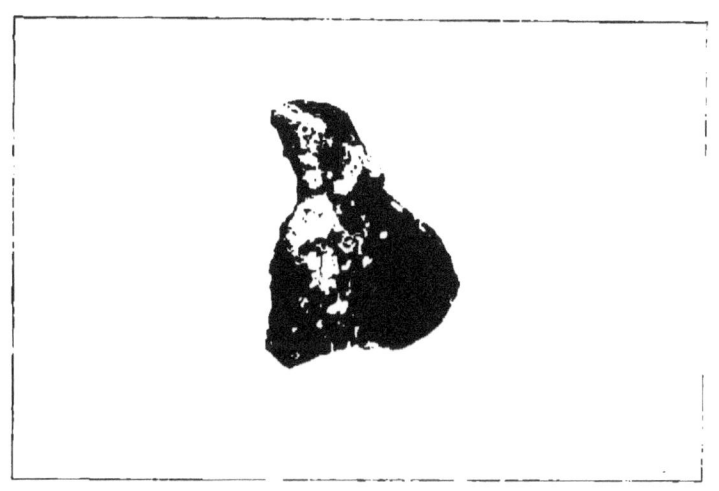

Portion of a minie-ball received at the battle of Boynton Road, Va., October 27th, 1864, by Major William H. Loyd, Eleventh New Jersey Volunteers. Extracted by Dr. R. M. Girvin, May 16th, 1896, at the Presbyterian Hospital, Philadelphia. The other part was extracted by Dr. John Neil, Surgeon, U. S. A., December, 1864. This photograph is exact size. Weight of bullet, one ounce. The wound has never healed from the first, and is still open.

MAJOR JOHN T. HILL was born in New Brunswick, N. J., July, 1836. He entered the service as a Captain in Company I, Eleventh New Jersey Volunteers, at its organization, and bore a conspicuous part in its first battle, December 13th, 1862, at Fredericksburg, Va. The following April he received a commission as Major of the Twelfth New Jersey Infantry, and joined that regiment a short time before the Chancellorsville campaign. After the rout of the Eleventh Corps, Colonel Willets being badly wounded in the early part of the fight, the command devolved upon Major Hill. At Gettysburg the regiment was also under his command, and its splendid achievements on that battlefield have been fully recorded in history. He remained in command until the latter part of the summer of 1863, when he was stricken down with inflammatory rheumatism, and, much against his will, he was honorably discharged for disability early in 1864. His enforced withdrawal from the service was regretted by all his comrades in arms. His record throughout was that of a brave and faithful officer, a trusted and honored commander.

T. O. DOANE enlisted as a private in Company B, August 16th, 1862; promoted to Corporal, October 1st, 1862; was present with the regiment at the battles of Fredericksburg and Chancellorsville, where he was slightly wounded. At Gettysburg he was wounded in the head, and remained in the hospital at Baltimore until December, 1863, when he was transferred to Company B, Twentieth Veteran Reserve Corps; was promoted to Sergeant, and was on special duty as detective on the staff of Mayor A. G. Brady, Provost Marshal, at Point Lookout; mustered out, July 29th, 1865. He now resides in Plainfield, New Jersey.

CYPRIAN H. ROSSITER entered the service as Corporal, in Company K, June 13th, 1862; Sergeant, July 1st, 1863; First Sergeant, August 1st, 1864; Second Lieutenant, Company B, September 18th, 1864; First Lieutenant, Company E, October 23d, 1864; Captain, Company F, June 13th, 1865, not mustered. Captain Rossiter was a brave and efficient officer. He was mustered out with the regiment, June 6th, 1865.

JOHN B. FAUSSETT first entered the service as Sergeant in Company A, three-months militia. Served in that capacity from April 27th, 1861, to July 31st, 1861. He was made First

Sergeant of Company C, Eleventh New Jersey Volunteers, August 15th, 1862; Second Lieutenant, March 6th, 1863; First Lieutenant, September 29th, 1863. Lieutenant Faussett received wounds both at Chancellorsville and Gettysburg. He was sunstruck while the regiment was on the March from its winter camp at Brandy Station to the Wilderness, and was discharged for disability, July 19th, 1864. He has resided since that time in Trenton, New Jersey.

CHARLES A. OLIVER was born in New Brunswick, New Jersey, September 8th, 1843. He enlisted as a private in Company I, Eleventh New Jersey Volunteers, August 11th, 1862; Corporal, September 7th, 1862; Sergeant, December 28th, 1862; Second Lieutenant, Company E, June 26th, 1863; First Lieutenant, Company A, October 23d, 1864; Captain, Company A, June 13th, 1865. Not mustered.

Captain Oliver was wounded at the battles of Gettysburg and the Wilderness. He was present with the regiment in all its battles, marches and skirmishes, and was, under all circumstances, a brave and efficient officer. In the night attack and re-capture of the picket-line at Fort Morton he bore a very prominent part. He now resides at New Brunswick, New Jersey.

LIEUTENANT EDWIN R. GOOD was mustered into the service as Second Lieutenant of Company F, August 13th, 1862; promoted to First Lieutenant, February 18th, 1863. Lieutenant Good was almost continuously in command of his company from the time of its entrance into active service. He was slightly wounded in the foot at the battle of Chancellorsville, but remained on the field, having been temporarily placed in command of Company B—Lieutenants Bloomfield and Reilly both having been killed and Captain Meeker prostrated by sunstroke soon after the battle. After the return to camp, he again took command of his own company. He received three wounds in the battle of Gettysburg—in the left arm and in the shoulder and elbow of his right arm. The bullet which entered his shoulder he still has in his possession. After an absence of sixty days, Lieutenant Good re-joined the regiment, but as his wounds were still unhealed, he was sent to Georgetown Seminary Hospital, and after remaining there some time was discharged for disability by order of the War Department. Lieutenant Good was a brave and valuable officer, and his loss was keenly felt both by his company and regiment. He now resides at Hamilton Square, New Jersey.

ALONZO B. SEARING enlisted in Company E, Eleventh New Jersey Volunteers, August 18th, 1862, and was, at the time of his entrance into the service, eighteen years of age. He was with the regiment during its entire term of service, being present at its muster-out, June 6th, 1865. Searing, like many others in the regiment, became a soldier when quite young, and the effective fighting element of the army was composed of just such men, the great bulk of them serving in the three-years volunteers of 1861 and 1862. At Gettysburg the two men on his immediate right were mortally wounded, while he escaped with a slight ankle wound. Searing was a faithful, brave and efficient soldier. Since the close of the war he has served five years in the National Guard of New Jersey. He now resides at Dover, New Jersey.

ALPHEUS ILIFF, entered the service as a Corporal in Company E, June 15th, 1862; Sergeant, July 1st, 1863; commissioned Second Lieutenant Company B, May 22d, 1865; not mustered; commissioned First Lieutenant Company A, June 13th, 1865; not mustered. Lieutenant Iliff was captured on the 10th of May, 1864, and for a time endured the sufferings and hardships of prison life. He rejoined the regiment before the close of the war, and was present when it was mustered out of the service June 6th, 1865. He rendered his country faithful, patriotic and conscientious service.

JAMES MCDAVITT, the subject of this sketch, was a member of Company E, and, previous to his enlistment, lived at Dover,

New Jersey. A man of splendid physique and fine soldierly bearing, he gave every evidence of rapid advancement and a brilliant future, but like many others he was taken soon after his enlistment, and the regiment lost the services of one of its bravest and most promising men. At the battle of Chancellorsville, when Captain Halsey was wounded, McDavitt went to his assistance, and while binding up the Captain's wound he was struck in the head and died a few minutes afterward. Like thousands of others, the place of his burial is unknown.

ALEXANDER BEACH, JR., enlisted May 30th, 1861, as a private in Company K, Second New Jersey Volunteers; was commissioned Second Lieutenant, Company B, Eleventh New Jersey Volunteers, August 16th, 1862; First Lieutenant, March 6th, 1863; Adjutant, August 26th, 1863; Captain, Company I, June 13th, 1865; wounded at Chancellorsville, May 4, 1863. Adjutant Beach was, under all circumstances, a thorough and reliable officer, and during his term of service, by his upright and manly bearing as a soldier, he commanded the respect and confidence of his superior officers. He received special mention for his gallant behavior at the battle of Locust Grove. He now resides in Newark, N J.

ANDREW H. ACKERMAN enlisted in the Second Regiment, New Jersey Volunteers, May 30th, 1861, as a private. Promoted First Lieutenant Company A, Eleventh Regiment, July 21st, 1862; Captain Company C, March 6th, 1863. He was killed while in command of his company, July 2d, 1863, at Gettysburg, Pa. He had won the respect and confidence of his superior officers by his coolness and bravery at Fredericksburg and Chancellorsville, and to be taken thus early in his military career deprived the regiment of the services of one of its most valuable and promising officers.

CAPTAIN DORASTUS B. LOGAN, the subject of this sketch, was a man of strong character and sterling worth. Of remarkable self-control and dignified presence, he was universally respected by his comrades in arms. He entered the service as Captain of Company H, August 14th, 1862; proved his value as an officer by his brave and efficient services at Fredericksburg and Chancellorsville. He was killed while in command of his company at Gettysburg, Pa., July 2d, 1863.

LIEUTENANT WILLIAM H. EGAN entered the service as First Sergeant of Company E, July 22d, 1862, and was promoted First Lieutenant of Company H, October 5th, 1863. He was killed at Spottsylvania Court House, Virginia, May 12th, 1864. The circumstances under which Lieutenant Egan was killed were most remarkable. The Second Corps in its successful charge on the enemy's line of entrenchments on the morning of May 12th was formed in three lines, the Eleventh Regiment being in the third line. A few minutes previous to the advance, Lieutenant Egan went to the Chaplain, handed him his watch and other articles, gave him his address and said that he would be killed by the first shot fired by the enemy. According to rebel history, on the day previous General Lee had sent away from the Angle twenty pieces of artillery, with positive instructions that they should return and be in position by daylight next morning. As the corps advanced at daylight on the morning of the 12th the artillery was galloping into position, but only had time to unlimber and fire two shots. The first one passed through the body of Egan, causing instant death. His loss was deeply felt. He was brave, reliable, and possessed the characteristics which combine to make a good officer.

The record of CAPTAIN SAMUEL T. SLEEPER, the subject of this sketch, was that of a brave, conscientious and upright soldier. Entering the service as First Lieutenant of Company I, August 6th, 1862, he was made the Captain of his company June 2d, 1863. He rendered valuable and distinguished services both at Chancellorsville and Gettysburg. He was killed in the great charge of the Second Corps at Spottsylvania Court House, Va., May 12th, 1864. Of a quiet and unassuming disposition and irreproachable character, his early death was greatly regretted by his comrades, and took from the regiment one of its most valuable officers.

CAPTAIN JOHN OLDERSHAW, the subject of this sketch, began his military life as First Lieutenant in Company K, August 19th, 1862. He was commissioned Captain of his company October 23d, 1863, and was mustered out with the regiment June 6th, 1865. Throughout his entire service Captain Oldershaw was conspicuous as a brave, reliable and efficient officer. He was much of the time on staff duty, both at Brigade and Division headquarters, and while occupying these positions frequently received mention and commendation for his bravery and efficiency.

WILLIAM HAND enlisted as a private in Company B, August 11th, 1862; Sergeant, February 1st, 1863; First Sergeant, July 1st, 1863; Second Lieutenant, Company I, October 13th, 1864; Acting Regimental Quartermaster, February 1st, 1865; First Lieutenant, Company E, June 13th, 1865. He was wounded in the right foot, at Gettysburg, July 2d, 1863; was present for duty in every engagement of the regiment, and was a brave, thoroughly capable and reliable officer. His present residence is in Plainfield, New Jersey.

SIDNEY M. LAYTON began his military life as First Lieutenant of Company D. He served faithfully in this position until July 3d, 1863, when he was promoted to the Captaincy of his company, *vice* Martin, killed. Captain Layton was killed in action near Petersburg, Va., June 16th, 1864. He was buried at City Point National Cemetery, Va.; section C, division 4, grave 73.

CHARLES F GAGE, whose services are fully recorded elsewhere in this history, enlisted as a Sergeant in Company F, Fifth

Regiment, New Jersey Volunteers, August 22d, 1861. He was early transferred to the Signal Service Department, and while serving in that capacity received a commission as First Lieutenant of Company G, Eleventh New Jersey Volunteers, dated December 5th, 1863. He was promoted to the Captaincy of Company F, June 26th, 1864, and brevetted Major for conspicuous gallantry April 9th, 1865. For coolness and intrepidity, Captain Gage had few equals. No duty was too hazardous for him to undertake, and his personal service in locating the rebel line after its night capture of our picket-line in front of Fort Morton, Va., has become a matter of history. He was mustered out with the regiment June 6th, 1865.

Titus Berry, Jr., the subject of this sketch, entered the service as a Corporal in Company E, August 9th, 1862; Sergeant, September 1st, 1863; Second Lieutenant, October 23d, 1864. He was commissioned Adjutant June 13th, 1865, but not mustered. Lieutenant Berry was a brave, faithful and deserving officer. He was mustered out with the regiment, June 6th, 1865.

Corporal Absalom S. Talmadge was mustered in with the regiment August 18th, 1862. He was present with his company in all its marches and battles up to the battle of Gettysburg, where he was severely wounded in the head. He remained in the hospital until February, 1864, when he rejoined the regiment at Brandy Station, Va. He was again wounded at the battle of the Wilderness and sent to the hospital at Washington, D. C. After his recovery he was detailed for duty in the Commissary Department, at Washington, where he remained until the close of the war, when he was mustered out with the regiment. Talmage was a brave and efficient soldier, and always had the confidence of his superior officers.

www.ingramcontent.com/pod-product-compliance
Lightning Source LLC
Chambersburg PA
CBHW020302240426
43673CB00039B/674